MASTERING MICROWAVE COOKING

Revised & Updated Edition

MASTERING MICROWAVE COOKING

Maria Luisa Scott

Jack Denton Scott

and the Editors of
Consumer Reports Books

CONSUMERS UNION

Mount Vernon, New York

Copyright © 1988 by Maria Luisa Scott and Jack Denton Scott and Consumers Union of U.S.,
Inc., Mount Vernon, New York 10553

Library of Congress Cataloging-in-Publication Data

Scott, Maria Luisa.
Mastering microwave cooking.
Includes index.
1. Microwave cookery.   I. Scott, Jack Denton,
1915–   .   II. Consumer Reports Books.   III. Title.
TX832.S39   1988   641.5′882   88–71034
ISBN 0-89043-268-6

Design by Joy Taylor

Originally published in 1976 by Bantam Books—revised and updated.

First printing, October 1988
Manufactured in the United States of America

CONTENTS

~~~~~~~~~~

PART ONE

ABOUT MICROWAVE OVENS

I

〰〰〰

THE TIME-SAVING APPLIANCE

IN OUR current culture of two-career families and latchkey children, fast convenience food, quickly defrosted meals, and 60-second servings have all been made possible by the labor-saving subject of this book.

It was born in an electronics laboratory in the Boston area in 1944. Dr. Percy Spencer of the Raytheon Company observed that the microwave energy generated by radar tubes had a heating effect on many objects. So he began to experiment. The result was the discovery of microwave cooking and a patent entitled "A Method of Heating Foodstuffs," filed with the U.S. Patent Office on October 8, 1945. That was the beginning. Dr. Spencer, who invented and developed mass production techniques for the magnetron tubes used in radar systems during World War II, was also responsible for a number of inventions that took the microwave oven from the laboratory to the restaurant kitchen. For many years fast-cooking microwave ovens were used primarily as a labor saving device only in restaurants and hospitals.

It didn't take long, however, for users to discover that microwave ovens have great capabilities. They cook much faster than electric or gas ranges because they cook with a different principle. There is no time or energy wasted in heating up the air. Microwave energy is converted directly to heat inside the food by a friction-like action. It is a moist cooking process with most food and tends to neither dry out the exterior nor to create much of a crust.

The growth of microwave ovens in America has been phenomenal, with

5.9 million bought in 1983, and twice that amount in 1985. In 1986 alone more than 12.4 million domestic-label ovens and 8.2 million imports were purchased. Today, about 70 percent of American families own microwave ovens; Americans now own more microwave ovens than toaster ovens, food processors, or dishwashers. Predictions are that by the turn of the century microwave ovens will appear in eight out of ten U.S. kitchens.

There has been an accompanying onslaught of cookbooks, with too many of them telling us that the microwave oven can do anything. It can't, and we want to make that clear from the start. One cookbook, to the alarm of manufacturers, even advises that we deep-fry in the microwave oven. This is a foolhardy suggestion, as deep frying is tricky even on the conventional stove. There are special deep fryers on the market to take most of the risk from this otherwise dangerous technique, but the microwave oven isn't one of them.

Aware of the importance of time to two-career families, every major company concerned with foods inside and outside the frozen food cabinet is at work on microwaveable products. In 1987 food companies introduced several hundred new food "products" specifically for the microwave-equipped, time-is-a-factor household, including 30-second hot fudge sundaes, two-minute linguine with clam sauce, four-minute cake mixes, and six-minute soup-and-sandwich combinations.

The new advances in packaging and food engineering mean that microwave fish can now be crisp, croissants can be browned without becoming soggy, and the quality of microwave cake mixes is just about as good as those prepared for regular ovens.

Retail sales of these microwave foods topped $760 million in the year between October 1986 and October 1987. One major company alone expects its sales to exceed $300 million in 1988, up from $172 million in 1987.

New "shelf-stable" entrees that have a shelf life of 18 months, do not require freezing, and can be prepared in the microwave oven in less than two minutes are ready to be marketed.

One problem in the past was that with some foods microwave ovens would not brown and crisp them and instead left them soggy. Special paperboard trays containing absorbent materials now prevent sogginess in microwave foods. To brown and crisp fish and pizzas properly, one company uses "susceptor plates" containing a thin layer of powdered aluminum laminated under plastic that absorbs microwave energy and heats to a high temperature.

To combat the confusion caused by the varying wattages among microwave ovens (what cooks perfectly in 15 seconds in one oven would be inedible after 15 seconds in another) some manufacturers are including very specific cooking instructions. One takes the guesswork out of heating microwave food with "microready indicators," in which a small colored strip on top of the plastic food container turns from blue and white to all blue as the food is properly heated.

Research reveals that 80 percent of microwave oven owners use their ovens for heating frozen or prepared foods, or for simple uncomplicated menus and entrees—with speed and simplicity paramount. Consequently (with few exceptions for weekend menus and perhaps guest cooking), we have concentrated on speed cooking and easy, problem-free recipes.

But before we get into actual recipes, let's take the mystery out of microwaves.

How Do Microwaves Work?

How can "waves" *cook*? Rub your hands together briskly. What is the result? Heat, caused by friction. That, more or less, is the way microwaves work. When they enter food, they cause the liquid or moisture molecules to vibrate 2,450 million times a second. That astoundingly fast friction forces the food to heat. The greater the moisture content, the faster the food will cook.

These waves do not use the *direct* application of heat, as all other cooking methods do. Electromagnetic waves from the magnetron power source (or tube, not unlike the one in your television set) are instantly absorbed into the food, becoming heat.

Microwaves are waves of energy with short wavelengths (from approximately $\frac{1}{10}$ inch to 40 inches) and high frequencies (300 million to 100 billion cycles per second), very much like those sent out by television and radio stations. They travel at the speed of light, about 186,000 miles per second.

Stated simply, the cooking occurs in five stages:

1. The magnetron tube sends microwaves into the oven cavity.

2. The metallic oven walls, floor, and ceiling reflect the waves (just as light is reflected by a mirror), bouncing them back and forth in irregular patterns.

3. These energy waves then strike a "stirrer" in the oven, a slowly revolving metal fan that reflects the power bouncing off the walls, ceiling, back, and bottom of the oven, distributing it so that it enters the food from all sides to cook evenly.

4. A dish of the proper material transmits the waves, allowing them to pass into the food. Microwaves pass through glass, paper, ceramic, and plastic without effect. These materials might warm up, but only because the heat transfers from the food. (We will discuss utensils later in this section.)

5. Food *absorbs* the microwaves, causing the food molecules to rub together so fast that friction results, heating the food. There is some misun-

derstanding about this function of microwaves, even among those who have been cooking with the waves for some time. Many believe that the food cooks from the inside out. Not so. It is cooked throughout at the same time, with more cooking on the exterior of the food. The waves penetrate only about ½ to 1½ inches, depending on the density of the food, and then the rest of the heating occurs through conduction or transference. This means, with proper timing, a roast can be cooked so that it is brown on the outside, and rare, medium, or well done on the inside.

Why Are Microwave Ovens Becoming So Popular?

Several factors are behind the boom, and energy and its spiraling cost may be among them. Microwave ovens *can* save energy, particularly when compared to conventional cooking methods. But the amount of energy you really save depends on how, and how often, you use your microwave. Since it cooks foods faster and more directly than a conventional oven, it saves energy. But defrosting in the microwave, a common use, uses energy that isn't used in ordinary defrosting in the refrigerator. Also, energy costs for cooking are only a small part of your total energy bill; it's therefore unlikely that you could save enough energy for a microwave oven to pay for itself.

Probably a more important factor behind the boom in microwave ovens is the time they save. Microwave ovens cook all foods in about a quarter of the time of any other method. Some take even less than that: a potato in four minutes, an acorn squash in seven, both of which take about an hour to bake in the conventional oven. With this speed a microwave oven peels hours off kitchen chores.

It will cook a large turkey to perfection at six or seven minutes a pound, whereas a conventional oven takes 35 minutes a pound. A family-size roast of beef takes only 40 minutes, a broiler chicken 15 minutes. You can scramble an egg in 45 seconds; bake a cake in 5 minutes; a cupcake in 30 seconds; heat a roll in 10 seconds; defrost and cook a lobster tail in 5½ minutes. A one-pound steak, frozen solid, is ready to cook in 3 to 5 minutes. Microwaves defrost frozen foods faster and more efficiently than any other medium. This means that you can come home from work and pop a frozen meal into the microwave oven and have it piping hot on the table in minutes.

Another wonderful aspect of the microwave oven is that it produces no heat. What a joy during the sweltering days of summer to have "cool" cooking for the entire meal. No hot kitchen, no exhausted cook.

Not long before we started work on this book, the East Coast had a heat wave, with temperatures in the mid-nineties, the air humid as a tropical forest. We found it no chore to cook a dinner in the microwave oven, cool drink in hand, in minutes. A roast chicken, a dish of fresh broccoli in white wine, a baked potato, a green salad, and a classic cheesecake (all recipes that are in this book). It took little more than a half hour and there was no hot kitchen to take the pleasure out of it.

The five steps we used in cooking this dinner may prove instructive. (1) The cheesecake was cooked first to allow it time to cool. It took 7 minutes. (2) Next came the chicken. After 15 minutes the chicken came out of the oven and "sat" wrapped in aluminum foil for the carry-over cooking time. (3) The potatoes were cooked in about 7 minutes. (4) While the potatoes were setting, we cooked the broccoli in 3½ minutes. (5) While the broccoli was setting, we whipped up a green salad. No wasted moments, and the entire dinner on that hot night required only 32½ almost effortless, heat-free minutes.

Also, the chicken was cooked on the serving platter, the broccoli in the dish in which it would be served, the baked potatoes on a paper towel. The leftover cheesecake in its glass dish went into the freezer. Dishwashing was a breeze that night!

Research among many owners of microwave ovens revealed that most of them had purchased their microwave oven because they believed it would provide easy, casual cookery: that all they would have to do is place a dish of food in the oven, press a button, and presto! in seconds, or minutes, it was ready without any further effort from them.

It *is* the easiest way to cook. But it is not completely casual. Not much effort is required. But some is. Dishes must be rotated. Food must be stirred. Accumulated liquid must be removed. You can't totally neglect what is cooking in the oven.

All of this is true of many microwave ovens. But now with some ovens, waves are evenly distributed by fans, which means the food cooks evenly without you having to move the cooking dish or stir the food. Also, with the introduction of the microwave/convection oven, breads will crust and pastry will brown. However, even if you do not have this new model, you can cook breads and pastries. They will be tasty and cooked well, but not as appealing to the eye.

A Word of Warning

The greatest harm you can do to a microwave oven is to operate it empty. Without the food to concentrate on, the microwaves can work on the glass or ceramic floor of the oven, fusing and even destroying it. Even the most expensive and integral part of the oven, the magnetron tube, could be damaged by operating an oven empty for a half hour or more. Keep a glass of water in your oven so you never run the risk of operating it empty.

What Are Some of the Drawbacks?

Without the convection feature, anything that remains in the oven less than 15 minutes cannot brown. This means that steaks, chops, hamburgers, and other small pieces of meat will not brown.

We have found that the microwave oven is perfect for cooking for two, or for four or six, but we use caution beyond that number. When you prepare large quantities of food, say for eight to ten or even more, then the cooking times are much longer and you also have to do more manipulation, turning, rotating, stirring, etc. You may find the conventional stove better for large feasts.

What Kind of Utensils Can I Use with the Oven?

You don't have to go out and buy a whole new line of cooking utensils for your microwave oven. But you will not be able to use *any* of your beautiful copper, or enameled cast-ironware. In fact, in most cases anything with metal is taboo. We often will suggest that you place small strips of aluminum foil on protruding areas, such as the ends of chicken legs and wings and the bone end of a roast, to prevent them from overcooking. Why? Metal reflects microwaves.

For years we have been advised never to use metal in microwave ovens. Today that situation is changing. One manufacturer is now using metal in its "active" appliances. Some of these metal components have a nonstick surface coating, and others are constructed of ferrite, a special metal composition that is more or less a microwave magnet. These new devices function effectively because of the form and shape of the metal.

The situation to avoid at all costs is metal touching metal. When metal comes in contact with other metal utensils or the metal wall of the oven, "arcing" will occur. Arcing is a sustained discharge of electricity, and can pit the wall of the oven.

We'd suggest not using copper, aluminum, or ironware pots. Try to use only the "professional" metal cookware created by microwave scientists and engineers.

When you do use metal, you must realize that it reflects microwaves, resulting in imperfect cooking. The waves cannot pass through metal. You should therefore be careful with frozen TV dinners that have aluminum trays. First, remove the top portion. Place the tray in the *direct center* of the oven. The metal sides of the tray will deflect the microwaves, but the waves will enter from the top, defrosting, then heating the food. This, of course, will take somewhat longer than it would if the tray were of special plastic or cardboard through which the microwaves could pass. We obtained best results from aluminum trays ¾ inch or less deep; they were shallow enough for the top action of the microwaves to penetrate quickly. With the trays placed in the center of the oven there is no arcing and no danger to the microwave oven.

A metal shish-kebab skewer covered with meat cubes does all right in the microwave oven, and so do metal clamps or clips placed on large chickens or turkeys.

When in doubt, it is always best to check with the manufacturer of your microwave oven.

In our recipes we recommend that you use a "glass casserole" to alert you to the fact that glass, not metal, should be used most often. We do not usually state a specific-sized dish, assuming that your eye will tell you what size cooking utensil to use, as it does in conventional cookery.

We suggest that you do not use an overly large utensil unless you are using quite a bit of liquid, in which case an oversize dish will prevent spillovers. Food, however, cooks better if it is not in a container with lost space. The old French chefs' admonition holds true for microwave cooking: "Cook in a pot just large enough to hold what you will cook." Common sense will tell you not to cook a stew in a shallow dish, place a game hen in a big pot, or a turkey in a small one.

If you are uncertain whether a dish is safe for microwave use, here is a simple test:

Place a glass of cool tap water in the dish you are testing. Heat for exactly two minutes. If the water is almost hot, and the dish cool, that dish is all right. If the dish is just slightly warm around the edges, use it only for a short period of cooking. If the water has remained cool and the dish hot, *do not use that dish.*

The food you are cooking should also be a determining factor. If you're cooking a food with a thick layer of fat (such as meat) or a high amount of sugar (such as icing or maple syrup), select a dish that can take higher heats. Heat-resistant glass is ideal. Use plastics with great caution.

The length of time that food is in the oven is important. When you warm food, it's in the microwave oven a short time, therefore a paper plate or a plastic cup is fine for warming leftovers or heating coffee. But if you're cooking food, such as baking a meat loaf or making gravy, you need a dish that will take hot food for a longer period of time. Once again, heat-resistant glass or glass-ceramic is a good choice.

The type of cooking you do will indicate the kind of dish to use. Sometimes foods require several methods of cooking; this is called complementary cooking. In such cooking, you'll need a dish that can take different types of heat. For instance, if you're browning the food on top of the range before putting it into the microwave oven, you'll need a dish that will take both direct heat and microwaves. Here's a job for a glass-ceramic dish—it saves transferring food from one dish to another and saves dishwashing time, too. Often the food can even be served in the same dish.

Here is a quick reference list of utensils that can be used in the microwave oven.

Plastics. Much has happened in the world of plastics. A chemical company recently created a tough, unbreakable thermoplastic resin made of polycarbonate. This material has complete transparency to microwave energy and low heat absorption, which permits food to cook more uniformly and about 20 percent faster than in ceramic or glass cookware. This plastic is dishwasher safe, requires no base of flour or grease, and can be flexed for easy removal of foods. The nonporous surface also makes it stain-resistant and easy to clean. Refer to the manufacturer's recommendations before using any "cooking" plastic. For example, some polycarbonates will dry or crack in temperatures over 350°.

Polypropylene should be used with caution: Heat above 230° can cause distortion. Any heat above the boiling point of water is not recommended. Fat of any kind will cause this plastic to melt.

Polysulphone is resistant to most distortion from high temperatures of foods.

Polystyrene can melt and distort when used in heat over 210°, so its use should be limited to heating sandwiches, some leftovers, and beverages.

Plastic picnic utensils, hard trays, thermal cups, mugs, bowls, foam cups and dishes are safe but just for short cooking periods at low temperatures— two minutes at the most. Plastic baby bottles with the nipple removed are fine for warming formulas or milk.

Plastic wrap can be used for short periods to warm up leftovers, soup, coffee, etc. Just remember to slit it before removing it or you risk a steam burn. Plastic cooking pouches work, too, but slit them also.

Melamine should not be used. It gets very hot and can burn you.

Paper. Paper towels, cartons, cups, and plates can be used for short periods for heating, defrosting, or absorbing moisture. For example, a hot dog in its bun can be wrapped in a paper napkin and be ready to eat in 40 seconds. The napkin will absorb some moisture and prevent the bun from becoming too soggy. The hot dog and bun will *almost* have that "ballpark" steamed flavor. Prolonged periods under microwaves can cause paper to scorch or even burn. Do not use plastic-coated paper as it can melt.

You can use wax paper; it helps prevent splattering.

Wood. You should avoid wood. Moisture in wood evaporates under microwaves and can cause the wood to crack. Many microwave-oven manufacturers say that wood can be used for *short* periods, but we advise against it.

Straw. There is really no reason to use straw in the microwave oven. But if you have a fancy straw basket for bread or rolls and want to serve them hot in that basket there is no reason why they can't be heated briefly in the basket.

More on dishes. Round dishes are most efficient, allowing microwaves to enter food from all sides equally. In a square or rectangular dish, food cooks faster in the corners, leaving the center undercooked.

Round dishes *without* a center, such as a ring mold, may be the best of all. Meat loaves cook perfectly in a ring mold. If you experiment, you'll find many recipes will work better in a ring mold.

Shallow dishes. Low-sided shallow dishes expose more food surface, and thus the food cooks more quickly.

Deep dishes. If you are cooking "soupy" recipes with milk, water, or stock base, there is every possibility that the superfast waves will cause a boil-over if you don't use a deep dish.

Racks. Racks elevate meat and poultry from their juices or drippings, preventing steaming or overcooking in places.

Using Dishes in Your Microwave Kitchen

Type of Utensils/Dishes	Microwave Oven	Conventional Oven	Top of Range	Broiler	Freezer	Dishwasher
Heat-resistant glass (without metal parts or decorations)	Yes	Yes	No	No	Yes	Yes
Glass-ceramic (without metals or plastic parts)	Yes	Yes	Yes	Yes	Yes	Yes
Pottery Earthenware Stoneware Fine china/porcelain	See manufacturer's directions or test	See manufacturer's directions	No	No	See manufacturer's directions	See manufacturer's directions
Paper	Yes (short time)	No	No	No	Yes	No (not reusable)
Straw/wood	Yes (short time)	No	No	No	No	No
Plastics	See manufacturer's directions (usually short time only)	No	No	No	See manufacturer's directions	See manufacturer's directions

Metal cookware/ bakeware	No	See manufacturer's directions	Yes	See manufacturer's directions	Yes	See manufacturer's directions
Metal decorations on glassware, dinnerware	No	See manufacturer's directions	See manufacturer's directions	See manufacturer's directions	See manufacturer's directions	See manufacturer's directions
Glazed glass/ ceramic dinnerware	No	Yes	No	No	Yes	Yes
Crystal/cut glass Antique glassware	No	No	No	No	Not recommended	See manufacturer's directions
Microwave browning dish	Yes	Yes	No	No	Yes	Yes

2

BUYING GUIDE TO MICROWAVE OVENS

SOME OF the smaller microwave ovens take up little more space than a toaster oven. The bigger microwave ovens can be much bulkier. The ovens are usually classed by capacity—as subcompact (an interior of 0.5 cubic foot or less), compact (0.6 to 0.7 cubic foot), mid-sized (up to 1 cubic foot), and full-sized (bigger yet). Although some companies specialize in a single size of oven, most manufacturers offer three or four different sizes, with as many as six or seven distinct models per size.

Size designations, however, are poorly defined, and often differ from one manufacturer to another. Furthermore, the interior size may not correspond with the space the oven occupies in your kitchen. For that reason, an oven's "space efficiency"—its ratio of capacity to external size—is a key judgment whenever you shop for microwave ovens.

Not only do an oven's outer dimensions have to fit the space available in your kitchen, its interior ought to fit your cookware. The cooking cavities of ovens with similar capacities can vary quite a lot in shape. You might want to take along a favorite casserole dish when you shop to help you check interior space.

The efficiency of an oven's design and the exact shape of its interior matter most among the small and medium-sized models. Any full-sized model will be spacious enough for just about anything you'd want to cook. It should also be a faster cooker. But even the most space-efficient big model occupies a lot of space.

How Fast Do They Cook?

Cooking time is a main selling point for microwave ovens. In general, the bigger the oven, the faster it will cook. Bigger ovens typically have a bigger magnetron. In the majority of full-sized ovens, the magnetron produces around 700 watts of power available for cooking. Subcompacts and compacts generally produce about 500 watts; we estimate that the average small oven takes about 30 percent longer than a full-sized model for the same job. There's a wide range of power among the smaller ovens, however, with some models producing only about 200 watts.

In small chores, such as baking one potato, those power differences may just mean a minute more or less in cooking time. But for multiple portions or a big dish like a casserole, the difference could be 10 or 15 minutes.

High power can also speed up defrosting or the partial cooking of large items. You can, for instance, speed up the roasting of a turkey by cooking it partially in a microwave oven, then transferring it to a regular oven to finish up and crisp the skin. Not every dish needs to be cooked at a high power setting, so high-powered ovens don't always have an edge.

Features to Consider

As the number of first-time buyers decreases, manufacturers aim their products more and more at the replacement market. That's where lots of fancy features come into play. Some models come loaded with things that are supposed to help you cook. Their controls present a level of complexity not typically found elsewhere in the kitchen, or perhaps in the whole house.

If you're considering the more elaborate models, you'll want to check the usefulness of their built-in "intelligence." Some of these models are smarter than others. If you don't want to use an oven's automatic features, you can also set it by hand, with the help of the instruction manual and the display.

Controls, displays. Exact timing is important in microwave cookery. Electronic controls are fortunately the norm. They let you set even the shortest cooking time exactly. Dial-type mechanical timers, typically found on less-expensive ovens, are less precise.

Control layouts are worth checking when you shop. Many of the full-sized models have electronic touch pads that give an audible signal when programmed, some with the numbers conveniently arranged like a push-button telephone's. A few models have setups that are less logical and easy to use—numbers laid out in a single column, for instance, or in a pair of columns for odd and even numbers. The digital electronic displays vary in helpfulness and in clarity.

The variety of programming steps among today's models include some niceties and some quirks. The displays in some models, for instance, will show you verbal prompts ("Time?", "Start?", or "Code?", say) to help you program them. One lets you program power-level and time commands in any order. Another must be set for high power whenever you want to cook that way; all others save you the extra step and cook at full power unless instructed otherwise.

Power levels. Most models provide 10 power levels, but 5 levels are quite sufficient for any cooking task.

Sensors, temperature probes. Here's where the ovens' intelligence shows. Several models include sensors that eliminate the need to figure cooking time and power levels. They do so by detecting moisture escaping from covered food.

If you were cooking broccoli, say, in an oven with a moisture sensor, you'd set the oven on automatic, look up broccoli's cooking code, enter that and perhaps additional codes indicating the weight or the doneness you prefer, and turn on the oven. The broccoli cooks automatically.

Sensors are especially handy for cooking vegetables and reheating foods. For cooking bulky foods such as meat loaf or large casseroles, a temperature probe works better. Probes are a common feature, especially among full-sized ovens.

A probe works rather like a meat thermometer. Attached to a cable that plugs into the oven wall, the probe skewers the food; the desired internal temperature is selected on the oven's key pad. You then set the appropriate power level; feedback from the probe controls the cooking.

The probes work best if slipped into food at an angle. A probe stabbed in vertically may get too close to the pan's bottom, where it can give a false reading.

Programs. Sensors and probes represent "intelligence" that gets feedback from the food. A more abstract form of machine intelligence lies in preprogrammed instructions. Some models come from the manufacturer already programmed with instructions for cooking common foods; you enter the weight and the kind of food, and the program sets the time and power level. Other models allow you to program your own instructions and store them in the oven's memory.

Turntable. Every oven distributes microwave energy in its own special pattern, with its own "hot spots." A turntable won't necessarily make food cook more evenly, but the cooking pattern will be more predictable. A trayful of turntable-cooked brownies, for instance, may cook in a bull's-eye pattern.

A turntable spares you the need to turn foods periodically as they cook, as some recipes demand. On the other hand, the turntable reduces an oven's capacity, a sacrifice that makes itself especially felt in a small oven. You really don't need one if you use your microwave for reheating foods and auxiliary cooking. You can always buy a wind-up turntable later on, if you change your mind.

Door. Check the door's convenience in the store. Look for a comfortable handle, in some cases with a release button or trigger on the door itself.

Now You're Cookin'

In-store checks, of course, tell you little about how an oven will perform. To pin that matter down, we ran some practical cooking tests, using the oven's sensor or probe where possible.

We set each oven at the power its maker recommended and made a simple meat loaf. If the oven came with a temperature probe, we set it at 160° before impaling the meat. When each loaf was done, we checked to see how evenly it had been cooked.

Some ovens required us to try several times, since their recommended power settings turned out not to be the best ones. That aside, the majority did a fine job. The loaves had dark (but not browned) outsides and medium-done insides; the slight burned area around the probe in many loaves was a very minor flaw. Several ovens, however, distributed their energy rather unevenly, leaving some areas overdone and others in need of further cooking.

The test also demonstrated the importance of letting foods sit after cooking. Internal heat redistribution during that "rest" period can mean the difference between an underdone dish and one that comes out just about right.

Reheating cold food (we put together a plate of meat loaf, green beans, and mashed potatoes) is one of the most common microwave chores, but only one did an outstanding job. In fact, that model did well with two dishes at a time, double-decked on its removable rack.

Thawing frozen food (we used meat loaf again) also turned up interesting differences. Most models have a special defrost mode or control. The three models that merely have you set a time and power level didn't do well in terms of speed and uniformity of results. But then, neither did some that have a special defrosting regime. However, even the poorest performers were satisfactory, though they tended to need considerable time (35 minutes or more). We had to turn the meat at least once in all models except those with a turntable.

Microwave ovens aren't the ideal medium for baking, but they can be used for brownies and other dense baked goods. Brownies, indeed, are a good index of an oven's energy distribution; uneven performers can easily over-bake until brownies are crumbly in spots.

One of the most popular supermarket items made specially for microwaving is popcorn. Even the best microwave ovens will leave a fair number of unpopped kernels.

Set for less than full power, a microwave oven cycles on and off to reduce the energy it delivers to food. With high-powered ovens, it's especially important that the oven throttle itself down adequately in the medium-to-low range. Otherwise, it may overcook heat-sensitive foods (such as those based on eggs) or slender items like turkey legs, or it may start to cook items you merely meant to defrost. It's also best if the oven cycles on and off frequently, rather than delivering a large blast of energy followed by a long rest period.

Looking at Safety

All the tested ovens were well within the U.S. Bureau of Radiological Health's standard for microwave-radiation leakage. A door seal on all recent models minimizes leakage even when slight gaps develop between the door and the oven. Furthermore, all the tested models have at least two interlocks that keep the oven from working if the door isn't tightly closed. If the tiny radiation leakage that remains concerns you, staying several feet away when the oven is working will minimize your exposure.

Microwave cookery doesn't heat up cooking utensils directly, but the hot food inside can. Pot holders are a good idea when removing food from the oven. When removing a lid or plastic wrap, be careful of escaping steam. As we mentioned in chapter 1, don't deep-fry in a microwave oven. And watch for hot spots in foods with fillings or mixed textures, such as fruit tarts and blueberry muffins.

Recommendations

The allure of a full-sized oven lies in its yawning food cavity, big enough for just about any dish, and the built-in cooking aids that many models provide. Among the full-sized models are several ovens with intelligent—and intelligible—controls and instructions. You would do well to also consider the manufacturer's reliability record for service; if you are considering a model that carries an extended warranty (more than the minimal one year for parts and labor), so much the better.

Even if your cooking needs dictate large capacity, a full-sized oven isn't the only answer. An intermediate model should be ample for most foods, with more than enough in power and features. Yet it won't overwhelm your kitchen counter, and it should be relatively easy on your purse.

If you want an oven merely for thawing frozen foods and reheating leftovers, a compact model may be all you need.

Which Have Been Most Reliable?

Fancy ovens like the ones we tested have lots of features to go wrong. To see which brands might hold up best, we asked readers, in our 1987 Annual Questionnaire, for their repair experiences with microwave ovens. The repair indexes here show how some 52,000 households fared with full-sized ovens with electronic touch controls, all bought new from 1983 to 1987.

As the chart shows, brands at the top have had a much better repair record than those at the bottom, as measured by the percentage of respondents whose ovens needed at least one repair. (Since appliances tend to need more fixing as they age, we adjusted the data to compensate for differences in oven age between brands.)

Differences in score of three points or less aren't meaningful, so there are a reasonable number of comparatively reliable brands to choose among. Note that Whirlpool and Litton, the makers of two of the ovens that performed best in our tests, came out significantly worse than any others on the list. Owners of an oven from the most reliable brands reported repairs at about a quarter to a third the rate needed by Whirlpool and Litton ovens.

You might expect controls, especially electronic ones, to be trouble spots. However, only 3 percent of the controls had ever needed to be fixed. Electronic controls were no more troublesome than manual ones, according to our readers.

Listings are in order of reliability, as published in a January 1988 report.

Repair Index

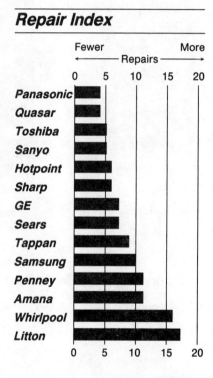

Note that our data apply only to brands—individual models may fare better or worse than the brand as a whole. And our data are historical—an important caveat in a market whose technology is changing swiftly. Companies can change ownership, improve or relax their quality control, or redesign their lines, all of which might affect a brand's long-term performance. The brand's past, then, doesn't inevitably predict a model's future. Still, we believe you can improve your odds of getting a reliable oven by choosing from brands near the top of this chart.

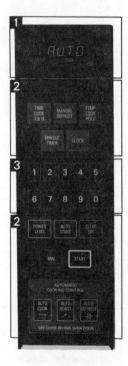

Litton 2494

Whirlpool
MW8900XS

General Electric
JE1465G

Approaches to Complicated Controls

1 Display. As the oven cooks, the display may show you your food's temperature during cooking, the power level in use, or the cooking mode you've selected. The displays of the Litton and the GE show you verbal prompts to help you program them or to instruct you to, say, turn a roast in the oven. When the oven's not in use, the display serves as a digital clock and can be used as a timer.

2 Command Pads. These tell the oven what to do, and in what order; many of them are used in combination with the number pads. A press of a command pad is often the first step in a sequence for entering cooking or defrost time, time of day, cooking temperature, power level, codes for automatic cooking, or a food weight for automatic defrosting.

3 Number Pads. You use the number pads to give the oven a time, a cooking power, or a food setting. We preferred the logical, telephone-style layout of the Whirlpool; the other setups are less familiar and require your fingers to move longer distances to set them.

Guide to the Ratings

Listed in order of estimated quality. Except where separated by heavy rule, quality differences between closely ranked models were slight.

1 Brand and model. We tested top-of-the-line models, for the most part. In most lines, however, you can find cheaper models with fewer features that should perform similarly to the ones we tested. See the Features table on pages 26 to 29.

2 Price. What CU paid for each oven, often much less than the maker's suggested retail price (see the Features table). + indicates shipping is extra.

3 Size. The key measurements for fitting a microwave oven into your kitchen, rounded to the next higher quarter-inch. If your oven is to be slipped under or beside a wall cabinet, note that some models require a bit of extra clearance for vents at the top. Pay attention to depth, too—set on a standard 24-inch-deep counter, the Litton allows only 4 inches of space in front of the oven on which to place a dish. The Whirlpool and KitchenAid, on the other hand, allow 8 inches.

None of these ovens are sylphs. Weights range from 43 to 69 pounds.

4 Capacity. The manufacturer's claimed figure, which was usually within one-tenth of a cubic foot of the oven's usable capacity as measured by CU. Exceptions are noted. They're all models whose turntables must be in place when the oven is used and whose usable capacity is the cylindrical space above the turntable.

5 Space efficiency. None of these models is much less bulky than the others. Still, some offer greater capacity for the space they occupy.

6 Automation. The help in cooking that the oven itself supplies. Models scored lowest here have only a temperature probe or automatic defrost; those a cut above offer both automatic defrost and a probe. Models that add to those features some built-in or user-programmable recipes scored in the middle (the Panasonic has a moisture sensor but no temperature probe). Models scored highest have a sensor keyed to a large number of recipes, as well as a temperature probe and automatic defrost.

7 Instructions. How much help the manufacturer provides in the user's manual.

8 Display. All were clear, but some had larger, brighter numbers than others. The Litton, GE, J.C. Penney 863-2820, and Hotpoint also display word prompts to help you program them. All displays can serve as countdown kitchen timers. However, with models that lack a special timer-control pad, you'd have to set the oven to run at zero power, causing the blower and oven light to be on while the timer works.

9 Speed. Based on our tests in heating measured amounts of water. The speedier models can cook about 10 percent faster than the slower ones. The minor difference isn't attributable to differences in magnetron power, since all models are rated at 700 watts; some models are particularly sensitive to where foods are placed in the oven.

10 Reduced power. Set for less than full power, the ovens cycle on and off to reduce the energy they deliver to food. It's important that high-power ovens like these throttle themselves down adequately at their medium-to-low settings. Otherwise, they would overcook delicate foods or slender items, or start to cook items you merely meant to defrost. Models that scored highest here were on about 10 percent of the time at Low, about 20 percent on their manual Defrost setting, and about 50 percent at Medium.

It's also best if the oven cycles on and off swiftly. Many foods could overcook if an oven reduced power by alternating large blasts of energy and long rest periods. The Advantages and Disadvantages columns note models with particularly good or bad cycling behavior at low settings.

11 Temperature probe. This test told us how evenly the ovens cooked when regulated by their probe. We cooked a two-pound meat loaf in each oven at the recommended power-level setting (usually Medium or Medium-High). The recommended probe settings varied from 150° to 170°; we used 160°. (In calibrating the probes, we found that some were off by as much as 17 degrees.)

12 Reheating. We warmed a plastic plateful consisting of a cold, ¼-pound slice of meat loaf, 24 green beans, and a scoop of mashed potatoes. We used an oven's reheat program, if it had one; otherwise, we set the oven as its maker recommended.

13 Defrosting. All but the Tappan, White-Westinghouse, and Frigidaire have a special defrost cycle. With some, you program in the weight of food and the oven defrosts it for a specific time. Or you set the time and let the oven change the power level automatically. There are some other

Ratings of Microwave Ovens

Ratings should be read in conjunction with the table of Features, as published in a **January 1988** report.

① Brand and model	② Price	③ Size, in.	④ Capacity, cu. ft.	⑤ Space efficiency	⑥ Automation	⑦ Instructions	⑧ Display	⑨ Speed
Litton 2494	$328	14 × 24 × 19¾	1.5	●	●	●	◔	●
General Electric JE1465G	329	15 × 23¾ × 16¼	1.4	◔	●	◔	◔	●
Whirlpool MW8900XS	335	15 × 24 × 15¾	1.3	●	◔	◔	●	○
KitchenAid KCMS135	385	15¼ × 24 × 15¾	1.3	●	◔	◔	●	○
J.C. Penney Cat. No. 863-2820	370+	14½ × 23¾ × 16¼	1.4	◔	○	●	◔	○
Amana Radarrange RS470P	350	14¼ × 21¾ × 17¾	1.2	●	○	○	●	●
J.C. Penney Cat. No. 863-1962	250+	14½ × 24¼ × 18①	1.4	●	●	●	●	○
Quasar MQ7796AW	245	15 × 24 × 17¼②	1.4	●	●	●	●	●
Sharp R9580	289	14½ × 24½ × 18¾	1.5③	○	●	●	○	●
Hotpoint RE1450	255	14½ × 24½ × 16¼	1.4	◔	●	◔	◔	○
Goldstar ER711M	229	14½ × 24½ × 18①	1.4	●	○	◖	○	○

variations, too. In tests with 2-pound meat loaves, we checked how fast the ovens defrosted and how well the food was unfrozen, without overwarm areas. The Whirlpool and KitchenAid were fastest (15 minutes, including some standing time for the food). The Sharp was nearly as fast (18 minutes) and gave even slightly better results. The slowest models took 35 minutes or more.

14 Popping corn. We used popcorn specially packaged for microwave use. Even the best ovens left a fair amount of unpopped kernels.

15 Baking brownies. We cooked a packaged microwave brownie mix in each oven and judged the brownies' evenness of cooking by their appearance, texture, and height.

16 Interior visibility. A coarse screen on the oven's window, especially if combined with a dim interior light, can make it hard to see inside.

17 Noise. All have a blower that works when the oven is on. The quietest are unobtrusive, but the noisiest could be annoying in an otherwise quiet kitchen.

18 Door opening. Our judgments of how easy the oven doors are to open. All doors swing to the left.

Better ◉ ◐ ○ ◑ ● Worse

Reduced power (10)	Temperature probe (11)	Reheating (12)	Defrosting (13)	Popping corn (14)	Baking brownies (15)	Interior visibility (16)	Noise (17)	Door opening (18)	Advantages	Disadvantages	Comments
◐	—	◐	◐	◐	◉	◑	○	◐	A,F,G	k	B,I
○	◐	◐	◐	◐	○	◐	◐	◐	—	—	I
○	◐	◉	◉	◐	○	○	◑	◐	E, F	—	E,H,I
○	◐	◐	◉	○	○	○	◑	◐	E	—	E,H,I
○	○	◐	◐	◐	○	○	○	◐	E	e	G,J
○	○	○	◐	○	◑	○	◑	◑	C	c	B,H,K
○	◐	◐	◐	◐	◑	◐	◐	◐	E	—	F,G
◔	◐	○	○	◐	◐	○	○	○	—	i	I,L
○	◐	◐	◉	◐	◐	◑	○	◑	G	d,g,k	A,I
◐	◐	◐	◐	○	◐	○	◑	◐	—	f	E
○	○	○	◐	◐	◑	○	◐	◐	E	—	E,F,M

Ratings of Microwave Ovens (continued)

① Brand and model	② Price	③ Size, in.	④ Capacity, cu. ft.	⑤ Space efficiency	⑥ Automation	⑦ Instructions	⑧ Display	⑨ Speed
Caloric MPS219	210	14¼ × 21¾ × 17¾	1.2	⊖	●	⊖	⊖	⊖
Panasonic NN7706	258	15 × 24 × 17[2]	1.4[3]	○	○	⊖	⊖	⊖
Sears Kenmore Cat. No. 87343	270+	15½ × 23¼ × 19	1.4	⊖	⊖	○	⊖	⊖
Maytag CME701	359	15 × 25¼ × 17¾[2]	1.2	○	⊖	○	○	○
Tappan 56-4477	249	15¾ × 23½ × 17¼	1.3	⊖	●	⊖	○	⊖
White-Westinghouse KM937K	225	15¾ × 23½ × 17¼	1.3	⊖	●	◐	○	○
Frigidaire MC1360E	250	15¾ × 23½ × 17¼	1.3	⊖	●	◐	○	○
Emerson AT1551	300	15¼ × 24¼ × 18[1]	1.4[3]	○	●	◐	○	○

[1]Vents at top rear; requires additional inch or so height clearance.
[2]Vents at top front; may require additional inch or so height clearance.
[3]Usable capacity significantly less than claimed.
[4]Lacks special defrost feature.

Specifications and Features

All: • Have touch pads that provide audible signal when programmed. • Have display that shows time of day when oven isn't in use. • Have interior light that goes on when oven is operated. • Operate at 120 v ac. • Have magnetron rated at 700 watts and drew 1270 to 1480 watts.

Except as noted, all: • Have reduced power settings that provide from 13 to 20 percent of full power at the lowest setting, 30 to 50 percent at Defrost and 53 to 61 percent at Medium. Oven cycles on for 4 to 5 sec. per cycle at lowest setting, 8 to 13 sec. at Defrost and 12 to 16 sec. at Medium. • Do not require that power level be programmed when cooking at full power. • Have control that lets display serve as a kitchen timer. • Have provision for keeping interior spills from running out. • Have a light-colored painted interior finish. • Have manufacturer's warranty for carry-in service.

Key to Advantages

A— Has shortest cycling times at Low and Medium of all models: 1 sec. at Low, 5 at Medium.

B— Defrost cycling time relatively short: 4 sec.

C— Reduces power at lowest setting by rapid cycling, so provides very even heating for delicate foods.

D— Cooking time and power level can be programmed in any order.

E— Number pad layout is similar to a push-button telephone's; judged logical and easy to use.

F— Reheating 2 dishes at once, using shelf, more uniform and quicker than most.

G— One of few that allows turning a 13½ × 9½-inch baking pan a quarter-turn.

Key to Disadvantages

a— Has turntable that doesn't use oven's entire floor width; large dishes may overlap turntable's raised edge.

b— Tended to cook less uniformly than most.

c— Door must be grasped at bottom to open, so may be harder to open than others, especially if user's fingers are big.

d— Requires a repair person to change interior light bulb.

e— User must program power when cooking at full power.

Reduced power (10)	Temperature probe (11)	Reheating (12)	Defrosting (13)	Popping corn (14)	Baking brownies (15)	Interior visibility (16)	Noise (17)	Door opening (18)	Advantages	Disadvantages	Comments
◓	●	●	●	○	◓	○	◓	●	B	f	D,N
○	—	○	●	○	◓	○	○	○	—	i	A,I,O
○	○	●	●	◓	◓	●	○	●	D,E	b,d	C,F
○	◓	●	◓	○	◓	●	○	◓	C,E	—	H
○	◓	○	○④	○	◓	○	◓	○	—	h	G
○	◓	○	○④	○	○	○	◓	○	—	h	G
○	◓	○	○④	○	○	○	◓	○	—	h,j	E,G
○	—	●	○	◓	○	○	○	●	—	a,h	F,G

f— Percentage of full power at lowest setting too high: 26 to 30 percent.

g— Cycling at all settings longer than most: 6 sec. on at Low, 12 at Defrost, 18 at Medium.

h— Number pads laid out in two columns, odd and even; less convenient than a telephone-style layout.

i— Uses "count-up" programming for time and power level, requiring repeated touches of same pad; judged less convenient than direct-entry system.

j— Contrast of numbers on touch pads judged poor.

k— Number pads arranged in single column, judged inconvenient

Key to Comments

A— Has built-in turntable, which improved cooking uniformity for some tasks but encroaches somewhat on usable space.

B— Flat ceramic interior bottom is easily cleaned but lacks lip to retain sizable spills.

C— Power levels can be entered as percentages, which requires punching two pads, or user can set 10 reduced-power levels with a single stroke, as most ovens do. Although 100 power levels are possible, settings below 10 percent are not reduced significantly.

D— Warranty provision for labor is responsibility of dealer; in-home or carry-in not specified.

E— Warranty is for in-home rather than carry-in service, without service travel charge.

F— Lacks special control for using display as kitchen timer; can be used as timer but oven light and blower may operate.

G— Warranty provides extra year of parts coverage without labor.

H— Warranty provides extra period of touch-panel replacement: 4 years (Whirlpool, KitchenAid); panel and other electronic components: 4 years (Amana), 3 years (Maytag).

I— Has moisture sensor that signals the oven to go into a programmed, final-cook sequence as soon as moisture is detected escaping from covered food.

J— According to manufacturer, replaced by catalog model 863-0725 (sold in stores as 1525).

K— According to manufacturer, replaced by model RS471P.

L— According to manufacturer, replaced by model MQ7797BW.

M— According to manufacturer, replaced by model ER761M.

N— According to manufacturer, replaced by model MPS229.

O— According to manufacturer, replaced by model MN7707.

Guide to Key Microwave-Oven Features

As published in a January 1988 report.

1 Brand and model. Models tested and a selection of those not tested, with each brand's line listed in order of increasing price. Based on the manufacturers' specifications, the untested models should perform similarly to the tested ones. Information on tested models (marked with ●) comes from CU; otherwise, data is from manufacturers. We have omitted models with mechanical controls and no reduced-power settings, a combination apt to overcook many dishes and hard to use for uniform defrosting. Cabinet color goes by brand: All are woodgrain except Caloric (solid brown), Frigidaire (gray), and KitchenAid (silver gray).

2 Price. Suggested retail, as quoted by the manufacturer, or the average price (indicated by *) when a range was quoted. Like other electronic gear, microwave ovens are heavily discounted. For an idea of possible discounts, compare these prices with those CU paid, noted in the Ratings.

3 Controls. Mechanical controls (M) set cooking times rather inexactly; they allow a maximum time of 30 to 35 minutes (entirely sufficient). Most electronic controls allow a maximum of 99 minutes 99 seconds. Count-up touch pads (TC) require you to hold a pad or repeatedly hit the key until the correct number is set. We prefer sequential pads (TS), which let you enter numbers as you'd write them.

4 Power levels. Five levels are plenty. Most models of this size have 10, which you generally set by punching in the desired number. Models with fewer levels typically have you enter the level with a special power-level touch pad. Ovens with 100 levels usually require you to punch in two digits.

5 Cooking stages. A stage is a specific set of time/power-level or temperature/power-level commands. Every oven can execute at least one; those

the effects of "hot" and "cold" spots. A turntable does that for you, at the cost of some interior capacity.

9 Special defrost. An automatic defrost cycle, in its fanciest form, varies the power as food defrosts. A simpler version may work only at a single power level.

10 Automatic short-cook. That manufacturers have invented this feature shows how complex the controls have become. At the press of a single pad, Automatic Short-Cook makes the oven work for a fixed time at high power. Some models vary the time, depending on how many times the pad is pushed. The feature is handy for heating foods whose time and power requirements aren't very fussy—foods with a lot of liquid, for instance.

11 Delay start. This lets you program an oven to turn on at a future time. An unimportant feature in an appliance renowned for speed.

12 Shelf. Ovens with a removable wire rack allow you to heat more plates than would fit on the oven floor alone. The racks, however, upset the energy distribution, so you have to exchange the location of plates during cooking. You should also stagger the plates, so that one doesn't "shade" the other.

13 Tray. A removable glass tray is handy for cleaning at the sink, but can break. Trayless models have ceramic bottoms that must be wiped out if dirtied.

14 Preprogrammed recipes. The number of foods listed in the instructions that are keyed to specific, built-in settings. There may be only a few such settings, but the manufacturer may note many foods that can be cooked at each setting.

with more than one stage can remember a number of stages and perform them in sequence. We count only actual cooking stages in this tabulation, not (as manufacturers sometimes do) delays, pauses, or defrost time.

6 Temperature probe. A skewerlike probe makes it easier to cook large dishes such as turkeys and casseroles. When the probe in the food reaches the programmed temperature, the oven signals and, usually, cycles into a Hold or Keep-Warm phase.

7 Sensor. On these models, sensors register moisture escaping from the food and signal the oven to go into a programmed final cooking sequence. Other ovens, not listed here, may have sensors that detect temperature directly.

8 Turntable. Since no microwave oven distributes its energy with absolute uniformity, many foods should be turned now and then to help reduce

15 Sensor recipes. The number of recipes in the instructions specifically keyed to the use of a sensor, if the oven has one. Cooking with a sensor requires you to set the oven for a specific food or task; in some cases, you must also key in the quantity and weight of the food. Ovens with only a few food categories are simpler to work than those with many choices. Either way, you'll have to rely on some guesswork and experimentation.

16 User-programmed recipes. The number of recipe programs of your own that you can enter into an oven's memory for use in the future.

17 Warranty. The basic terms for the whole unit and the coverage on the magnetron, as stated by the manufacturer. Any additional terms for tested models are noted in the Comments column of the Ratings. Most warranties explicitly include labor for the initial period, whether in factory service centers or by arrangement with dealers. Caloric leaves you to dicker with the dealer about labor coverage.

1 Brand and model	2 Price	3 Controls	4 Power levels	5 Cooking stages	6 Temperature probe	7 Sensor	8 Turntable	9 Special defrost	10 Automatic short cook	11 Delay start	12 Shelf	13 Removable glass tray	14 Preprogrammed recipes	15 Sensor recipes	16 User-programmed recipes	17 Warranty, basic/mgn.
Amana																
RS415T	$220	TS	10	1	—	—	✓	—	—	✓	—	—	—	—	—	1/5 yr
RS458P	250	TS	10	2	✓	—	✓	—	—	✓	—	—	—	—	—	1/5
• RS471P [1]	300	TS	10	1	✓	—	✓	✓	✓	✓	—	—	10	—	—	1/5
Caloric																
MPS218	240	TS	10	1	—	—	✓	—	—	✓	—	—	—	—	—	1/5
• MPS229 [1]	260	TS	10	4	—	—	✓	✓	✓	[2]	—	—	✓	—	—	1/5

① Brand and model	② Price	③ Controls	④ Power levels	⑤ Cooking stages	⑥ Temperature probe	⑦ Sensor	⑧ Turntable	⑨ Special defrost	⑩ Automatic short cook	⑪ Delay start	⑫ Shelf	⑬ Removable glass tray	⑭ Preprogrammed recipes	⑮ Sensor recipes	⑯ User-programmed recipes	⑰ Warranty, basic/mogn.
Emerson																
• AT155I	280	TS	10	2	—	✓	✓	—	✓	—	—	—	—	—	—	1/8
Frigidaire																
MCT1310E	[3]	M	5	—	—	—	—	—	—	—	—	—	—	—	—	1/10
MCI330E	[3]	TS	10	—	—	—	—	—	—	—	—	—	—	—	—	1/10
• MCI360E	[3]	TS	10	✓	—	—	—	✓	✓	—	✓	—	—	—	—	1/10
General Electric																
JE425G	264*	TS	10	2	—	—	—	✓	✓	✓	—	—	—	2	—	3/3
JE435G	294*	TS	10	2	—	—	—	✓	✓	✓	—	—	—	2	—	3/3
JE445G	294*	TS	10	2	—	—	✓	✓	✓	✓	—	—	—	2	—	3/3
JE455G	304*	TS	10	2	—	—	✓	✓	✓	✓	—	—	—	2	—	3/3
• JE465G	319*	TS	10	2	✓	—	✓	✓	✓	✓	—	—	30	—	—	3/3
Goldstar																
• ER76/M [1]	330	TS	10	2	—	—	✓	—	✓	✓	✓	—	—	4	—	2/8
Hotpoint																
RE1440	244*	TS	10	—	—	—	✓	—	✓	✓	—	13	—	—	—	1/5
• RE1450	284*	TS	10	—	—	—	✓	✓	✓	✓	✓	53	—	—	—	1/5
J.C. Penney																
• Cat. No. 863-1962	340+	TS	10	3	✓	—	✓	—	✓	✓	✓	30	—	60	—	1/3
• Cat. No. 863-0725 [1]	350+	TS	10	3	✓	—	✓	✓	✓	✓	✓	6	—	3	—	1/3
KitchenAid																
KCMS132	450	TS	10	2	✓	—	✓	—	[2]	—	—	—	—	—	—	1/10
• KCMS135	475	TS	10	3	✓	—	✓	—	✓	—	—	—	80	—	—	1/10
Litton																
2494	430	TS	10	4	✓	—	✓	—	✓	✓	—	—	40	1	—	1/10

Model	Price	Type																								Rating
Maytag																										
CME301	290*	M	9	—	—	—	—	—	—	—	—	—	—	—	—	—	—	—	—	—	—	—	—	—	—	2/5
CME501	330*	TS	10	—	—	—	—	—	—	—	—	—	—	—	—	—	—	—	—	—	—	—	—	—	2/5
CME601	360*	TS	10	2	✓	✓	✓	—	—	—	—	—	—	✓	—	—	—	—	—	—	—	—	—	—	2/5
•CME701	390*	TS	10	4	✓	✓	✓	✓	✓	✓	✓	—	✓	✓	—	—	—	—	—	—	—	—	—	2/5
Panasonic																										
NN7606	300	TC	6	3	✓	—	✓	✓	—	✓	✓	—	✓	—	—	—	—	—	—	—	—	—	—	1/5
•NN7707 [1]	340	TC	6	3	—	✓	✓	✓	✓	✓	✓	✓	✓	—	—	—	—	—	—	—	8	—	—	1/5
Quasar																										
MQ7757BW	220	TC	6	1	—	—	—	—	—	✓	✓	—	—	—	—	—	—	—	—	—	—	—	—	1/5
MQ7767BW	240	TC	6	3	✓	—	✓	—	—	✓	✓	✓	—	—	—	—	—	—	—	—	—	—	—	1/5
•MQ7797BW [1]	300	TC	6	3	✓	—	✓	—	—	✓	✓	✓	—	—	—	—	—	11	—	11	—	—	—	1/5
Sears																										
Cat. No. 87144	220+	TS	100	2	—	—	✓	—	—	✓	✓	—	—	—	—	—	—	[4]	—	—	—	[4]	—	1/5
Cat. No. 87245	350+	TS	100	3	✓	✓	✓	✓	✓	✓	✓	—	✓	—	—	—	—	25	—	—	—	[4]	—	1/5
•Cat. No. 87343	390+	TS	100	4	✓	✓	✓	✓	✓	✓	✓	✓	✓	✓	—	—	—	10	—	—	—	3	—	1/5
Sharp																										
R9280	300	TS	5	—	—	—	✓	✓	—	✓	✓	—	—	—	—	—	—	9	—	—	—	—	—	2/7
R9480	370	TS	5	3	✓	✓	✓	✓	✓	✓	✓	—	✓	—	—	—	—	9	—	11	—	—	—	2/7
•R9580	400	TS	5	3	✓	✓	✓	✓	✓	✓	✓	✓	✓	✓	—	—	—	—	—	10	—	—	—	2/7
Tappan																										
56-3357	[3]	M	5	—	—	—	—	—	—	—	✓	—	—	—	—	—	—	—	—	—	—	—	—	1/10
56-4277	[3]	TS	10	—	—	—	✓	—	—	—	✓	—	—	—	—	—	—	—	—	—	—	—	—	1/10
•56-4477	[3]	TS	10	—	✓	✓	✓	✓	—	✓	✓	✓	✓	—	—	—	—	—	—	—	—	—	—	1/10
Whirlpool																										
MW8500XS	200	TS	5	—	—	—	✓	—	—	—	—	—	—	—	—	—	—	9	—	—	—	—	—	1/10
MW8650XS	280	TS	10	5	—	✓	✓	✓	✓	✓	✓	✓	✓	—	—	—	—	—	—	—	—	1	—	1/10
•MW8900XS	405	TS	10	3	✓	✓	✓	✓	✓	✓	✓	✓	✓	✓	—	—	—	—	—	80	—	—	—	1/10
White-Westinghouse																										
KM935K	[3]	TS	10	—	—	—	—	—	—	—	✓	—	—	—	—	—	—	—	—	—	—	—	—	1/10
•KM937K	[3]	TS	10	—	✓	✓	✓	✓	—	✓	✓	✓	✓	—	—	—	—	—	—	—	—	—	—	1/10

[1] Replaces tested model; see Ratings. [2] Optional. [3] Not stated by manufacturer. [4] Has feature; manufacturer does not state number of recipes.

3

~~~~~~~~

THE MICROWAVE/CONVECTION OVEN

THE MICROWAVE/CONVECTION oven is a combination that we think is a solid, dependable cooking machine, with many advantages and few disadvantages. With more manufacturers adding the capacity for convection cooking to their microwave lines, we feel that the combination is probably here to stay, giving microwave ovens great, and needed, versatility.

First, let's explain what convection cooking is and how it differs from both the microwave oven and the conventional oven. Since the 1960s the convection oven has been the professional chef's secret weapon for cooking pastry, poultry, and meat to perfection. Pastries and meats come out beautifully brown and crusty. Meats and poultry are moist inside, picture perfect on the outside.

Convection ovens are simply more efficient versions of conventional ovens. No new cooking techniques are required as for the microwave oven. The secret of the convection oven is the noiseless fan that constantly circulates the heated air around the inside of the oven, surrounding and cooking the food. Think of it as a rotisserie in reverse: the heat is turning, not the meat. This type of heat eliminates the "hot spots" that occur in conventional ovens and vary internal temperatures by as much as 50 degrees.

Moreover, the conventional oven uses more energy and is more time-consuming than the convection oven. The convection oven, with a smaller cavity, uses only 1,200 to 1,500 watts, as compared with a conventional oven's 3,000 watts. Normally a convection oven doesn't have to be preheated, but if it is, the small cavity heats quickly. It costs less than five cents an hour to operate a convection oven.

While the moving heat is cooking all surfaces of the food simultaneously, not only is it doing so in about one-third less time than the conventional oven, but also at temperatures 25 degrees to 50 degrees lower than required by an ordinary oven.

But the main reason professional chefs swear by convection cooking is that the technique not only cooks meat uniformly on top and all sides, but quickly sears it, thereby sealing and retaining the natural juices, and making the outside evenly brown and very crisp. (This saves further money by preventing meat shrinkage.)

Therefore, you can use a microwave/convection oven in four ways: as a straight microwave oven; as a straight convection oven; by cooking first with microwave, then switching to convection; or in its most valuable way as a combination microwave/convection. This means that food is being zapped with the fast waves while at the same time, or alternately, the convection cooking is also browning and crisping. In reality, this gives you four ovens in one.

Use the microwave oven for all the energy- and time-saving speedy jobs: defrosting, warming up leftovers, or fast-cooking any food.

Use the convection oven for baking bread, pies, cakes, cookies—all of the floury foods that the convection oven cooks as well as any other appliance can.

Use the microwave/convection combination on all roasts and poultry. Not only do they cook quickly but they come out brown and crusty on the outside and juicy and moist inside.

This brief chapter is not intended as the last word on microwave/convection cooking. But here are a few simple recipes that we have developed to show the versatility of this unique oven and cooking method.

HERB-BUTTERED CHICKEN

Microwave, then convection

½ cup (¼ pound) butter or
  margarine, softened
1 large garlic clove, minced
½ teaspoon dried oregano
¼ teaspoon dried rosemary

¼ teaspoon dried thyme
1 teaspoon salt
½ teaspoon pepper
One 4- to 4½-pound chicken

Place everything except the chicken in a bowl and blend well. Insert 1 tablespoon of the herb butter inside the cavity of the chicken. Truss the chicken. Evenly coat the entire chicken with the remaining herb butter. Place in a shallow casserole. (*Note:* In convection cooking, best results are obtained by cooking in shallow cookware, which enables the fan-driven heat to reach more of the food.) Insert the metal rack in middle guide, or center position. Cover the chicken with waxed paper to prevent splattering. Set microwave on high power for 15 minutes. Remove waxed paper and switch to convection cooking. Cook for 35 minutes at 350°, basting twice.

Test for doneness. An instant-read thermometer should read 165°. Or prick the thickest part of the thigh; if the liquid runs clear, the chicken is done; if yellow, cook another 10 minutes. Let the bird set for 10 minutes, wrapped in foil, before carving. *Serves 4.*

TOMATOES STUFFED WITH BROCCOLI-CUSTARD

Microwave, then convection

4 large, ripe (but not overripe) tomatoes	3 tablespoons water
1 medium-sized onion, minced	Salt and pepper
2 tablespoons butter or margarine	1 teaspoon lemon juice
Small bunch of broccoli (about 1 pound)	¾ cup grated cheddar cheese
	1 egg, plus 1 egg yolk
	⅔ cup medium cream

Cut a thick slice from the top of each tomato. Discard or save for some other purpose. Scoop out the seeds and center pulp from the tomato, leaving enough pulp on the sides to make a substantial shell. Lightly salt the insides and invert to drain.

Cook the onion in the butter for 1 minute on microwave. Separate broccoli and peel stems. Arrange in glass baking dish with buds in center, stems pointing out. Cook in microwave oven with water for 3 minutes. Turn broccoli over and cook 3 minutes more. Let set, covered, for 3 minutes.

In a bowl combine the onion, broccoli, salt, pepper, lemon juice, two-thirds of the cheese, egg, egg yolk, and cream. Blend well. Fill tomatoes with broccoli mixture. Sprinkle with the remaining cheese. Arrange in a shallow baking dish and microwave on full power for 40 seconds. Place on rack in center position and cook on convection, uncovered, for 15 minutes, or until the custard is set, puffed, and golden. *Serves 4.*

LEMON CREAM ROULADE

Convection

Sponge Roulade

4 eggs, separated
⅔ cup sugar
¾ cup sifted flour

¾ teaspoon baking powder
1 teaspoon vanilla
Grated rind of 1 lemon

Beat the egg yolks until light and lemony in color. Gradually beat in the sugar, flour, baking powder, vanilla, and lemon rind. In a separate bowl beat the egg whites with a clean, dry beater until stiff, then fold them into the egg-yolk mixture. Butter a jelly-roll pan. Line it with waxed paper and butter the paper. Pour the batter into the pan. Preheat the convection oven to 350° for 10 minutes. Bake roulade on center-rack position for 10 minutes, or until the top is golden and a toothpick inserted comes out clean. Cover with a moist towel and cool.

Lemon Cream Filling

¾ cup sugar
¼ cup cornstarch
¼ cup flour
1½ cups boiling water

Grated rind and juice of 2 lemons
4 tablespoons butter
4 egg yolks, slightly beaten

In the top of a double boiler, combine the sugar, cornstarch, and flour. Mix well. Gradually add boiling water, stirring. Bring to a simmer on the heat, then cook over hot water for 20 minutes, or until thick. Remove top pan from heat. Stir in the lemon rind and juice. Quickly mix in butter and egg yolks. Place the pan back over the hot water. Continue cooking, stirring until thick and smooth. Cool thoroughly in refrigerator.

To Assemble

Roulade   Lemon cream filling   Confectioners' sugar

Sprinkle confectioners' sugar over the roulade. Lay waxed paper over it. Invert the pan to turn the roulade out onto the waxed paper. Carefully peel off the waxed paper from the bottom of the roulade. Spread the thoroughly cooled lemon filling over the sponge, and roll, using the waxed paper to help. Just before serving, sprinkle with confectioners' sugar. The roulade can be garnished with whipped cream and candied violets and roses, if desired. *Serves 6 to 8.*

PART TWO

~~~~~~~~

MICROWAVE RECIPES

4

~~~~~~~~~

HOW TO USE THE RECIPES

IMPORTANT: Read this introduction before using the recipes. The time given at the beginning of each recipe is total cooking time. The speed-cook setting will be recommended most often.

Just as you experimented with your conventional stove, learning its assets and its limitations, becoming aware of its idiosyncrasies, its uneven baking or broiling results, so will you tinker with your microwave oven—and learn. Consider it your reliable kitchen aid that seldom, if ever, lets you down.

You will note that, unlike other cookbooks for this medium, we have listed cooking time at the top of each recipe, so at a glance you can see approximately how much time a recipe takes, and whether we think it should be cooked on high ("speed-cook") and/or simmered or "slo-cooked" at half power.

All recipes in this book were cooked in a 675-watt microwave oven, with all the up-to-date settings including automatic defrost and slo-cook, besides being computerized.

If you already have an oven, you will have received a book of instructions with it that will key you in on cooking times. Read this manual carefully, following instructions and heeding the hints and suggestions. However, to put everything in one place, here are some of our own helpful hints:

If you own a 500 to 600 watt oven, add about 15 percent to the cooking times for the recipes in this book.

If your oven is in the 400 to 500 watt category, about 35 percent should be added.

In other words, if you have a 500 to 600 watt oven, and you are cooking a recipe in this book that takes 1 minute, you would cook a total of 1 minute 9 seconds. If you are cooking food that takes 5 minutes in this book, it would cook 5 minutes 45 seconds. If the recipe cooks 20 minutes here, you would cook 23 minutes.

If your oven is from 400 to 500 watts, an item that we cook here at 3 minutes would take 4 minutes 3 seconds. Our 20-minute cooking time for your oven would be 27 minutes.

Here is a simple test that will quickly help determine if you need extra cooking time in your oven for these recipes. Pour 6 ounces of water run cold from the tap into a glass. Bring it to a boil in the oven. It should take 2 minutes, or perhaps 2 minutes 15 seconds at most. If the water isn't boiling in this time, you will need at least 1 more minute of cooking time. If it boils more quickly, then, of course, you subtract about a minute.

As you will discover as you use these recipes, cooking times are approximate, and will vary according to power output in your community, and to your own personal tastes.

The commonsense rule of thumb is to *undercook* and *test*. This is mainly what you do with your conventional stove, so cooking by microwave shouldn't take much adjustment. Here is a chart to help you translate cooking times. Cooking times in minutes have been rounded off to the nearest half minute.

	600–700 watt*	500–600 watt add 15%	400–500 watt add 35%
TIME	15 sec.	17 sec.	20 sec.
	30 sec.	35 sec.	41 sec.
	1 min.	1 min.	1.5 min.
	2	2.5	2.5
	3	3.5	4.0
	4	4.5	5.5
	5	6.0	7.0
	6	7.0	8.0
	7	8.0	9.5
	8	9.0	11.0
	9	10.5	12.0
	10	11.5	13.5
	11	12.5	15.0
	12	14.0	16.0
	13	15.0	17.5

600–700 watt*	500–600 watt add 15%	400–500 watt add 35%
14	16.0	19.0
15	17.5	20.5
16	18.5	21.5
17	19.5	23.0
18	20.5	24.5
19	22.0	25.5
20	23.0	27.0
21	24.0	28.5
22	25.5	29.5
23	26.5	31.0
24	27.5	32.5
25	29.0	34.0
26	30.0	35.0
27	31.0	36.5
28	32.0	38.0
29	33.5	39.0
30	34.5	40.5
31	35.5	42.0
32	37.0	43.0
33	38.0	44.5
34	39.0	46.0
35	40.5	47.5
36	41.5	48.5
37	42.5	50.0
38	43.5	51.5
39	45.0	52.5
40	46.0	54.0
41	47.0	55.5
42	48.5	56.5
43	49.5	58.0
44	50.5	59.5
45	52.0	61.0
46	53.0	62.0
47	54.0	63.5
48	55.0	65.0
49	56.5	66.0
50	57.5	67.5
51	58.5	69.0
52	60.0	70.0
53	61.0	71.5
54	62.0	73.0

600–700 watt*	500–600 watt add 15%	400–500 watt add 35%
55	63.5	74.5
56	64.5	75.5
57	65.5	77.0
58	66.5	78.5
59	68.0	79.5
60	69.0	81.0

*Recipes in this book were cooked at this wattage.

The great enemy of most kitchen creations is dryness. With conventional heat we often underestimate the amount of liquid to add and overestimate cooking time. One of these hazards, drying out, is almost eliminated with microwaves. This is *moist* cookery. So you do not add as much liquid as you would in conventional cooking. But again we warn, you can overcook and that can be catastrophic. So go easy. Don't be a spendthrift with microwave speed. Like adding too much salt which cannot be removed, neither can you save a chop, chicken, or a roast that has been under the microwaves too long. We've used restraint with our recipes, timing them on the short rather than the long side.

You'll be reading this so often that you'll probably be sick of it: Food continues to cook after it is out of the microwave oven, so you *must* allow for that carry-over cooking.

Our recipes are mainly for four to six people. If you want to cook for two, cut the recipe and cooking time in half. But watch it carefully, and undercook. For example, although the amount of food may be 50 percent less, it doesn't always follow that the cooking time should also be *exactly* 50 percent less. Play it safe, make it 60 percent less, then add that other 10 percent of cooking time after testing to see if the food is right for your taste.

We have been generous in our amounts, usually allowing half a pound of meat or fish per person. If you wish to reduce that, then, of course, reduce the cooking time.

Read the recipes that you plan to use first. Reading them *twice* is even better. Then plan. For example, if the recipe calls for chopped onions, do the chopping, all the time-consuming chores, first. Then assemble. Gather everything you need in one place so you won't have to hop all over the kitchen.

Place a trivet or a wooden board near the microwave oven on which you can place the hot dish or browning skillet when you take it from the oven. Have pot holders handy, also the spoon or the fork you need for stirring, the spatula for turning food over.

Tips

You do not have to learn how to cook all over again with a microwave oven. But, as with everything, from riding a bicycle to needlepointing a canvas, there are pointers and hard facts that help. Common sense is your best guide.

We find that canned soups make excellent sauces and thickeners. Commercial soups, if properly used, are an asset to many dishes where tasty thickeners or quick sauces are needed.

This is moist cookery. And very fast. Frequently, liquid does not have time to cook down and thicken. If dishes cooked with liquid do not seem thick enough, also use other thickeners besides soups to get the right consistency. Tomato paste, flour and butter blended, cornstarch, arrowroot, eggs and cream, sour cream, and heavy tomato puree are excellent. With a little experimentation, you'll quickly discover what works best for you. As an example, check our recipe for *Sausage alla Pizzaiola,* page 157. Usually that is cooked with tomatoes, not tomato puree. But with microwaves we found the sauce too watery. Tomato puree gave it perfect consistency.

Other books recommend that to prevent splatter you cover food with a paper towel. Fine. But first *smell* that paper towel. One manufacturer does produce special "microwave towels," yet many other standard rolls seem to come impregnated with an unpleasant chemical odor. We do not know what it is, but quite often that chemical odor will be there, and it can be transmitted to the food via microwaves. We once cooked a chicken draped with a paper towel and it ended up tasting as if it had been basted with cough syrup. Waxed paper is safer and an excellent splatter-guard. Plastic wrap is also excellent for quick-cooking foods; it keeps the heat in and aids steaming for even cooking. But do not use it for periods of over 3 or 4 minutes, as it is likely to melt, or at least get sticky and gummy.

You will need to test, rotate, turn, or stir the food from time to time. When you open the door, the cooking stops immediately. When you close the door, the time will take up where it left off so you do not have to add extra time.

If the food isn't hot enough for your taste after the "setting" times that we advise, simply put it back into the oven. But briefly.

Stews and braised meats such as pot roasts are more tender if cooked with the simmer or "slo-cook" setting, which cuts the power 50 percent, and increases the time. However, the slo-cook setting is still fast, cooking in half the time of your conventional stove.

Always place the dish in the center of the oven, thick pieces of food to the outside, thin inside.

If you like food brown and crusty, place it briefly under the broiler of your conventional stove. Or, better still, use your convection setting, if you have one.

Always test for tenderness *after* the "setting" time, for the food will continue to cook for some time after it is out of the oven.

When we say "let set, covered," we mean with aluminum foil, unless otherwise specified.

Test for doneness as you always have, by sight and by touch. A toothpick inserted in the center of a cake will tell if it is done.

As explained, microwaves are drawn to the moisture in food; they take the path of least resistance. Because of the composition of the food itself, there is a higher concentration of heat in certain places. To distribute this heat and assure more even cooking, it often is necessary to change the position of the dish, or of the food itself. Some food should be stirred occasionally; always stir from the outside in. The waves work on the outside first; by stirring "in," the food will cook more evenly.

When heating pastries or a hot dog in a bun, wrapping them in a napkin reduces moisture and sogginess and distributes the heat more evenly.

Vegetables will cook more effectively if the container is covered. Glass, plastic, or paper are good, but we have found if the cooking time is short, plastic is the best because it holds the steam in more effectively, which means the vegetables will be cooked more evenly.

In stews or other dishes requiring various meats and vegetables cooked together, try to cut the meats and vegetables so they are similar in size and shape. Otherwise the smaller pieces will be overdone before the larger ones are cooked.

Temperatures affect cooking. Refrigerated goods take longer than foods that are at room temperature when they are cooked. Warm foods need mere seconds to become very hot.

Arrangement of food is also important. Even cooking results when all food is placed on the same level. For example, spread out lima beans or peas in a single layer in a large dish. Do not stack food. Always have the thicker parts

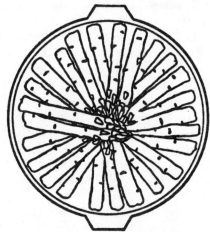

of food toward the outside, the thinner toward the inside. All of this is spelled out in the pertinent chapters.

Standing time (we call it "setting" time) is needed for all food cooked under microwaves. As we have stated and will state again, allowance must be made in the original timing for this carry-over cooking time. Early in our cooking experience we followed to the letter one cookbook's recipe for roasting two game hens, each weighing 1 pound: "12 minutes breast down, then 12 minutes breast up," plus 10 minutes standing time were the instructions. To our taste, the birds were badly overcooked. Now we cook them in exactly 12 minutes, and let them set, wrapped in aluminum foil, for 15 minutes. For us, they are perfect. You will have to experiment, too.

Types of food and the density of food require different cooking times. Ground meat has less density than a steak, thus the steak will take longer to cook. Bread and pastry, which are light and porous, take less time than other compact food of the same weight.

As the volume is increased, so is the time. If you place twice the amount of food in a dish, it usually will take almost twice as long to cook it. But you must experiment with this.

Size and shape of food also are important. Boned roasts fare better than those with the bone because they are more uniformly shaped and will cook more evenly. Trussed poultry cooks more evenly than poultry that is not trussed. Slender, protruding portions will cook more quickly than large, compact areas. Small strips of aluminum foil can be used to cover tips of wings, legs, and the bone end of the leg of lamb, shielding them, reflecting the microwaves, and lessening the cooking.

Be warned that herbs are more powerful in this cookery. Their flavors are not diluted and are almost instantly fixed. Too much dill or oregano on your fish or chicken and you will be eating dill or oregano and won't taste the meat or fish.

About defrosting: You will have received an instructional booklet when you bought your microwave oven. Read it carefully. If you have a new oven, then probably you will have an automatic defrosting setting, which means that you merely have to use that setting and the food will defrost, with heating and setting periods automatically alternated.

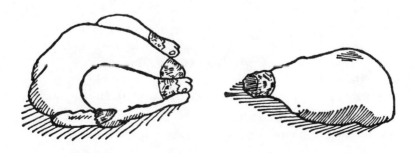

To perform this manually, for each 8 ounces of frozen cooked food, heat 1 minute and let stand 1 minute. If possible, always do this with the icy side up so that as it melts it will conduct heat downward. Continue until there are just a few ice crystals left. After thawing, heat 1½ minutes per cup of food.

The manufacturer of your oven will have included a chart for the defrosting and heating of convenience foods. Many of the food companies are also printing microwave cooking instructions on their packages.

These charts are for your convenience and quick reference. The modern microwave ovens with variable power, built-in computers, sensing probes, etc., operate with almost pinpoint accuracy and come with their own instructional booklets and charts. Regardless, we suggest testing and working on the low side, adding the additional seconds or minutes if needed.

Basic Timings

This chart will give you a good idea of, and will be a quick checkpoint for, most cooking times. We suggest, however, that you read the instructional booklet that came with your oven for other amounts. Be warned that all timings do not increase proportionately when you cook larger amounts of food. It depends on the kind of food.

Poultry

6 minutes per pound, let stand, covered, 10 minutes.

Fish and Shellfish

4 minutes per pound for fish. It is done when easily flaked with a fork.

Shrimp and other shellfish should be just firm, not hard or soft.

Test both fish and shellfish at 3 minutes and let both stand, covered, 2 minutes after cooking.

Beef

Roasts, bone in, 2-rib roast, 5 minutes per pound, rare
                              6 minutes per pound, medium
                              8 minutes per pound, well done
Let stand, covered, 25 minutes.
Same cooking time for 4-rib, but let stand, covered, 40 minutes.

Roasts, rolled, sirloin tip, rolled, rump,
    5½ minutes per pound, rare

7 minutes per pound, medium
8 minutes per pound, well done
Let stand, covered, 20 minutes.

Steaks. Check the instructional booklet that came with the browning skillet (if you will use it, and we advise that you do). One-inch-thick choice steaks take less than 1 minute on each side. Check at 40 seconds.

Veal

Roasts, 7½ minutes per pound, medium
        9 minutes per pound, well done
Let stand, covered, 20 minutes

Chops. See recipes.

Lamb

Rolled, 7½ minutes per pound, medium
        8½ minutes per pound, well done
Let stand, covered, 25 minutes.

Shoulder with bone, 8 minutes per pound, medium
                9 minutes per pound, well done
Let stand, covered, 30 minutes.

Leg, pink, French style, 6 minutes per pound
        American style, 8½ minutes per pound, well done
Let stand, covered, 35 minutes.

Chops. See recipes.

Pork

Fresh roasts, loin, shoulder, fresh ham, etc., 9 minutes per pound.
Let stand, covered, 25 minutes.
Cured, canned, precooked ham, etc., 5 minutes per pound.

Thermometer Readings After Standing Time

All poultry and meats should have a standing time to let the carry-over cooking time finish. If you like to use a meat thermometer (never in the oven, unless it is especially designed for microwave cooking), here is a quick-reference chart. While poultry and meats rest, temperature may rise as much as 20 percent. Always use the thermometer *after* the standing time.

Meat	Internal Temperatures
Beef (rib, rolled rib,	110° to 115° (rare)
rib-eye, tenderloin)	115° to 120° (medium rare)
	130° to 135° (medium)
(boneless rolled rump)	145° to 150° (well done)
Veal (leg, loin, rack,	
boneless shoulder)	160° (well done)
Lamb (leg, shoulder,	125° to 130° (medium rare)
boneless cushion, rib)	145° to 150° (well done)
Fresh pork (loin, leg, ham)	165° to 170° (well done)
Poultry (chicken, turkey,	
goose, duck)	160° to 170°

Quick-Reference Charts for Other Cooking, Heating, and Defrosting

Defrosting meats: 2 to 3 minutes per pound, depending upon size. Check your defrosting instructional booklet.

Heating precooked meats: 30 seconds per serving, depending upon amount

Heating casseroles: 2 minutes per cup

Fresh vegetables: 6 to 7 minutes for 4 servings

Frozen vegetables: the vegetables prepared in sauces, such as eggplant Parmesan and scalloped potatoes, take 5½ to 8 minutes for a 12-ounce package. Stir before serving.

Baked potatoes: 4 minutes for a 7-ounce potato

Warming dinner rolls: 1 to 3, 15 to 30 seconds
                   4 to 6, 30 to 60 seconds

One 1-pound loaf of frozen sliced bread in wrapping: remove metal twist and heat 1½ minutes, rotating one-quarter turn every 30 seconds

Doughnuts: 1 to 3, 15 to 30 seconds
           4 to 6, 30 to 45 seconds
           Box of 12, heat 1 minute, rotate box one-half turn at 30 seconds

Coffee cake, 13-ounce package: remove aluminum foil, heat, icing side up, 2 minutes, rotate dish one-half turn at 1 minute. Let stand 2 minutes.

Heating desserts: such as pie, coffee cake, etc., 15 seconds per serving

Heating milk or water: 2 minutes for 6 ounces

Other Uses of the Oven

The microwave oven will prove to be your most versatile piece of kitchen equipment. You'll find many uses as you let your imagination take over. For example, read how we opened clams in the oven, then went on to prepare an unusual appetizer (page 50). Here are a few bonuses, arranged alphabetically by food item, that we discovered:

Appetizers: All appetizers, your own from the refrigerator or the convenience packages from the grocer, take only seconds to heat, and not much longer to defrost if frozen.

Brown sugar: Soften that stubborn, hard brown sugar. Place it in a small glass bowl with a small slice of apple. Cover with plastic wrap. Heat 15 seconds. The steam from the apple softens the sugar.

Butter: To soften refrigerated butter, unwrap and place ¼ pound or 1 stick on a glass dish. Heat 15 seconds. Let set 5 minutes before using. If the stick is frozen, heat 30 seconds, let set 10 minutes. To melt: heat 1½ minutes. To clarify butter, place ¼ pound in a measuring bowl. Heat 2½ minutes, or until it is melted and boiling. When bubbly, take from the oven. The clear (clarified) butter will float to the top. Pour it off. Discard the rest.

Cheese: Cheese is at its best at room temperature. How often have you forgotten this and brought it out to serve with drinks, finding its personality deadened by the refrigerator? No more. Just pop it into the oven for 15 seconds, or 20, or even 25, depending upon the size of the piece of cheese.

Place a slice of cheese on a piece of apple pie. Heat for 15 seconds, or until it starts to melt.

Cheese sauce for vegetables: Spoon out your choice of processed cheese from the jar into a measuring cup. Heat 1 minute, or until you can stir it, or until it is soft enough to pour over the vegetables.

Chestnuts: To roast 2 dozen raw chestnuts, slash nuts in four places. Arrange in 1 layer in a shallow container. Cook 1 minute, uncovered, stirring at 30 seconds. Nuts should be soft when squeezed. Don't be tempted to cook another minute or they will be overcooked.

Chocolate: To melt: Unwrap a 3-ounce package of squares. Heat in a glass dish 2 minutes. Chocolate curls for pastry: Place unwrapped block of chocolate in the oven. Heat 7 seconds. Scrape the curls off with a vegetable scraper.

Coffee: Don't throw that good perked coffee away. The microwaves will renew it. Store in a measuring cup in the refrigerator. Heat 1 minute per cup, or until hot.

Crêpes: To make them more flexible and easier to handle, place them in a damp towel and heat until just pliable. Time depends upon the number. If they are frozen, time will double.

Croutons: Arrange 4 cups of bread cubes in one layer in a suitable dish, and dry for 6 minutes. Stir every 2 minutes.

Dough: Frozen dough defrosts rapidly, so watch it. Try 10 seconds, then 5 seconds more, depending upon the amount. It should be cold yet pliable.

Egg Whites: Frozen egg whites can be defrosted in the oven.

Fruit: To get more juice from oranges or lemons, heat 1 lemon or orange for 15 seconds. To peel peaches, heat a large peach 20 seconds. Let stand 5 minutes. Peel. Warm up chilled refrigerated fruit such as apples, oranges, or grapes for 15 seconds. They are juicier and more palatable after the chill is off. Quickly rehydrate dried fruits such as apricots or prunes: Place in a bowl, barely cover with water, heat 5 minutes. Let stand 5 minutes.

Herbs: To dry out, place washed and dried fresh herbs on a piece of doubled paper towel. Heat 1½ minutes, or until they can be crumbled. Cool and store in jars with screw tops.

Ice cream: To soften, place 1 pint package on a dish. Heat 15 seconds. Heat 1 quart, 30 seconds; half a gallon, 45 seconds.

Frozen ice-cream pies and cakes: Slice. Heat each portion 10 seconds, perhaps 15, depending upon size. Fresh pie also heats in this length of time.

To defrost frozen puddings: Heat one 4¾-ounce package 30 seconds. Stir, let stand 5 minutes.

Meat bones: Defrost frozen bones for soup or stock.

Milk: Take the chill off milk. It has no flavor coming right out of the refrigerator. Fifteen seconds should do it.

Nuts: To toast 1 cup of raw peanuts: In a shallow glass dish, paper or pie plate, arrange the nuts in one layer. Cook, 6½ minutes, uncovered, stirring every 50 seconds. To toast 1 cup of raw cashews: Arrange in one layer in a shallow container. Cook 9 minutes, uncovered, stirring every 30 seconds. To toast ½ cup of raw whole almonds: Arrange in one layer in shallow container. Cook 7 minutes, uncovered, stirring every 60 seconds.

Spreads and Toppings: Cream cheese (foil wrap removed), cheese, or other appetizer spreads in glass jars (after the metal cover is removed) can be made soft and spreadable in 15 seconds. To warm up maple syrup, remove metal top and heat 40 seconds. Dessert toppings for ice cream can go into the oven right in their glass jars (no metal tops) for 15 to 20 seconds until they are warmed and softened.

Waffles: Heat frozen waffles 35 seconds.

5

~~~~~~~~~

APPETIZERS

An example of the might and the magic of the microwave oven was put into motion one evening when a friend, Roger Gayat, who had moved to Prudence Island, off the coast of Rhode Island, dropped in with three dozen clams that he had gathered that very morning. Fresh clams, from what he claimed were unpolluted waters off his little island, were a rare treat and had to be sampled immediately. But fresh clams are stubborn and very difficult to open. The three of us had a unique idea: We placed six clams in the microwave oven for 30 seconds. Sure enough, they obligingly opened their shells wide enough to accept a clam knife. In seconds we had incomparable clams on the half shell. But more. We also whipped up a tasty appetizer, Clams Oreganato (page 50) and put dinner on the table, all in about 17 minutes.

We had planned to have chicken florentine, but when our friend unexpectedly arrived we learned that this Frenchman, who doesn't cook, but who is married to a Texan who cooks like a Frenchwoman, had had chicken three times that week. So what to do? No problem. The freezer plus the microwaves produced Pasta Bolognese (page 161). We had on hand some frozen ground sirloin, some chicken livers, and a little *filetto* sauce, a tomato sauce with white onions and basil. We defrosted three ground-meat patties in 40 seconds, a half pound of chicken livers in 30 seconds, the pasta sauce in 3 minutes. We sautéed garlic in olive oil under the microwaves, added and cooked the ground sirloin for 2 minutes, then stirred in the pasta sauce. Two minutes later, the chicken livers were added and cooked for 1 minute. The sauce set, covered, while we cooked the pasta under microwaves. *Ecco!* In slightly more than 15 minutes, dinner was ready.

Here is the clam appetizer that proved that it pays to experiment with microwaves:

CLAMS OREGANATO

Speed-cook; 4 minutes

2 garlic cloves, minced
2 tablespoons olive oil
2 small ripe tomatoes, peeled, seeded, and chopped
½ teaspoon salt
¼ teaspoon pepper
1 teaspoon dried oregano
2 tablespoons chopped fresh parsley

2 tablespoons coarsely chopped pine nuts
1 tablespoon minced raisins
3 dozen shucked cherrystone clams, minced (reserve 3 tablespoons of the liquid)
8 tablespoons grated Parmesan cheese
8 tablespoons bread crumbs

In a glass casserole, cook the garlic in the oil 1 minute. Stir in the tomatoes, salt, pepper, oregano, parsley, pine nuts, and raisins. Cook 2 minutes. Stir in the clams and the clam liquid. Cook 1 minute. Blend well. Spoon equal portions into 8 scallop shells, large clam shells, or ramekins. Sprinkle each serving with 1 tablespoon each of cheese and bread crumbs. Place under the broiler of a conventional stove 2 minutes, or until the cheese has melted and the bread crumbs are crusty brown. *Serves 8.*

ELEANOR STONE'S MINI PIZZAS

Speed-cook; 40 seconds

Two 7-ounce cans tomato paste
1 tablespoon Italian seasoning
1 teaspoon dried oregano
30 slices party rye bread, toasted

½ pound Genoa salami, chopped
1 cup grated Parmesan cheese or slivered mozzarella cheese

In a small bowl, blend the tomato paste, Italian seasoning, and oregano. Spread each toasted bread slice with the tomato paste mixture. Sprinkle on a layer of salami, then one of cheese. Place paper towels in the oven and arrange 10 slices in a circle on the towels. Cook for 40 seconds, or until the cheese begins to bubble and melt. Cook the remaining slices 10 at a time. Serve hot. These freeze well and can be popped under the microwaves right from the freezer. If you do this, increase the cooking time to 55 seconds. *Serves 10.*

MAURICE BROCKWAY'S DATE-BACON DELIGHTS

Speed-cook; 7 minutes

20 pitted dates   10 slices bacon, cut in half
Bourbon

Cover the dates in bourbon and soak for at least 24 hours; 48 is better. Drain. Wrap each date in one-half slice of bacon and fasten with a toothpick. On a glass or paper plate, place four layers of paper towels. Arrange the date-bacon rolls on the towels and cover with one layer of paper towels. Cook in the center of the oven 3 minutes. Turn the rolls over. Rotate the plate a half turn. Cook 4 minutes. Blot off any remaining fat. Serve immediately. *Serves 8 to 10.*

CREVETTES

Speed-cook; 3½ minutes

½ cup mayonnaise   1 teaspoon salt
2 tablespoons ketchup   ⅓ cup beer
2 tablespoons brandy   ⅓ cup water
1 tablespoon minced onion   1 pound small, fresh shrimp,
1 garlic clove, crushed   shelled and deveined
1 tablespoon chopped fresh   4 crisp inner leaves of Boston
  parsley   lettuce
1 tablespoon seafood seasoning

In a large bowl, blend the mayonnaise, ketchup, brandy, onion, garlic, and parsley. Set aside. In a glass measuring cup, blend the seafood seasoning, salt, beer, and water. Cook 2 minutes, or until boiling. Pour the hot liquid into a glass pie plate large enough to hold the shrimp in one layer. Add the shrimp and cook in the center of the oven 45 seconds. Turn the shrimp. Cook 45 seconds. Turn the shrimp again and let set, covered, for 2 minutes. They should be pink and firm, but not hard—be careful not to overcook. When the shrimp are cool, add them to the mayonnaise sauce and mix well. Refrigerate 2 hours. Remove the garlic clove. Serve on lettuce leaves on individual plates. To multiply number of servings, cook the shrimp in 1-pound batches for every 4 guests. *Serves 4.*

RALPH GUIDETTI'S MUSHROOMS TRIFOLATI

Speed-cook; 6 minutes

This is a tasty, "different" Italian first course or appetizer.

4 large garlic cloves, minced
½ cup olive oil
1 pound mushrooms, thinly sliced
Salt and pepper to taste
¼ cup dry white wine
Juice of 2 lemons

3 tablespoons chopped fresh
  parsley
Four ½-inch-thick slices white
  bread (crusts removed), fried in
  butter or margarine, or toasted
  and buttered

In a glass casserole, cook the garlic in the olive oil in the center of the oven for 1 minute or until soft. Stir in the mushrooms and season with salt and pepper. Cook 2 minutes, stirring after 1 minute. Stir in the wine. Cook 2 minutes, stirring after 1 minute. Stir in the lemon juice and parsley and cook 1 minute. Remove from the oven. Stir and let set, covered, 3 minutes. The mushrooms should look "wilted." Spoon them with some of the sauce over the fried or toasted bread slices and serve hot. *Serves 4.*

KIELBASA SAUSAGE CANAPÉS

Speed-cook; 3 minutes 20 seconds

½ cup (¼ pound) butter or
  margarine, softened
3 tablespoons mustard

24 slices party rye bread, toasted
½ pound smoked kielbasa sausage
  in one piece, skinned

In a small bowl, blend the butter or margarine and mustard. Spread the toasted bread with the mixture. Place the sausage on three layers of paper towels in the center of the oven. Cook 2 minutes. Turn the sausage over and cook 1 minute. Remove from oven. Let set, covered, for 3 minutes. Cut the sausage into ¼-inch-thick slices (or any thickness you prefer). Place a round of sausage on each slice of bread, then heat under microwaves, 12 at a time, for 20 seconds. Serve immediately, while the sausage is warm. *Serves 8.*

SPANISH SHRIMP

Speed-cook; 3½ minutes

4 tablespoons butter or margarine
1 garlic clove, minced
⅓ cup dry sherry
1 pound small shrimp, shelled and
   deveined

Salt and pepper to taste
2 tablespoons chopped fresh
   parsley
Toast strips

In a glass pie plate large enough to hold the shrimp in one layer, melt the
butter or margarine. Add the garlic and cook in the center of the oven for 1
minute, or until the garlic is soft. Stir in the sherry. Arrange the shrimp in a
layer and sprinkle with salt and pepper. Cook 45 seconds. Turn the shrimp.
Cook 45 seconds and turn again. Sprinkle with the parsley and cook 1 minute.
Let set, covered, 2 minutes. Shrimp should be pink and firm, but not hard.
Serve the shrimp warm in the sauce, in ramekins. Pass the toast strips so that
guests can soak up the shrimp sauce. Number of servings can be multiplied;
cook 1-pound batches. *Serves 4.*

SHRIMP IN VERMOUTH

Speed-cook; 10 minutes

*Vermouth, a fortified wine, becomes vermouth when a number of secret
herbs are added, giving it its unique flavor. It is superb for cooking
seafood.*

½ cup dry white vermouth
⅓ cup clam broth
2 small white onions, thinly sliced
1 small celery rib, thinly sliced
1 small carrot, thinly sliced
¼ teaspoon dried thyme

6 whole black peppercorns
1 tablespoon chopped fresh
   parsley
1 pound small shrimp, shelled and
   deveined

In a glass casserole, combine all the ingredients except the shrimp. Cook,
covered, in the center of the oven 5 minutes. Stir in the shrimp. Cook, uncovered, 3 minutes. Stir. Cook 2 minutes. Let set, covered, 5 minutes. The
shrimp should be pink and firm, but not hard. Serve them on toothpicks.
Serves 4.

POACHED SCALLOPS

Speed-cook; 6 minutes

½ cup dry white wine
¼ cup water
1 medium-size white onion, sliced
3 sprigs parsley
⅛ teaspoon dried tarragon
1½ pounds scallops
Salt to taste

Crisp leaves of Boston lettuce
½ cup Green Mayonnaise (recipe
  following)
2 hard-boiled eggs, sliced
2 tablespoons chopped fresh
  parsley

In a glass casserole, combine the wine, water, onion, parsley sprigs, and tarragon. Cook in the center of the oven 2 minutes. Stir in the scallops and sprinkle lightly with salt. Cook 2 minutes; stir; cook 2 minutes. Stir, then let set, covered, 5 minutes. The scallops should be firm but not hard. Let the scallops cool in their liquid. Do not refrigerate. Drain and serve in individual dishes on lettuce leaves with a dollop of Green Mayonnaise atop, garnished with egg slices and chopped parsley. *Serves 6 to 8.*

Green Mayonnaise

In a bowl, blend well ½ cup mayonnaise, 1½ tablespoons chopped fresh parsley, and 1½ tablespoons chopped watercress.

TUNA BAUSERMAN

Speed-cook; 3 minutes

William Bauserman has topped the oysters Rockefeller people with this one. We like it as a first course, but it also makes an excellent appetizer.

1 cup finely chopped fresh spinach
¼ cup finely chopped fresh parsley
2 tablespoons finely chopped
  watercress
2 tablespoons minced celery
½ teaspoon salt
¼ teaspoon dried tarragon
Pinch of cayenne pepper

Pinch of paprika
½ cup mayonnaise
¼ cup butter or margarine, melted
3 tablespoons lemon juice
Two 7-ounce cans tuna, drained
  and flaked
2 tablespoons buttered bread
  crumbs

In a glass casserole, mix all of the ingredients except the tuna and buttered bread crumbs. Cook in the center of the oven 3 minutes, stirring after each minute. Stir in the tuna, blending well. Spoon into 6 scallop shells or ramekins. Sprinkle with the bread crumbs and place under the broiler of a conventional stove until the bread crumbs are crisp and the sauce bubbles. *Serves 6.*

6

SOUPS

"THE ARMY," said Napoleon, "doesn't travel on its stomach. It travels on soup."

With a microwave oven you can feed an army or just your own family in no time at all. But it isn't only speed that is an asset. Soups are especially savory cooked under microwaves. The rapid penetration of seasonings in soups is unequaled by any other method of cookery. Flavors are released and fixed in a flash. Vegetables in your homemade soup will have a much fresher taste than the old-fashioned soups that simmered for hours, losing flavor, freshness, and vitamins along the way. Microwave cooking ensures that these vitamins are retained.

Frozen soups can be heated in minutes. Canned soups, poured into the serving bowl or cup, are ready in 2 minutes.

Use an extra-large glass bowl or casserole when making soups, especially those with a lot of liquid. This will prevent spillovers. Common sense and your own judgment will see to this—you won't try to make a quart of soup in a 1½-quart dish.

Microwaves will tempt you to be inventive. Mix canned soups, or speedily create your own version of minestrone or Chinese egg drop. Convert your old soup recipes into new taste delights, in a fourth of the time, and with a freshness and flavor that no other method of cooking can match.

EGG AND LEMON SOUP

Speed-cook; 11 minutes

5 cups hot beef broth
6 tablespoons rice
3 small eggs
¼ cup lemon juice

Salt and pepper to taste
1 tablespoon chopped fresh
   parsley

In a glass bowl, bring 1 cup of the hot broth to a boil. Add the rice and cook in the center of the oven 4 minutes. Let set, covered, 5 minutes. The rice should be tender but firm. In a glass casserole, bring the remaining hot broth to a boil (this will take about 5 minutes). Stir the rice into the boiling broth. In a bowl, beat the eggs until they are light and fluffy. Adding a small amount at a time, beat the lemon juice into the eggs. Gradually beat 1 cup of the hot soup into the egg–lemon juice mixture. Stir this diluted egg mixture into the casserole with the hot broth and rice. Season with salt and pepper. Cook 2 minutes, or until it begins to simmer, stirring after 1 minute. Let set, covered, 5 minutes. Sprinkle each serving with parsley. *Serves 4.*

CHEDDAR CHEESE SOUP

Speed-cook; 14 minutes

4 slices bacon
2 tablespoons butter or margarine
1 medium-size white onion, minced
2 tablespoons flour
2 cups warm milk

1½ cups warm chicken broth
1½ cups grated sharp cheddar
   cheese
¼ teaspoon paprika
Salt and pepper to taste

Place 2 paper towels on a plate. Space the bacon evenly on top. Cover with a paper towel. Cook in the center of the oven 4 minutes, rotating the plate a half turn after 2 minutes. Pat the fat from the bacon with a paper towel. Let cool, then crumble. Set aside. In a glass casserole, in the center of the oven, melt the butter or margarine. Add the onion and cook 3 minutes, or until soft, stirring after 1½ minutes. Stir in the flour. Cook 1 minute, then stir until you have a smooth paste. Stir in the warm milk, a little at a time, stirring constantly until you have a smooth sauce. Stir in the warm broth. Cook 3 minutes, or until the sauce begins to thicken, stirring every 30 seconds. Strain the sauce and return to the casserole. Stir in the cheese, paprika, salt, and pepper. Cook 3 minutes, or until the cheese melts and the soup is simmering, stirring after 1½ minutes. Let set, covered, 5 minutes. Serve hot in soup bowls, garnishing each serving with the crumbled bacon. *Serves 6.*

FINNISH FISH CHOWDER

Speed-cook; 13 minutes

⅓ cup finely diced salt pork
1 large celery rib, scraped and
  chopped
1 medium onion, chopped
Two 10½-ounce cans cream of
  potato soup
2 cups milk
1 cup sliced cooked carrots

One 8-ounce can whole corn
  kernels, drained
1 small bay leaf
¼ teaspoon pepper
Pinch of dried tarragon
1 pound ocean perch fillets, cut
  into 1-inch squares
Salt to taste

Place the salt pork in a glass casserole, cover with waxed paper, and cook in the center of the oven 3 minutes, stirring after 1½ minutes. Add the celery and onion. Cook 3 minutes, or until soft, stirring after 1½ minutes. Stir in remaining ingredients. Cook 4 minutes. Stir. Cook 3 minutes. Stir. Let set, covered, 5 minutes. Remove bay leaf. The chowder is ready when the fish flakes easily with a fork. Taste for seasoning. *Serves 6 to 8.*

QUICK CLAM BISQUE

Speed-cook; 8 minutes

4 tablespoons butter or margarine
1 medium onion, minced
1 cup heavy cream
1 cup milk

¼ teaspoon hickory-smoked salt
¼ teaspoon celery salt
Two 8-ounce cans minced clams
  (undrained)

In a glass casserole, in the center of the oven, melt 2 tablespoons of the butter or margarine and cook the onion 3 minutes, or until soft, stirring after 1½ minutes. Stir in the cream, milk, smoked salt, and celery salt. Cook 3 minutes, stirring after 1½ minutes. Stir in the clams and their liquid and cook 2 minutes. Taste for seasoning. Stir in the remaining butter or margarine and serve piping hot. *Serves 4.*

FAST GREEN CRAB SOUP

Speed-cook; 6 minutes

One 10½-ounce can condensed
   green pea soup
2 cups chicken broth
One 7-ounce can crabmeat, well
   picked over and flaked

2 tablespoons light rum
Salt and pepper to taste
1 cup heavy cream, whipped
1 tablespoon chopped fresh chives

In a glass casserole, combine the pea soup and chicken broth. Cook in the center of the oven 4 minutes, or until boiling, stirring after 2 minutes. Stir in the crabmeat, rum, salt, and pepper. Cook 2 minutes, stirring after 1 minute. Stir in the whipped cream. Taste for seasoning. Serve hot in bowls and garnish with chopped chives. *Serves 4.*

SHRIMP AND CORN SOUP

Speed-cook; 9 minutes

2 tablespoons cornstarch
1 tablespoon soy sauce
1 tablespoon water
5 cups chicken broth
2 cups cooked fresh or frozen corn

½ teaspoon salt
2 eggs, beaten
½ cup coarsely chopped cooked
   shrimp

Blend the cornstarch, soy sauce, and water and set aside. In a glass casserole, heat the chicken broth in the center of the oven 7 minutes, or until simmering. Stir in the corn; cook 30 seconds. Stir in the cornstarch mixture and salt and cook 30 seconds. Stir until the soup thickens. Quickly stir in the eggs. Cook 1 minute. Serve hot in soup bowls, garnished with chopped shrimp. *Serves 6.*

BOULA

Speed-cook; 8 minutes

Two 10½-ounce cans condensed
   green pea soup

Two 6½-ounce cans green turtle
   soup

Salt and pepper to taste
2 tablespoons butter or margarine
1 cup dry sherry

½ cup heavy cream, whipped
2 tablespoons grated Parmesan
  cheese

In a glass casserole, combine the soups. Stir until smooth. Season with salt and pepper. Cook in the center of the oven 3 minutes. Stir. Cook 3 minutes. Stir in the butter and sherry. Cook 2 minutes. Stir. Pour into heated oven-proof soup bowls. Top each serving with a dollop of whipped cream. Sprinkle with the cheese and brown lightly under the broiler of a conventional stove. *Serves 4 to 5.*

CREAMED ASPARAGUS SOUP

Speed-cook; 25 minutes

1½ pounds fresh asparagus
4 cups chicken broth
4 tablespoons butter or margarine
1 medium onion, chopped

1 large celery rib, chopped
1 cup heavy cream
Salt and pepper to taste

Break off and discard the tough ends of the asparagus stems. With a vegetable peeler, peel the stems. Cut off the tips, then cut the stems into 1-inch pieces. Put the asparagus tips and ¼ cup of the chicken broth in a glass bowl. Cook in the center of the oven 5 minutes, or until the tips are barely tender. Drain, reserving the liquid, and set aside. In a glass casserole, in the center of the oven, melt the butter or margarine. Stir in the asparagus stems, onion, and celery; cook 3 minutes, stirring after 1½ minutes. Pour in ¼ cup of the chicken broth and cook 7 minutes, or until the vegetables are soft, stirring every 2 minutes. Pour in the reserved chicken broth in which the asparagus tips cooked. Add the remaining 3½ cups chicken broth. Cook 5 minutes, stirring after 1½ minutes. Let cool slightly, then pour contents of the casserole into a blender and puree. Return to the casserole and cook in the center of the oven 4 minutes, or until simmering. Stir in the heavy cream. Cook 1 minute. Season with salt and pepper. Let set, covered, 5 minutes. Serve garnished with the asparagus tips. *Serves 4 to 6.*

PO VALLEY POTATO SOUP

Speed-cook; 11 minutes

3 tablespoons butter or margarine
1 tablespoon olive oil

1 medium-size white onion,
  chopped

2 small carrots, scraped and
    coarsely chopped
2 celery ribs, scraped and coarsely
    chopped
1 garlic clove, crushed
Salt and pepper to taste
1 cup tomato sauce

4 cups hot beef broth
1 large boiled potato, skinned and
    put through a ricer
2 tablespoons chopped fresh
    parsley
Grated Parmesan cheese

In a glass casserole, heat the butter or margarine and oil. Stir in the onion, carrots, celery, and garlic. Cook in the center of the oven 4 minutes or until the vegetables are soft, stirring after 2 minutes. Remove the garlic. Stir in the salt, pepper, tomato sauce, beef broth, and potato. Cook 7 minutes, or until simmering, stirring after 3 and 5 minutes. Let set, covered, 5 minutes. Serve with the parsley and Parmesan cheese sprinkled atop. *Serves 6.*

HEARTY ZUCCHINI SOUP

Speed-cook; 15 minutes

4 tablespoons butter or margarine
2 small white onions, thinly sliced
1 large celery rib, scraped and
    thinly sliced
1 large carrot, scraped and thinly
    sliced
3 cups chicken broth

3 medium zucchini (unpeeled), cut
    into quarters lengthwise, then
    thinly sliced
Salt and pepper to taste
Grated Parmesan cheese
Heavy cream (optional)
Sour cream (optional)

In a glass casserole, melt the butter or margarine. Stir in the onions, celery, and carrot and cook in the center of the oven 3 minutes or until soft, stirring after 1½ minutes. Stir in ¼ cup of the chicken broth, and the zucchini. Cook 8 minutes or until the zucchini are tender, stirring every 2 minutes. Stir in the remaining chicken broth, and salt and pepper. Cook, covered, 4 minutes, or until simmering, stirring after 2 minutes. Taste for seasoning. Let set, covered, 10 minutes. Serve hot as is, with the cheese sprinkled atop. Serve buttered crusty bread as an accompaniment.

The soup also can be served cold without the cheese. Let cool and puree in a blender. Just before serving, stir in 1 tablespoon of heavy cream for each individual bowl and top with a dollop of sour cream. *Serves 4 to 6.*

OLD-TIME VEGETABLE SOUP

Speed-cook; 45 minutes

On a conventional stove, this soup would take about 3 hours. Micro-waves not only cook it in a fourth of the time, but the old-fashioned version never had the fresh flavor of this one.

1 pound lean beef brisket, cut into
  ½-inch cubes
1 pound beef shinbone with meat
8 cups boiling beef broth
2 small white onions, coarsely
  chopped
2 small carrots, scraped and
  coarsely chopped
2 small celery ribs, scraped and
  coarsely chopped
One 1-pound can plum tomatoes,
  broken up

1 tablespoon chopped fresh
  parsley
¼ teaspoon dried basil
¼ teaspoon dried marjoram
1 teaspoon salt
½ teaspoon pepper
½ cup fresh or defrosted frozen
  peas
½ cup fresh or defrosted frozen
  baby lima beans

In a large casserole, place the beef cubes, shinbone, and boiling beef broth. Stir in remaining ingredients except peas and lima beans. Cover and cook in the center of the oven 10 minutes. Stir. Rotate the casserole half a turn. Cook 10 minutes. Stir. Rotate half a turn. Cook 10 minutes. Stir in the peas and lima beans. Cover and cook 5 minutes. Stir; cook 5 minutes, then stir again and cook 5 minutes longer. Let set, covered, 15 minutes. Before serving, skim off any fat. Remove the shinbone, dice the meat, and stir it back into the soup. *Serves 8 to 10.*

7

EGGS

In 1945, when scientist Percy L. Spencer discovered microwave cookery partly by accident, one of the experimental food items that he placed before a radar horn antenna was a raw egg—in its shell. It exploded.

Forty-three years later, raw eggs in their shells still explode in microwave ovens. That lightning-fast heat of the microwaves expands the air inside the shell of the egg, forcing it to burst. Therefore, cook hard-boiled eggs on your conventional stove; it will be much less messy! We also suggest that you use a conventional stove for fried eggs and omelettes. You can cook them under microwaves in the browning skillet, but we think that the conventional stove prepares them just as well, perhaps better. But for scrambled eggs, poached eggs, even baked eggs, microwaves are nothing short of marvelous.

Egg cookery under microwaves, however, is a delicate operation that requires attention to detail—and precise timing.

As all cholesterol watchers know, the egg yolk has more fat than the white, thus it cooks faster. Especially under microwaves. If you have a choice, scramble the eggs. This produces the most even results. Use butter, but be aware that in microwave cookery it gives more flavor and less is needed. The reason: Conventional heat breaks down fats. Microwaves are so speedy this does not happen, so scrambled eggs cooked in butter are softer and tastier.

When scrambling eggs, stir them often, fluffing them with a fork. This will result in a lighter texture.

For any method other than scrambling make certain that you carefully puncture the surface of the yolk twice with the tines of a fork, the sharp point of a knife, or even a toothpick. This will break the membrane encasing the yolk and prevent the egg from popping or exploding. Do it *carefully*. It is only the thin outer skin surrounding the yolk that you want to break.

Always make sure that eggs to be poached are completely covered with water, or whatever liquid they are to be cooked in. The liquid slows down the cooking and evens the heat.

Cooking times will vary from half a minute to 2 or more minutes, depending on the size of the egg, its temperature, and the number of eggs to be cooked.

All food cooked under microwaves continues to cook after being removed from the oven. Teach yourself to take egg dishes from the microwaves *before* they are completely cooked, even if only by seconds. Then you can let them set, covered, depending upon how well done you like them, to complete the cooking. This is an important technique and can be impressed upon you only through trial and error. Now that salmonella has been traced to egg yolks, the USDA has begun to stress the importance of cooking eggs thoroughly— to avoid hot and cold spots or runny, underdone eggs. On the other hand, overpoach an egg and it's a bullet; bake an egg too long and you can use it to play Ping-Pong; cook scrambled eggs too long and you've got rubber. The microwaves are so fast that a minute, sometimes only 30 seconds, can make all the difference. People who like 3-minute eggs, sunny-side up and "lightly poached," take care. We repeat: This is sensitive cookery!

POACHED EGG

Speed-cook; 2 minutes, 45 seconds, including boiling the water

Start your microwave egg cookery simply. Poach a single egg. It will be a graphic lesson in the importance of timing. If you like your poached egg softer than we do, perhaps only 30 seconds will be enough time. Invest in a dozen eggs and run a series of tests. It will be time and money well spent.

1 cup water	1 large egg at room temperature
½ teaspoon white vinegar	Salt and pepper to taste

In a measuring cup, in the center of the oven, combine the water and vinegar (it helps set the egg white) and bring to a boil, about 2 minutes. A 10-ounce custard cup or a small heat-resistant skillet make perfect egg poachers. Break the egg into either one. With a fork or a toothpick, carefully pierce the surface of the yolk twice, puncturing the membrane. Pour the boiling water around the egg. Cover with plastic wrap and cook in the center of the oven 45 seconds. Place the egg in its cooker on a plate on the table and let it set, covered, 30 seconds, so you can educate yourself by watching the carry-over cooking at work. Season with salt and pepper. *Serves 1.*

SCRAMBLED EGGS

Speed-cook; 2 minutes

Scrambled eggs cooked under microwaves are superb: soft, creamy, done to perfection—provided your timing is right. We again remind you that, as with all food subjected to this sensitive style of cooking, you must be careful not to overcook. A minute too long and your scrambled eggs will be hard and dry. Start off with this simple recipe for two, then experiment and expand your repertoire as you go along.

4 eggs
¼ cup light cream

¼ teaspoon salt (optional)
2 tablespoons butter

In a bowl, beat the eggs, cream, and salt. In a glass pie plate, in the center of the oven, melt the butter. Pour in the beaten eggs. Cover with waxed paper and cook 1 minute. Stir. Cook 30 seconds. Stir. Cook 30 seconds. Stop cooking the eggs while they still look underdone. *Serves 2.*

EGGS WITH CHICKEN LIVERS

Speed-cook; 7 minutes

4 tablespoons butter or margarine
2 small white onions, chopped
½ pound chicken livers, each cut
  into 4 pieces
8 small eggs

1 teaspoon salt (optional)
½ teaspoon pepper
1 tablespoon chopped fresh
  parsley

In a glass casserole, in the center of the oven, melt 2 tablespoons of the butter or margarine. Add the onions and cook for 2 minutes, or until soft. Stir in the chicken livers. Cook 1 minute. Turn the livers and cook 1 minute. In a bowl, beat the eggs with the salt and pepper until frothy. Melt the remaining butter or margarine in the dish with the onions and livers. Pour in the beaten eggs and cook 1 minute. Stir. Cook 1 minute. Stir. Cook 1 minute. Let set, covered, 2 minutes. Sprinkle with the parsley. *Serves 4.*

HAM AND CHEESE SCRAMBLE

Speed-cook; 6 minutes

2 tablespoons butter or margarine
1 tablespoon olive oil
1 small sweet red pepper, cored,
   seeded, and chopped
1 medium-size white onion,
   chopped

½ cup chopped cooked ham
One 11-ounce can condensed
   cheddar cheese soup
8 small eggs, beaten

In a glass casserole, in the center of the oven, heat the butter or margarine and oil. Add the pepper and onion and cook 3 minutes, or until they are soft, stirring after 1½ minutes. Stir in the ham. In a bowl, stir the soup until smooth. Blend in the beaten eggs. Pour the soup-egg mixture into the casserole with the ham and vegetables. Cover with waxed paper and cook 1 minute. Stir. Cook 1 minute. Stir. Cook 1 minute. Let set, covered, for 2 minutes. *Serves 4.*

BAKED HAM AND EGGS

Speed-cook; 3 minutes

2 cups soft ¼-inch bread cubes
1½ cups ground cooked ham

One 10½-ounce can condensed
   cream of celery soup
4 large eggs

In a bowl, mix the bread cubes, ham, and soup. Divide the mixture among four 1½-cup glass baking dishes. Break 1 egg into the center of each. With a fork, carefully pierce the surface of the egg yolk twice, puncturing the membrane. Place the small dishes in a large baking dish in the center of the oven. Cover with waxed paper and cook 2 minutes. Rotate the dish half a turn. Cook 1 minute. Let set, covered, 2 minutes. *Serves 4.*

MEXICAN EGGS

Speed-cook; 8½ minutes

2 tablespoons butter or margarine
2 small white onions, minced

2 medium-size ripe tomatoes,
   peeled, seeded, chopped, and
   drained in a strainer

1 tablespoon minced fresh parsley
1½ teaspoons chili powder

8 small eggs and 1 teaspoon salt,
beaten well with a fork

In a glass casserole, melt the butter or margarine. Add the onions and cook in the center of the oven for 2 minutes, or until soft. Stir in the tomatoes, parsley, and chili powder. Cover with waxed paper and cook 4 minutes. Stir in the beaten eggs. Cook 1½ minutes. Stir. Cook 1 minute. Stir. Stop cooking while the eggs still look slightly underdone. Let set, covered, 2 minutes. Eggs should be soft and creamy. *Serves 4.*

EGGS POACHED IN MUSHROOM SAUCE

Speed-cook; 5 minutes

2 tablespoons butter or margarine
One 10½-ounce can condensed
    cream of mushroom soup
½ cup milk

4 large eggs
Salt and pepper to taste
2 English muffins, split, toasted,
    and buttered

In a shallow glass casserole, in the center of the oven, melt the butter or margarine. Stir in the soup and milk. Cover with waxed paper and cook 2 minutes, or until simmering. Stir. Break the eggs, one at a time, into a small dish. With a fork, pierce the surface of each egg yolk twice, puncturing the membrane. Slide the eggs into the sauce, making sure the eggs are covered with the sauce. Season with salt and pepper. Cover with plastic wrap and cook 2 minutes. Rotate the dish half a turn. Cook 1 minute. Baste the eggs. Let set 2 minutes. Serve the eggs on the English muffins, with the mushroom sauce spooned atop. *Serves 4.*

EGGS WITH SCALLIONS

Speed-cook; 7 minutes

4 tablespoons butter or margarine
1 tablespoon olive oil
10 whole scallions, chopped
1 tablespoon flour

8 small eggs
½ cup heavy cream
1 teaspoon salt (optional)

In a glass casserole, in the center of the oven, heat the butter or margarine and oil. Add the scallions and cook 3 minutes, or until soft, stirring after 1½ minutes. Sprinkle with the flour. Cook 1 minute. Stir. Cook 1 minute. Stir.

In a bowl, beat the eggs, cream, and salt until frothy. Pour into the casserole with the scallions. Cook 1 minute. Stir. Cook 1 minute. Stir. Let set, covered, 2 minutes. *Serves 4.*

SCRAMBLED EGGS WITH SHRIMP

Speed-cook; 4 minutes 20 seconds

4 tablespoons peanut oil
½ pound medium shrimp, shelled,
    deveined, and each cut into 4
    equal pieces

8 small eggs, beaten
4 whole scallions, chopped
1 teaspoon salt (optional)

In a glass pie plate or shallow casserole, in the center of the oven, heat 2 tablespoons of the oil 30 seconds. Stir in the shrimp and cook 20 seconds, or until the shrimp begin to turn pink. Remove the shrimp and drain the liquid from the cooking dish. In a bowl, blend the eggs, scallions, and salt. In the cooking dish heat the remaining oil 30 seconds. Add the egg mixture. Cook 1 minute. Stir. Cook 1 minute. Stir in the shrimp. Cook 1 minute. Let set, covered, 2 minutes. *Serves 4.*

EGGS BAKED ON SPINACH BED

Speed-cook; 10 minutes

One 10-ounce package frozen
    chopped spinach
½ teaspoon salt (optional)
4 large poached eggs (see Poached
    Egg, page 64, but cook eggs
    only 30 seconds)

One 10½-ounce can condensed
    cream of mushroom soup
½ cup grated cheddar cheese

Place the spinach in a glass dish. Sprinkle with the salt, cover, and cook in the center of the oven 3 minutes. Separate unthawed portions. Rotate the dish half a turn. Cook 3 minutes. Drain well. Arrange the spinach in a baking dish. Make 4 depressions for the eggs and place the poached eggs in the "nests" you have prepared. Pour the soup into a glass measuring cup. Cover with waxed paper and cook 2 minutes. Stir. Cook 1 minute, or until very hot. Spoon the soup over the eggs and spinach and sprinkle with the cheese. Cover with plastic wrap and cook 30 seconds. Rotate the dish half a turn. Cook 30 seconds. Let set, covered, 1 minute. *Serves 4.*

MARIA LIMONCELLI'S EGGS POACHED IN TOMATOES

Speed-cook; 14 minutes

3 tablespoons olive oil
2 small white onions, chopped
1 garlic clove, minced
One 1-pound can plum tomatoes,
  pushed through a food mill
1 tablespoon chopped fresh
  parsley

½ teaspoon salt (optional)
¼ teaspoon pepper
Pinch of dried marjoram
4 large eggs

In a glass casserole, in the center of the oven, heat the olive oil and cook the onions and garlic 2 minutes, or until soft. Stir in the tomatoes, parsley, salt, pepper, and marjoram. Cover with waxed paper and cook 10 minutes, stirring every 2 minutes. Break the eggs, one at a time, into a small dish; with a fork, carefully pierce the surface of each yolk twice to break the membrane, then slip the eggs into the sauce. Spoon the sauce over them. Cover the casserole with waxed paper and cook 1 minute. Baste the eggs with the sauce. Rotate half a turn. Cook 1 minute. Let set, covered, 2 minutes. *Serves 4.*

EGGS WITH VEGETABLES, YUGOSLAVIAN STYLE

Speed-cook; 10½ minutes

2 tablespoons butter or margarine
1 tablespoon olive oil
1 medium green pepper, cored,
  seeded, and chopped
1 small white onion, chopped
1 small hot chili pepper, cored,
  seeded, and finely chopped

1 medium-size ripe tomato, peeled
  and cut into eighths
8 small eggs
½ cup large-curd cottage cheese,
  well drained
1 teaspoon salt (optional)

In a glass casserole, in the center of the oven, heat the butter or margarine and olive oil. Stir in the green pepper, onion, and chili pepper and cook 3 minutes, stirring after 1½ minutes. Stir in the tomato. Cook 5 minutes, carefully stirring after 1¼ minutes. In a large bowl, beat together the eggs, cottage cheese, and salt. Stir in the vegetable mixture. Pour the mixture into the casserole. Cook 1 minute. Stir. Cook 30 seconds. Stir. Cook 30 seconds. Stir. Cook 30 seconds. When you stop cooking, the eggs should be slightly softer than desired for serving. *Serves 4.*

8

~~~~~~~~~~

FISH AND SHELLFISH

FISH LEAD the list of foods overcooked by new owners of microwave ovens. Overcooked fish is dry, without flavor. The temptation, regardless of instructions received with the new microwave oven, is to play it on the safe side and "give it just one more minute." That minute equals four, maybe five on your conventional stove. Few of us would gamble that much extra time in ordinary cookery to make certain that the fish is ready—at least, those of us who like fish and respect the rules used in cooking it.

Fish have very fragile connective tissue and can easily be overcooked, using any medium. We remind you again that in microwave cookery there is carry-over cooking time. Whatever comes out of the microwave oven will continue cooking for a short period while it is out of the oven. Nothing can stop that action. But you can foresee, plan ahead and undercook, allowing for that carry-over cooking.

Don't let these warning tips discourage you. The reward is great. Fish properly cooked in a microwave oven is unexcelled—moist, flaky, tender, with an unusually delicate flavor that other cookery somehow seems to diminish.

It is advised to cook fish about 4 minutes per pound. We cook it 3 minutes per pound, sometimes even less. Many claim that because of its irregular shape and uneven weight, you cannot successfully cook a whole fish. We have cooked whole bluefish, red snapper, and bass. The head and tail aren't eaten anyway—at least not by us—and the remainder is deliciously moist and tender.

But to play it safe (if you aren't an experimenter), cook just the fillets and steaks. They are uniform in size and are the best parts of the fish anyway.

No fat is needed with microwave fish cookery, thus cholesterol-minded cooks get a double benefit, for the fish itself has little fat. You can use butter, margarine, or oil if you wish, but it isn't necessary. We happen to like butter and sauces.

Remember to keep the thicker parts of the fish toward the outside of the cooking dish.

Covering the fish with plastic wrap or waxed paper while cooking will contain the steam, thus accelerating the cooking time.

Test! When the fish is easily flaked with a fork it is cooked. We remove our fish before it flakes easily, when it still has some resistance. Then we let it set, covered, for 1 or 2 minutes. The carry-over time produces a fish that does flake easily and isn't overcooked.

When defrosting frozen fish fillets or steaks, place them in their package on a paper towel (except those wrapped in aluminum foil). Only partially defrost fish. Overlong heating of frozen fish will cook the outer areas; when you cook the fish they will certainly be overdone. Defrost 1 pound of fillets only 2 minutes on the regular cycle (4 minutes on the stop-and-go automatic defrost), turning the package every 30 seconds. Separate the partially thawed pieces under cold running water. And always cook defrosted fish *soon*. Depending upon the size of the fish, a glass pie plate is excellent for cooking fillets and steaks.

BLUEFISH FILLETS WITH TOMATOES AND VERMOUTH

Speed-cook; 13 minutes, including sauce

1 teaspoon salt (optional)	6 tablespoons olive oil
½ teaspoon pepper	2 bluefish fillets (about 1½
Juice of 2 lemons	pounds), cut into 4 equal pieces

In a bowl, blend the salt, pepper, lemon juice, and olive oil. Place the fillets in one layer in the bottom of a glass dish. Pour the marinade over the fillets, cover and let marinate 3 hours, turning several times. Remove the fish from the marinade and pat dry. Next, prepare the following ingredients:

2 tablespoons butter or margarine	One 1-pound can plum tomatoes,
1 tablespoon cooking oil	broken up
2 medium white onions, minced	2 garlic cloves, cut into slivers

½ teaspoon dried oregano   ¼ teaspoon pepper
½ teaspoon salt (optional)   ½ cup dry white vermouth

In a skillet on a conventional stove, or in a preheated browning skillet, heat the butter or margarine and oil, and brown the bluefish fillets evenly. Transfer to a shallow glass baking dish just large enough to hold them. In a glass bowl, blend the onions, tomatoes, garlic, oregano, salt, pepper, and vermouth. Cover with waxed paper and cook in the center of the oven 2½ minutes. Stir. Cook 2½ minutes. Stir. Spoon the tomato mixture evenly over the bluefish fillets. Cover the dish and cook in the center of the oven 4 minutes, rotating the dish half a turn at 2 minutes. Cook 4 minutes, rotating, half a turn at 2 minutes. Let set, covered, 3 minutes. The fish is ready when it flakes easily with a fork. *Serves 4.*

WHOLE BLUEFISH IN WAXED PAPER

Speed-cook; 7 minutes

Here's the perfect recipe for the bluefish that a friend drops off and you're doubtful about how to handle. Scale and clean it, but leave it whole; it makes a dramatic presentation.

One 3- to 3½-pound whole   4 tablespoons Herb Butter,
   bluefish, scaled and cleaned   softened (page 129)
Seasoned salt

Sprinkle the inside of the fish with seasoned salt. Place it on a large sheet of waxed paper on an inverted plate or two saucers (to hold it above any liquid that may collect in the bottom of the dish) in a shallow glass baking dish. Spread the Herb Butter evenly over the fish. Fold the edges of the waxed paper together, making the seam above the top of the fish (for easier testing). Cook in the center of the oven 4 minutes. Rotate the dish half a turn. Cook 3 minutes. Let set, still wrapped in the paper, 5 minutes. Test. The fish is ready when it flakes easily with a fork. *Serves 4 to 6.*

CODDLED COD

Speed-cook; 10 minutes, including the poaching liquid

½ cup bottled clam juice   2 tablespoons white wine vinegar
½ cup water   2 small white onions, thinly sliced
3 tablespoons lemon juice   1 celery rib, chopped

2 garlic cloves, coarsely chopped
1 small bay leaf
4 whole cloves
1 teaspoon salt (optional)

¼ teaspoon dried thyme
4 cod steaks (6 to 8 ounces each)
Hollandaise sauce or Green
    Mayonnaise (page 54)

Blend all the ingredients except the cod steaks in a glass dish or bowl. Cover with waxed paper. Cook in the center of the oven 6 minutes, stirring after each 3 minutes. Strain. Place the cod steaks in one layer in a shallow glass baking dish. Pour the strained liquid over them. Cover with waxed paper and cook in the center of the oven 2 minutes. Carefully turn the cod steaks over. Cook 2 minutes. Let set, covered, 2 minutes. Fish is ready when it flakes easily with a fork.

This dish can be served hot or cold. If served hot, remove from the liquid and serve with melted parsley butter or margarine. If served cold, let it cool in its liquid, then drain and serve with Hollandaise sauce or Green Mayonnaise. *Serves 4.*

MACKEREL FILLETS À LA FRANÇAISE

Speed-cook; 9 minutes, including sauce

This is a French classic that converts a mackerel into a morsel that trout fishermen would resent and envy. Caution: Make certain that the mackerel are fresh; otherwise, they will taste too "fishy." Clear, unclouded eyes mark fresh fish.

4 mackerel fillets (about 1½
    pounds)
Salt and pepper to taste
2 tablespoons fresh lemon juice
¼ cup dry white wine

4 tablespoons butter or margarine
1 medium-size white onion, minced
4 small fresh mushrooms, sliced
2 tablespoons tomato sauce
½ cup bread crumbs

Season the fillets with salt and pepper. Arrange them in a buttered, shallow glass baking dish just large enough to hold them in one layer. Pour the lemon juice and wine over the fish. Cover with plastic wrap, puncturing the center to permit the steam to escape. Cook in the center of the oven 4 minutes. Rotate the dish half a turn at 2 minutes. Let set, covered, 3 minutes. In a glass bowl, melt 2 tablespoons of the butter or margarine and cook the onion 2 minutes. Stir in the mushrooms; cook 1 minute. Stir in the tomato sauce. Drain or siphon off the cooking liquid from the fillets into a glass measuring cup. Cook 2 minutes. Stir it into the bowl with the onions and mushrooms. Pour this sauce over the fillets in their dish. Sprinkle with the bread crumbs, dot with the remaining butter or margarine, and place under the broiler of a conventional stove until the butter or margarine melts and the crumbs brown. *Serves 4.*

OCEAN PERCH FILLETS IN CELERY SAUCE

Speed-cook; 5 minutes

1½ pounds ocean perch fillets
Salt and pepper to taste
One 10½-ounce can condensed
  cream of celery soup
⅓ cup shredded sharp cheddar
  cheese

1 tablespoon chopped fresh
  parsley
½ cup bread crumbs

Place the fillets side by side in a shallow glass baking dish just large enough to hold them in one layer. Lightly season with salt and pepper. Stir the soup well and spoon it over the fish. Cook in the center of the oven 3 minutes. Rotate half a turn. Cook 2 minutes. Sprinkle the cheese, parsley, and bread crumbs over the fillets and place under the broiler of a conventional stove until the cheese melts and bread crumbs are brown. *Serves 4.*

CREAMED SALMON WITH PEAS

Speed-cook; 6 minutes

2 tablespoons butter or margarine
1 medium onion, chopped
4 medium mushrooms, thinly
  sliced
One 10½-ounce can condensed
  cream of mushroom soup

⅓ cup medium cream
2 cups canned red salmon,
  drained, picked over, and flaked
1 cup cooked fresh or frozen peas
2 tablespoons lemon juice
Salt and pepper to taste

In a glass bowl or casserole, melt the butter or margarine and cook the onion in the center of the oven for 2 minutes, or until soft. Stir in the mushrooms and cook 1 minute. Add the remaining ingredients, stirring well. Cover with waxed paper and cook 3 minutes, stirring after each 1½ minutes. Let set, covered, 3 minutes. Taste for seasoning. This is excellent over creamy mashed potatoes. *Serves 4.*

JAMBALAYA

Speed-cook; 26 minutes

Here's a party-dish surprise from the Deep South that will please the palates of your guests.

½ pound pork loin, shredded
½ pound smoked ham, shredded
2 tablespoons cooking oil
½ pound bulk pork sausage
1 medium-size white onion, chopped
2 garlic cloves, chopped
1 cup canned plum tomatoes, broken up

1 teaspoon chili powder
1 cup chicken broth
1 tablespoon chopped fresh parsley
1 tablespoon mixed pickling spices
1½ pounds medium shrimp, shelled and deveined
Salt and pepper to taste
Hot cooked rice

In a large glass casserole, in the center of the oven, cook the pork and ham in the oil 4 minutes, stirring after 2 minutes. Add the sausage and cook 4 minutes, stirring after 2 minutes. Stir in the onion, garlic, and tomatoes. Cook 2 minutes, stirring after 1 minute. Stir in the chili powder, chicken broth, parsley, and pickling spices. Cook 15 minutes, stirring after each 5 minutes. Stir in the shrimp. Cook 1 minute, or until the shrimp are pink but firm. Stir. Let set, covered, 5 minutes. Test for seasoning. Serve over rice. *Serves 6 to 8.*

SCROD STEAKS LOUISIANA

Speed-cook; 14 minutes

Scrod, tender young codfish, is too often overlooked in our fish cookery.

4 scrod steaks (6 to 8 ounces each)
2 tablespoons butter or margarine
1 medium-size white onion, chopped
1 small sweet red pepper, cored, seeded, and chopped

1 large celery rib, scraped and chopped
2 garlic cloves, minced
One 1-pound can stewed tomatoes
Salt and pepper to taste
1 tablespoon red wine vinegar

Arrange the scrod steaks side by side in a buttered, shallow glass baking dish. In a glass bowl or casserole, heat the butter or margarine. Add the onion, sweet red pepper, celery, and garlic and cook 4 minutes, stirring after 2 minutes. Stir in the tomatoes, salt, pepper, and vinegar. Cook 2 minutes. Stir. Cook 2 minutes. Stir. Pour this sauce over the fish. Cover with waxed paper and cook, in the center of the oven, for 3 minutes. Rotate the dish half a turn. Cook 3 minutes. Let set, covered, 3 minutes. Fish is ready when it flakes easily with a fork. *Serves 4.*

RED SNAPPER FILLETS WITH HERB BUTTER

Speed-cook; 4 minutes

This is a fine-textured fish with a delicate flavor that needs little except its own personality in the preparation.

2 red snapper fillets (each about 1 pound)
1 teaspoon salt (optional)
½ teaspoon pepper

½ teaspoon paprika
4 tablespoons butter or margarine
4 cubes Herb Butter (page 129)

No need to use a casserole for this; you can cook the fish on its serving platter. Place the fillets on the platter. Sprinkle with the salt, pepper, and paprika. Dot with butter or margarine. Cook, uncovered, 2 minutes. Rotate platter half a turn. Cook 2 minutes. Let set, covered with aluminum foil, 5 minutes. If it flakes easily with a fork, it is cooked. Serve with a cube of the Herb Butter melting atop each offering. *Serves 4.*

MEXICAN SNAPPER

Speed-cook; 11 minutes

Here, from Yucatán, is a red snapper dish with a fascinating character.

4 red snapper fillets (6 to 8 ounces each)
Salt and pepper to taste
1 medium-size white onion, chopped
2 tablespoons olive oil
¼ cup coarsely chopped green olives

¼ cup coarsely chopped pimiento
2 tablespoons chopped fresh parsley
⅓ cup orange juice
Juice of 1 lemon
1 hard-boiled egg, coarsely chopped

Place the fillets side by side in a shallow glass baking dish. Season lightly with salt and pepper. In another glass dish or casserole, cook the onion in the oil in the center of the oven for 2 minutes, or until soft. Stir in the olives, pimiento, parsley, orange juice, and lemon juice. Cook 3 minutes, stirring after 1½ minutes. Spoon over the fillets. Cover with waxed paper and cook in the center of the oven 3 minutes. Rotate dish half a turn. Cook 3 minutes. Let set, covered, 3 minutes. Fish is ready when it flakes easily with a fork. Serve in the sauce, sprinkled with the chopped egg. *Serves 4.*

FILLETS OF SOLE WITH CRABMEAT

Speed-cook; 12 minutes

Microwaves give you the extra time to get fancy, once in a while, with a company dish. Don't let this list of ingredients deter you. The recipe isn't complicated.

⅓ cup dry white wine
⅓ cup bottled clam juice
1 small celery rib with leaves,
    coarsely chopped

1 small bay leaf
¼ teaspoon dried thyme

In a glass bowl, combine all of the above ingredients. Cook in the center of the oven 4 minutes. Strain and reserve the liquid.

3 tablespoons butter or margarine
4 medium mushrooms, thinly
    sliced
2 tablespoons flour
½ cup grated Parmesan cheese
¼ cup dry sherry

¼ cup heavy cream
One 8-ounce can crabmeat, picked
    over and flaked
Salt and pepper to taste
4 sole fillets (about 1½ pounds)

In a glass bowl, melt the butter or margarine and cook the mushrooms in the center of the oven 1 minute. Remove with a slotted spoon and reserve. Stir the flour into the liquid in the bowl. Cook 1 minute, or until you have a smooth paste, stirring every 30 seconds. Gradually add the reserved wine-clam juice, stirring into a smooth sauce. Stir in the mushrooms, half the cheese, the sherry, cream, and crabmeat. Cook 2 minutes, stirring after 1 minute. Season with salt and pepper; blend well. Cover the bottom of a large, shallow baking dish with half the sauce. Arrange the fillets side by side in the dish and cover with the remaining sauce. Sprinkle the remaining cheese over the sauce. Cover with waxed paper and cook in the center of the oven 4 minutes, rotating the dish half a turn after 2 minutes. Let set, covered, 3 minutes. The fish is ready when it flakes easily with a fork. Place under the broiler of a conventional stove until a golden brown crust has formed. *Serves 4.*

FILLET OF SOLE DUGLÈRE

Speed-cook; 10 minutes

4 sole fillets (about 1½ pounds)
Salt and pepper to taste
3 tablespoons butter or margarine
1 medium-size white onion,
  chopped
2 tablespoons flour
¼ cup Chablis
¼ cup chicken broth

¼ cup heavy cream
2 medium tomatoes, peeled,
  seeded, coarsely chopped, and
  drained in a strainer
½ cup bread crumbs, lightly
  browned in butter
¼ cup grated Swiss cheese

Arrange the fillets side by side in a buttered shallow glass baking dish. Season with salt and pepper. In a glass casserole, in the center of the oven, melt the butter or margarine and cook the onion 2 minutes, or until soft. Stir in the flour. Gradually add the wine and chicken broth, stirring into a smooth sauce. Cook 1 minute, stirring after 30 seconds. Slowly stir in the cream. Cook 1 minute, stirring after 30 seconds. Stir in the tomatoes. Cook 2 minutes, stirring at 1 minute. Spoon the sauce over the fillets. Cover with waxed paper. Cook in the center of the oven 4 minutes, rotating the dish half a turn at 2 minutes. Let set, covered, 3 minutes. The fish is ready when it flakes easily with a fork. Sprinkle the bread crumbs and cheese atop and brown quickly in a conventional oven broiler. *Serves 4.*

SOLE WITH YOGURT

Speed-cook; 4 minutes

4 sole fillets (about 1½ pounds)
1 tablespoon prepared horseradish
1 tablespoon Dijon mustard
2 tablespoons fresh lemon juice
2 tablespoons grated Gruyère
  cheese

⅓ cup plain yogurt
2 tablespoons butter or margarine,
  softened

Place the fillets side by side in a shallow glass baking dish. In a bowl, blend the remaining ingredients and spread evenly over the fillets. Cover with waxed paper and cook in the center of the oven 2 minutes. Rotate the dish half a turn. Cook 2 minutes. Let set, covered, 3 minutes. Fish is ready when it flakes easily with a fork. *Serves 4.*

FILLETS OF SOLE ONE STEP AHEAD

Speed-cook; 3 minutes

Microwaves are unequalled for getting the host or hostess out there with the guests. One step of the cooking (of just about every kind of food) can be done early in the day, the rest quickly finished under the microwaves minutes before you are ready to have dinner. In Copenhagen, a Danish fisherman taught us this simple way of cooking sole. The fillets are liberally dipped in beaten egg, then in bread crumbs, then sautéed in butter or margarine until both sides are crusty. The fisherman's secret was not to eat the bread-crumb crust, but to slide this off, and eat the moist, delicate fish underneath.

4 sole fillets (about 1½ pounds)
Salt and pepper to taste
2 eggs, beaten

About 2 cups bread crumbs
3 tablespoons butter or margarine
1 tablespoon cooking oil

Lightly sprinkle the fillets with salt and pepper. Dip them in the beaten egg, then dredge with bread crumbs. On a conventional stove or in a preheated browning skillet, heat the butter or margarine and oil and brown the fillets until crusty. (If you use a browning skillet, use half the butter and oil and cook only 2 fillets at a time; pour off any liquid left in the pan after browning, then add the remaining butter or margarine and oil.) Arrange the fillets on a serving platter and wrap with waxed paper. Let cook; they should be at room temperature when placed under the microwaves hours later. Cook on the serving platter in the center of the oven 3 minutes. Rotate the platter half a turn at 1½ minutes. Let set, covered, 2 minutes. Fish is ready when it flakes easily with a fork. *Serves 4.*

STRIPED BASS STUFFED WITH SHRIMP

Speed-cook; 14 minutes

One 3- to 3½-pound whole striped
    bass, scaled and cleaned
Juice of 2 lemons

1 tablespoon butter or margarine

1 garlic clove, minced
1 tablespoon flour
½ cup hot beef broth
½ teaspoon salt (optional)
½ teaspoon black pepper
Dash of cayenne pepper
½ teaspoon dry mustard

½ pound shrimp, shelled, deveined, and chopped
4 medium mushrooms, chopped
1 tablespoon chopped fresh parsley
2 egg yolks, beaten
4 thin slices larding pork

Marinate the bass in the lemon juice 1 hour, turning two or three times. Melt the butter or margarine in a glass bowl. Add the onion and garlic and cook in the center of the oven 2 minutes, or until soft. Stir in the flour. Cook 1 minute, then stir in the beef broth 1 minute or until the sauce is smooth and thickened. Let cool, then mix in the salt, pepper, cayenne pepper, mustard, shrimp, mushrooms, parsley, and egg yolks. Stuff the bass with this mixture and close the cavity with toothpicks. Place the bass on 2 inverted saucers in a glass baking dish. Arrange the larding pork atop the bass. Cover loosely with waxed paper and cook in the center of the oven 5 minutes. Baste with the juices. Rotate the dish half a turn. Baste. Cook 5 minutes. Let set, covered, 5 minutes. Do not overcook. The fish is ready when it flakes easily with a fork. *Serves 4 to 6.*

SWORDFISH STEAKS WITH MAÎTRE D'HÔTEL BUTTER

Speed-cook; 4 minutes

Four ¾-inch-thick swordfish steaks
　(each about 6 ounces)
2 tablespoons cooking oil

Salt and pepper to taste
Maître d'Hôtel Butter (page 81)

Brush both sides of the steaks with the oil; sprinkle lightly with salt and pepper. We like a 9½-inch browning skillet for this dish, but you can use a shallow baking dish. To use a browning skillet: Preheat the pan 4½ minutes. Cook the fish 2 minutes on each side. Let set, covered, 2 minutes. The fish is ready when it flakes easily with a fork. If you use a shallow glass baking dish, place the oiled steaks in the dish and cook in the center of the oven 3 minutes on each side. Let set, covered, 3 minutes. Top each steak with a dollop of soft Maître d'Hôtel Butter, and serve.

Salmon steaks can be substituted for the swordfish. *Serves 4.*

Maître d'Hôtel Butter

½ cup unsalted butter or
   margarine, softened
½ cup minced fresh parsley

1½ tablespoons fresh lemon juice
¼ teaspoon pepper

In a bowl, blend all of the above ingredients.

STUFFED BROOK TROUT

Speed-cook; 12½ minutes

4 slices bacon
2 tablespoons butter or margarine
2 shallots or 1 small white onion,
   minced
2 tablespoons tomato sauce
1 tablespoon chopped fresh
   parsley
1 cup bread crumbs
12 raisins, chopped

½ teaspoon salt (optional)
½ teaspoon pepper
2 teaspoons Madeira
Dash of hot sauce
4 whole brook trout (each 6 to 8
   ounces), cleaned
Paprika
1 lemon, quartered and seeded

Place 2 or 3 paper towels on a plate and arrange the bacon on them in one layer. Cover with a paper towel and cook in the center of the oven 3½ minutes. Pat off the fat. Let cool, then finely crumble. In a glass bowl, melt the butter or margarine and cook the shallots or onion 2 minutes, or until soft. To this bowl add the bacon and remaining ingredients except the trout, paprika and lemon. Blend well. Divide the mixture into 4 parts and stuff the trout; close the cavities with toothpicks. Place the trout on a serving platter or in a shallow glass baking dish. Sprinkle with paprika and cover loosely with waxed paper. Cook 4 minutes. Rotate the dish half a turn and cook 3 minutes. Let set, covered, 2 minutes. The trout are ready when they flake easily with a fork. Serve garnished with the lemon wedges. *Serves 4.*

SPEEDY SHRIMP CURRY

Speed-cook; 8 minutes

1 pound medium shrimp, shelled
   and deveined

¼ cup hot water
1 small celery rib, sliced

1 small white onion, quartered
2 tablespoons lemon juice

1 teaspoon salt (optional)
½ teaspoon pepper

Place the seven ingredients in a glass casserole. Cook in the center of the oven 2 minutes, stirring after each minute. Drain shrimp and set aside.

2 tablespoons butter or margarine
1 medium-size white onion, minced
1 tablespoon curry powder
One 10-ounce can frozen
    condensed cream of shrimp
    soup, thawed

One 10½-ounce can condensed
    cream of mushroom soup
Salt and pepper to taste
Hot cooked rice

In a glass casserole, melt the butter or margarine and cook the onion in the center of the oven 2 minutes, or until soft. Stir in the curry powder and the soups, blending well. Cook 2 minutes, or until simmering. Stir. Taste for seasoning, adding salt and pepper, if necessary. Stir in the shrimp and cook 2 minutes. Stir. Shrimp should be firm but not hard. Serve spooned over rice, and pass the chutney. *Serves 4.*

TUNA OR SALMON LOAF

Speed-cook; 6 minutes

6 ounces potato chips, broken up
Two 7-ounce cans chunk tuna or
    salmon, drained and flaked

One 10½-ounce can condensed
    cream of mushroom soup
1 tablespoon chopped pimiento

In a bowl, mix all the ingredients thoroughly. Butter a glass loaf dish and spoon the mixture evenly into it. Cook in the center of the oven 4 minutes. Rotate the dish half a turn and cook 2 minutes. Let set, covered, 5 minutes. *Serves 4.*

TUNA SCALLOP

Speed-cook; 9 minutes

2 tablespoons butter or margarine
1 medium-size white onion,
    chopped
1 celery rib, scraped and chopped
1 garlic clove, minced

1 small sweet red pepper, cored,
    seeded, and chopped
Two 7-ounce cans fancy white
    chunk tuna, drained and flaked

2 tablespoons chopped fresh
  parsley
½ teaspoon salt (optional)
¼ teaspoon pepper

1 cup coarse, unsalted cracker
  crumbs
¼ cup light cream
2 eggs, beaten

Melt the butter or margarine in a bowl. Add the onion, celery, garlic, and sweet red pepper and cook in the center of the oven 3 minutes, or until soft, stirring after 1½ minutes. Let cool slightly, then add all the remaining ingredients. Mix well. Spoon the mixture into a buttered glass casserole, dot the top with butter, and cook in the center of the oven 4 minutes. Rotate the dish half a turn. Cook 2 minutes. Let set, covered, 5 minutes. *Serves 4 to 6.*

WHITING WITH CLAMS

Speed-cook; 8 minutes

4 whiting (each about ½ pound
  after cleaning)
3 tablespoons olive oil
Salt and pepper to taste
2 garlic cloves, minced

2 tablespoons minced fresh parsley
¼ cup fresh lemon juice
1½ cups dry white wine
12 clams, scrubbed

Roll the whiting in the oil, coating them well. Place them side by side in a large glass casserole. Sprinkle lightly with salt and pepper. Sprinkle on the garlic, parsley, and lemon juice. Pour the wine around the fish to a depth of ½ inch. Cook, covered, in the center of the oven, 2½ minutes. Turn the fish. Cook 2½ minutes. Arrange the clams around and between the fish. Cook, covered, 3 minutes, or until the clams open and fish flakes easily with a fork. Discard unopened clams. Serve in warm deep plates with the broth. Pass warm buttered crusty bread for dunking. *Serves 4.*

COQUILLES ST. JACQUES

Speed-cook; 6 minutes

2 tablespoons butter or margarine
1 medium-size white onion, minced
1 garlic clove, minced
1 tablespoon chopped fresh
  parsley

1 pound whole bay scallops or cut-
  up ocean scallops
⅓ cup dry white wine
One 10½-ounce can condensed
  cream of mushroom soup

½ cup grated Gruyère cheese
2 tablespoons flour blended with ¼
   cup water

Salt and pepper to taste
½ cup bread crumbs
Paprika

In a glass casserole, in the center of the oven, melt the butter or margarine. Add the onion, garlic, and parsley. Cook 2 minutes, or until the onion is soft. Stir in the scallops and wine. Cook 2 minutes. Stir. Blend in the soup and cheese. Stir in the flour-water mixture, blending well. Cook 2 minutes. Stir. Season with salt and pepper. Test scallops. They should be just firm, but not hard. Place mixture in individual scallop shells or ramekins. Sprinkle with bread crumbs and paprika. Place under the broiler of a conventional stove until the bread crumbs are brown. *Serves 4.*

9

~~~~~~~~~~

POULTRY

ALTHOUGH most foods do well under microwaves, we believe that poultry does best. Whereas other methods of cooking tend to remove moisture, microwaves seem to moisten and tenderize everything from Cornish game hen to turkey.

There are some points to keep in mind, however, when preparing poultry. We will be repeating ourselves at the beginnings of some chapters, for we think that it is pertinent to state the facts where they will be helpful and not refer the reader back to other pages, except where it is necessary.

Even if you have a defrost setting on your microwave oven, your roast poultry will be more satisfactory if you let them defrost slowly in their wrappings in the refrigerator for 24 hours; turkeys, depending upon their size, probably will take twice that long. The defrosting capabilities of the microwave oven, as stated elsewhere, are unequalled for emergencies. If you must defrost fast, by all means do so, following the outlined routine carefully. There is a proper defrosting time, followed by a resting time, which ensures that the meat will not be overcooked on the outside and undercooked on the inside, where defrosting wasn't complete. There's no trick to it and it's a great help. But why use microwaves to defrost if you don't have to?

Most microwave experts state that poultry should be cooked 7 minutes to the pound. We disagree. We cook ours perfectly at 6 minutes to the pound. Why? Heat equalization in microwave cookery always must be taken into consideration. The cooking will continue while you cover the bird and let it set.

We further discuss the method of "resting" or "setting" the bird in our roast turkey recipe (page 105).

Little or no reference is made in other microwave cookbooks about the importance of proper trussing. We stress this. Protruding legs, thighs, wings, anything "akimbo," will be dried out quickly by the superfast microwaves. A well-trussed bird should be as tight and compact as a clenched fist. This skillful trussing will keep it moist and tender, permitting more even cooking.

The French needle system is the best by far. We offer a diagram to help you learn the technique which, at first glance, may appear a bit complicated but which proves to be simple once you put your mind to it.

A long trussing needle, similar to a mattress needle, draws the cord through, not around, the bird. They are available in most shops that sell sophisticated cooking equipment.

There are only two tie positions: near the tail, to truss the legs and drumsticks; and through the thighs, which also ties in the wings and neck skin.

The needle passes through the lower carcass, comes back over (not through) one leg, *through* the tip of the breast bone, and *over* the second leg. The cord is then tied tightly. In the second tie, using a new piece of cord, the needle is pushed through the apex of the second joint and the drumstick, emerging at that same point on the opposite side. The bird is then turned over, the wings are folded back, and the needle is pushed through one wing. The needle's emerging point catches the loose neck skin and passes through the other wing. The cord is again drawn as tightly as possible and tied. The diagram will take you through these simple steps to a better bird.

After the bird is trussed (your way or our way) we like to brush it with Herb Butter (page 129). Melt enough to yield one tablespoon and brush the bird well with it.

Next, place pieces of aluminum foil on protruding wing tips and legs, and on the part of the breast adjacent to the cavity. These should not be large pieces of foil. They should cover only those "akimbo" portions that will dry out quickly unless they are shielded from the microwaves. Make certain that this foil does not touch the sides of the oven as it may pit them. Some authorities suggest that you remove this foil after half the cooking time has elapsed. We leave it on, however, throughout the cooking period.

Do not salt any large piece of poultry or meat. The salt will draw moisture to the surface, forming a crust that will slow microwave penetration. (You will note that our Herb Butter contains unsalted butter or margarine.)

The bird to be cooked also must be placed on an inverted saucer, plate, or nonmetal trivet, to keep it above the juices. But that is not enough. You also should siphon off with a bulb baster or spoon off any liquid that accumulates. Baste the bird each time you do this; save some for gravy if you wish and discard the rest. This is moist cookery and you will find that liquid continually accumulates. Liquid absorbs microwaves, and if you do not get rid of it, it will throw off your timing; even with carry-over cooking when the bird sets, covered, you may end up with undercooked poultry.

The bird also must cook evenly. One way to do this is to *turn* the bird. Start it off on one side, then breast down, then the other side, then breast up. Recipes will give you the timing for these steps.

If you are cooking poultry pieces, make sure the thicker portions are near the outside of the casserole or dish, the slender or thinner portions nearer the center.

You'll find that the microwave oven can be a great help if you are going

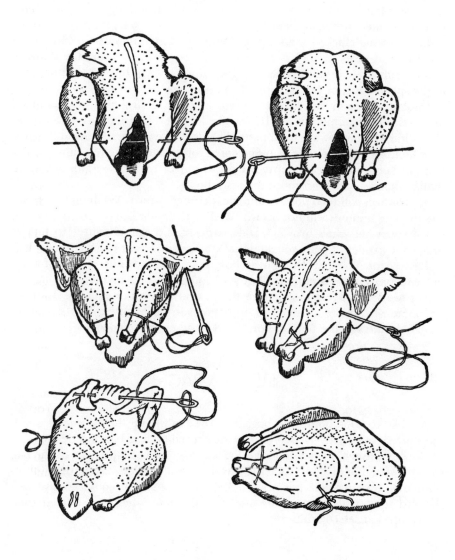

to have a barbecue feast for a number of people, and plan to cook the chicken pieces outside over a charcoal grill. You can precook the chicken in minutes under microwaves, then bring them to crisp perfection over charcoal. The chicken will be evenly cooked; charcoal-barcecued chicken too often is very crisp and brown on the outside and underdone on the inside.

To prevent splatters, cover the poultry loosely with waxed paper. It will not prevent browning.

We also remind you that each chicken or turkey or duck probably will vary in cooking time according to its age, diet, and the length of time it was frozen or stored. A tender, coddled chicken will cook fast (so will one that has been held overlong in cold storage); a tough one will take longer. Primer rules, true, but timely tips. For example, we use frying chickens for any stew-type dish. A stewing chicken is an old bird and tough. It cannot tenderize in the short time it takes to cook a bird under microwaves. By using the slo-cook timer we have successfully poached a stewing chicken, but if you attempt it in the speed-cook, or fast, setting, it will be chewy.

Cooking times in this book are predicated on the fact that the food is at or close to room temperature. If you take it right out of the refrigerator and pop it into the microwave oven naturally it will take longer. To avoid the possible buildup of salmonella or other dangerous bacteria, we recommend that you not keep uncooked poultry (or meat) out of the refrigerator for more than an hour—and *never* more than two hours.

Microwaves will turn poultry and meat golden brown. Anything that cooks less than 18 minutes will not brown. We like the color of microwave poultry, but if you want yours browner and crisper it is a simple matter to slide it under the broiler of your conventional stove, or use your convection setting.

Last words: Watch it. Don't overcook. You can always microwave for a few more seconds or even minutes. But you cannot uncook anything.

Let food set, covered, to permit the heat and juices to equalize. Internal temperature can rise as much as 40 degrees in 20 minutes. This is why we cook 6 minutes to the pound, not 7 or 8 as others recommend.

BIRD IN A BAG

If you like to cook poultry in bags, microwaves will do the job nicely. Place the stuffed, seasoned, trussed bird in the special poultry bag and tie the neck of the bag. Punch 5 small holes all the way around near the neck of the bag to allow steam to escape. Place the bird in a shallow glass baking dish. Allow 6 minutes cooking time per pound, and to make sure it cooks evenly, turn the bird at intervals, first on one side, then the other, then breast down, then breast up. Let set 10 minutes.

CREAMED CHICKEN BREAST CASSEROLE

Speed-cook; 16 minutes

5 tablespoons butter or margarine
6 large mushrooms, thinly sliced
3 tablespoons flour
1 cup chicken broth
½ cup dry white wine

½ cup heavy cream
Salt and pepper to taste
2 large whole chicken breasts, cut
    into halves

In a skillet on a conventional stove, or in a preheated browning skillet, melt 2 tablespoons of the butter or margarine and lightly brown the mushrooms. Remove and reserve them. Heat the remaining butter or margarine in the skillet and stir in the flour, blending into a smooth paste. Add the chicken broth, a small amount at a time, stirring until you have a thickened smooth sauce. Stir in the wine and cream, simmering and stirring until well blended. Season with salt and pepper. Stir in the mushrooms. Place the chicken breasts in a glass casserole, skin side down, in one layer, thicker parts near the edge of the casserole. Pour the sauce over them. Cover with waxed paper and cook in the center of the oven 8 minutes, rotating the casserole half a turn at 4 minutes. Turn the breasts over, spoon the sauce over them, and cook 8 minutes, rotating half a turn at 4 minutes. Let set, covered, 10 minutes. Test for tenderness and seasoning. *Serves 4.*

CHICKEN WITH ARTICHOKE HEARTS

Speed-cook; 18 minutes

Here is a fancy one that is easier than fried chicken.

One 3½-pound chicken, cut up
Salt and pepper to taste
⅛ teaspoon dried thyme
3 tablespoons butter or margarine
1 tablespoon cooking oil
2 tablespoons flour

1 cup chicken broth
2 tablespoons Madeira
8 small mushrooms, cut into halves
One 15-ounce can artichoke hearts
    packed in water, drained

Sprinkle the chicken pieces with salt, pepper, and the thyme. In a skillet on a conventional stove, or in a preheated browning skillet, heat the butter or margarine and oil and brown the chicken. Place in a glass casserole, skin side down, in one layer, thicker parts near edge of the dish. Stir the flour into the skillet; pour in the broth and wine, simmering and stirring into a smooth sauce. Arrange the mushrooms and artichoke hearts between the chicken pieces. Pour the sauce over the ingredients in the casserole. Cover and cook in the center of the oven 9 minutes. Turn the chicken over and rotate the dish half a turn. Cook, uncovered, 9 minutes. Let set, covered, 10 minutes. Test for tenderness. *Serves 4.*

CHICKEN BOMBAY

Speed-cook; 10 minutes

This is a fine spicy chicken we enjoyed in Bombay. We had it hot, nestled in rice, and also cold, served with a salad heavy with mangoes.

⅛ cup chicken broth
Juice of 3 limes
Juice of 2 lemons
1 teaspoon tomato paste
2 teaspoons ground cardamom
1 teaspoon sugar
½ teaspoon salt

⅛ teaspoon hot chili powder
2 large whole chicken breasts, cut into halves and skinned (make several slashes in each breast with a sharp knife to allow the chicken to absorb more of the marinade)

In a glass casserole large enough to hold the chicken breasts in one layer, blend well all of the ingredients except the chicken. Add the chicken breasts and, turning them several times, marinate in the refrigerator 2 hours. Remove the chicken breasts from the marinade 1 hour before cooking and let them sit at room temperature. When you are ready to cook, place the casserole with the marinade in the center of the oven. Bring to a simmer. Add the breasts in one layer, the thicker parts near the edge of the casserole. Cook, covered, 5 minutes. Rotate the dish half a turn. Cook 5 minutes. Let set, covered, 5 minutes. Test for tenderness and seasoning. This dish is very easy to overcook. The breasts will still be cooking in the hot marinade after the casserole is removed from the oven. *Serves 4.*

BREAST OF CHICKEN IN LEEK SAUCE

Speed-cook; 14 minutes

2 tablespoons butter or margarine
½ tablespoon cooking oil

2 large whole chicken breasts, cut into halves

Salt and pepper to taste
One 2¾-ounce envelope dry leek
  soup mix
⅛ cup chicken broth

⅓ cup light cream
¼ cup dry sherry
2 tablespoons brandy
4 large pitted black olives, sliced

In a skillet on a conventional stove, or in a preheated browning skillet, heat the butter or margarine and oil and brown the chicken breasts. Season with salt and pepper and place in a glass casserole, skin side down, in one layer, thicker parts near the edge of the casserole. In the skillet in which the breasts browned, stir in the leek soup mix, chicken broth, cream, sherry, and brandy. Simmer, stirring until well blended into a smooth sauce. Pour the sauce over the chicken breasts. Cook in the center of the oven, covered, 5 minutes. Turn the breasts over. Cook 5 minutes. Rotate the casserole half a turn. Cook 4 minutes. Let set, covered, 10 minutes. Test for tenderness and seasoning. Serve with the leek sauce spooned over each breast, topped with sliced black olives. (They should be black truffles. But who can afford them?) *Serves 4.*

ROAST BUTTERY CHICKEN

Speed-cook; 18 minutes

One 3½-pound chicken
Seasoned salt
1 large white onion, cut into
  quarters

½ cup (¼ pound) *unsalted* butter or
  margarine, softened
½ teaspoon pepper

Liberally sprinkle the cavity of the bird with seasoned salt. Add the onion and truss the chicken. Coat it well with the butter or margarine and sprinkle with the pepper. Cover the ends of the legs and wings with small strips of aluminum foil. Also cover the breast tip at the cavity, so that small portion will not overcook. Place the chicken on its side on an inverted saucer in a glass baking dish. Cover loosely with waxed paper to prevent splatter. Cook in the center of the oven 6 minutes. Baste. Siphon or spoon off any liquid. Turn the chicken on its other side; each time you turn the bird, do it carefully so you do not dislodge the foil strips. Cook 6 minutes. Baste. Siphon or spoon off any liquid. Turn the bird breast up. Baste. Cook 6 minutes. Turn breast side down and let set, covered with foil, for 15 minutes. Test for tenderness. Prick the thick part of the thigh with a fork. If the juices run clear, the chicken is done; if yellowish pink, it will need about another 3 minutes. The bird will be golden brown. Season to taste with salt. If you want it browner or crisper, place it under the broiler of your conventional oven or use your convection setting. *Serves 4.*

CHICKEN CACCIATORE

Speed-cook; 21 minutes

Most chicken cacciatore recipes are heavy on tomatoes and red wine. Here is a white one with a delicious taste difference.

One 3½-pound chicken, cut up
Salt and pepper to taste
5 tablespoons olive oil
2 medium-size white onions,
    chopped

2 celery ribs, scraped and chopped
2 garlic cloves, minced
1 small bay leaf
¼ teaspoon dried oregano
1 cup dry white wine

Season the chicken with salt and pepper. In a skillet on a conventional stove or in a preheated browning skillet, heat 3 tablespoons of the olive oil and brown the chicken. Place it in a glass casserole, skin side down, in one layer, the thicker parts near the edge of the dish. In a glass bowl heat the remaining olive oil. Add the onions, celery, and garlic and cook in the center of the oven 3 minutes, or until soft. Add the bay leaf, oregano, and wine. Mix well; bring to a simmer and pour over the chicken in the casserole. Cook in the center of the oven, covered, 10 minutes, turning the chicken over at 5 minutes. Cook 8 minutes, rotating the casserole half a turn at 4 minutes. Let set, covered, 10 minutes. Test for tenderness and seasoning. *Serves 4.*

COUNTRY CHICKEN WITH CORN

Speed-cook; 16 minutes

This quick Brunswick stew is so simple and speedy that it seems to take mere seconds, yet its succulence will surprise you.

2 small whole chicken breasts, cut
    into halves
4 chicken thighs
One 10¾-ounce can condensed
    chicken gumbo soup

One 10-ounce package frozen
    whole kernel corn, defrosted
1½ teaspoons Worcestershire sauce
Salt and pepper to taste

In a skillet on a conventional stove or in a preheated browning skillet, brown the chicken pieces. Place them in one layer in a glass casserole, skin side down, with thicker parts near edge of dish. In a bowl, blend the soup, corn, Worcestershire sauce, salt, and pepper. Pour the mixture over the chicken.

Cover and cook in the center of the oven 8 minutes. Turn the chicken parts over, spooning the sauce over them, and rotate the dish half a turn. Cook 8 minutes. Let set, covered, 10 minutes. Test for tenderness and seasoning. *Serves 4.*

CHICKEN CURRY WITH ALMONDS

Speed-cook; 14 minutes

4 chicken legs
4 chicken thighs
One 10½-ounce can condensed
   cream of chicken soup

½ cup dry sherry
1 teaspoon curry powder
1½ tablespoons chopped pimiento
⅓ cup slivered almonds, toasted

In a skillet on a conventional stove or in a preheated browning skillet, brown the chicken pieces. Place them in a glass casserole, skin side down, in one layer, thicker parts near the edge of the dish. In a bowl, blend the soup, sherry, curry powder, and chopped pimiento. Pour over the browned chicken. Cook, covered loosely with waxed paper, 5 minutes. Rotate the dish half a turn. Cook 4 minutes. Turn the chicken pieces over and spoon the sauce over them. Cook 4 minutes, rotating the dish half a turn at 2 minutes. Sprinkle with the almonds. Cook 1 minute. Let set, covered, 10 minutes. Test for tenderness and seasoning. *Serves 4.*

CHICKEN OR RABBIT FRANÇAISE

Speed-cook; 16 minutes

This is a favorite recipe, one usually made with domestic rabbit, available in many supermarkets.

1 cup flour
1½ teaspoons salt (optional)
½ teaspoon pepper
½ teaspoon dried thyme
One 3½-pound chicken or rabbit,
   cut up

2 tablespoons butter or margarine
1 tablespoon cooking oil
4 garlic cloves
1 cup chicken broth
⅓ cup dry white wine

Blend the flour, salt, pepper, and thyme. Dredge the chicken pieces with the seasoned flour. In a skillet on a conventional stove or in a browning skillet, heat the butter or margarine and oil; add the garlic and chicken pieces and brown them. Place the chicken in a glass casserole, skin side down, in one layer, thicker parts near the edge of the dish. Pour off the oil and liquid from the skillet, leaving the garlic and the browned specks. Stir in the chicken broth and wine, scraping the bottom of the skillet. Bring to a boil. Pour this and the garlic over the chicken. Cook, covered, in the center of the oven 10 minutes. Rotate the casserole half a turn. Turn the chicken over, spooning some liquid over it, and cook, uncovered, 6 minutes. Let set, covered, 10 minutes. Remove the garlic. Test for tenderness and seasoning. *Serves 4.*

FAST COQ AU VIN

Speed-cook; 20 minutes

This is a French classic. We've skipped a few steps without any loss of flavor.

¼ pound lean salt pork, cut into ½-inch cubes
One 3½-pound chicken, cut up
Salt and pepper to taste
12 small white onions, root ends scored
8 medium mushrooms, sliced
2 garlic cloves, crushed

2 ounces brandy
½ cup dry red wine
½ cup beef broth
⅛ teaspoon dried thyme
1 small bay leaf
2 tablespoons butter or margarine blended with 2 tablespoons flour

In a skillet on a conventional stove or in a preheated browning skillet, lightly brown the salt pork. Season the chicken pieces with salt and pepper; add to the skillet with the salt pork and brown. Place the chicken in a glass casserole, skin side down, in one layer, thicker parts near the edge of the dish. Add the salt pork cubes, onions, mushrooms, and garlic. In a glass bowl, blend the brandy, wine, beef broth, thyme, and bay leaf. Bring to a simmer, stir, and pour over the chicken and vegetables. Cook, covered, in the center of the oven 10 minutes, rotating the casserole half a turn at 5 minutes. Turn the chicken over and cook 10 minutes, rotating half a turn at 5 minutes. Add the blended butter or margarine and flour to the liquid in the casserole, stirring until it has thickened. Let set, covered, 10 minutes. Remove garlic and bay leaf. Test for tenderness and seasoning. *Serves 4.*

GARLIC CHICKEN SURPRISE

Speed-cook, 16 minutes; slo-cook, 32 minutes

This unique dish will come as a surprise to guests. Garlic cooked this way is sweet, not overwhelming, imparting a singularly delicious flavor. Even if you are cautious with garlic, give this a try.

⅛ cup olive oil
24 large garlic cloves
1 celery rib, thinly sliced
2 tablespoons chopped fresh
   parsley
½ teaspoon dried tarragon

1½ teaspoons salt (optional)
½ teaspoon pepper
Pinch of ground nutmeg
4 large chicken legs
4 large chicken thighs

The marinating stage can be done early in the day, but marinate the chicken parts in the refrigerator for at least 3 hours. In a glass casserole that will hold the chicken in one layer, combine the oil, garlic, celery, parsley, tarragon, salt, pepper, and nutmeg. Stir well. Add the legs and thighs and mix well with your hands, coating all the chicken pieces. Turn several times during the marinating period. Remove the chicken from the marinade 1 hour before cooking and let it sit at room temperature. Then heat the marinade separately, bringing it to a simmer. When you are ready to cook the chicken, place waxed paper snugly over the casserole. Place the casserole lid over the waxed paper. To speed-cook, cook in the center of the oven 4 minutes. Rotate the casserole half a turn. Cook 4 minutes. Rotate half a turn. Cook 4 minutes. Rotate half a turn. Cook 4 minutes. Let set, covered, 15 minutes. To slo-cook, rotate the dish half a turn every 8 minutes. Serve the chicken with slices of good bread and "butter" them with the soft garlic. *Serves 4.*

FRIED CHICKEN

Speed-cook; 4 to 6 minutes for each skilletful

With the invention of the browning skillet, this all-American favorite now can be cooked speedily and succulently in the microwave oven. For the best fried chicken, select birds no larger than 2½ pounds; 2-pounders are even better. Inasmuch as the chicken will be cooked with simple seasonings, quality and freshness are important. It also is important not to crowd the pieces in the browning skillet. If necessary, fry them in batches, and keep them warm in a 200° conventional oven. Remember to fry the legs and thighs first. Wings and breast pieces won't take as much time. You can use either flour or bread crumbs as a coating to keep the chicken moist and tender inside and crisp outside. We like both but use flour more often.

This may seem to be an overconcentration on such a simple dish as fried chicken. But it is everyone's favorite, and, until the advent of the browning skillet, chicken was not successfully fried under microwaves. One more point: Arrange the thicker parts of the chicken pieces toward the outside of the skillet, the thinner parts nearer the center.

1 clean brown paper bag
1½ cups flour
1½ teaspoons salt (optional)
½ teaspoon pepper
¼ teaspoon dry mustard
Juice of 1 lemon
Two 2-pound fryers, cut up (do
    not use the backs or wing tips)

4 tablespoons butter or margarine
    (or more, if needed)
4 tablespoons cooking oil (or
    more, if needed)
Paprika

Combine the flour, the salt, pepper, and mustard in the paper bag and mix well. Sprinkle the chicken pieces with the lemon juice. Place the chicken, a few pieces at a time, in the paper bag and shake until they are lightly coated. Remove the chicken from the bag and lightly shake the pieces free of excess flour. They should be coated, but not too thickly. Heat the browning skillet in the center of the oven 4½ minutes. Remove from the oven, add 2 table-spoons of the butter or margarine and 2 of the oil, then add the thighs and legs (do not crowd), skin side down, thicker parts near the edge of the skillet. Loosely cover with waxed paper to prevent splattering. Cook in the center of the oven 3 minutes. Turn the chicken pieces over and lightly sprinkle with paprika. Cook 3 minutes. Test for tenderness. Place the cooked chicken on a platter, covered with foil, in a conventional 200° oven to keep warm while you cook the other pieces. If you are cooking only one batch, let the chicken set, outside the oven, covered with foil, 5 minutes. Pour all liquid from the browning skillet and reheat it 2½ minutes. Add 2 tablespoons butter or mar-garine and 2 of oil and repeat the frying procedure, reheating the skillet 2½ minutes each time and adding more butter or margarine and oil, if necessary. Cook the wings and breasts 4 minutes, turning the pieces at 2 minutes. *Serves 4.*

Note: You can approximate fried chicken in the microwave oven even without a browning skillet. Cook cut-up chicken in a casserole in butter or margarine (6 minutes per pound), turning the chicken pieces over midway through cooking. The chicken then can be crisped and browned under the broiler of a conventional stove, or use your convection oven setting.

CHICKEN WITH ONIONS, GREEK STYLE

Speed-cook; 26 minutes

1 clean brown paper bag
½ cup flour
1½ teaspoons salt (optional)
½ teaspoon pepper
One 3½-pound chicken, cut up

5 tablespoons olive oil
6 medium-size white onions,
    chopped
3 garlic cloves, minced
1 cup chicken broth

In the paper bag, combine the flour, salt, and pepper. Shake, then add the chicken pieces. Shake them until they are evenly coated with flour. Remove the chicken and shake off any excess flour. In skillet on conventional stove or in preheated browning skillet, brown chicken in 2 tablespoons of oil. Place in a glass casserole, skin side down, in one layer, thicker parts near the edge of the dish. In a glass dish, in the center of the oven, cook the onions and garlic in 3 tablespoons of oil 4 minutes, or until soft. Pour in the chicken broth. Blend well. Bring to a simmer; this should take about 4 minutes. Pour the onion sauce over the chicken. Cook in the center of the oven, covered, 18 minutes, rotating the dish half a turn at 4 minutes and turning the chicken at 9 minutes. Spoon the sauce over the chicken after turning. Let set, covered, 10 minutes. Test for tenderness and seasoning. *Serves 4.*

HUNGARIAN CHICKEN MAGYAR

Speed-cook; 19 minutes

4 chicken legs
4 chicken thighs
3 medium-size white onions,
    minced
2 garlic cloves, pushed through a
    garlic press
Salt and pepper to taste
3 tablespoons chopped fresh dill
    or 1 tablespoon dried dill weed

½ cup chicken broth
⅓ cup dry white vermouth
2 tablespoons good paprika,
    preferably Hungarian
3 tablespoons tomato sauce
⅓ cup sour cream

Place the chicken pieces in a glass casserole, skin side down, in one layer, with thicker parts near the edge of the dish. Sprinkle the onions, garlic, salt, pepper, and half the dill over the chicken. Add the chicken broth and vermouth. Cook in the center of the oven, covered, 4 minutes. Rotate dish half a turn. Cook 4 minutes. Turn the chicken pieces over, spooning the sauce over them.

Cook 4 minutes. Rotate dish half a turn. Cook 4 minutes. Let set, covered, 10 minutes. Test for tenderness. Transfer the chicken to a deep, warm serving platter, cover with foil and keep warm. Simmer the liquid in the casserole 2 minutes, stirring. Blend in the paprika and tomato sauce. Cook one minute, or until just simmering. Stir in the sour cream. Spoon the hot sauce over the warm chicken on its serving platter. Sprinkle with the remaining dill. *Serves 4.*

CHICKEN ROMANO

Speed-cook; 12 minutes

This longtime favorite was discovered in a little trattoria *in Rome.*

4 large chicken thighs
3 tablespoons olive oil
1 teaspoon salt
½ teaspoon pepper
¼ teaspoon dried basil
¼ teaspoon dried oregano

1 cup bread crumbs
2 medium potatoes, peeled and
  quartered lengthwise, with the
  ends squared for evenness in
  shape and size
Paprika

In a bowl, place the chicken thighs, olive oil, salt, pepper, basil, and oregano. Mix well, coating the chicken. Let set 2 hours: 1 in the refrigerator, 1 at room temperature. Remove the chicken and dredge with bread crumbs. Place in a glass baking dish, skin side down, in one layer, thicker parts near the edge of the dish. Dry the potatoes and roll them in the liquid remaining in the bowl the chicken marinated in, adding more oil if necessary to coat them lightly. Space the potatoes in a circle around the chicken. Cook, loosely covered with waxed paper, in the center of the oven 5 minutes. Turn the chicken and potatoes over. Sprinkle the chicken lightly with paprika. Cook 2½ minutes. Rotate the dish half a turn. Cook 2½ minutes. Rotate the dish half a turn. Cook 2 minutes. Let set, covered with aluminum foil, 5 minutes. Test for tenderness. You can place the dish under the broiler of a conventional stove until the chicken and potatoes brown, but it will not improve the flavor. *Serves 4.*

CHICKEN CÔTELETTES POJARSKI

Speed-cook; 15 minutes

You'll probably be sorry if you don't double this recipe. Guests always ask for more, and these delicate côtelettes are delicious served cold the next day. They are also fine picnic fare.

4 slices white bread, crusts
  removed
1 cup chicken broth
¼ cup butter or margarine, melted
1½ pounds skinned, boned chicken
  breasts, ground
1½ pounds skinned, boned chicken
  thighs, ground

2 small eggs, beaten
Salt and pepper to taste
4 tablespoons dill weed
Flour for dredging
5 tablespoons butter or margarine
2 tablespoons olive oil
2 cups heavy cream

Break up the bread in a bowl and stir in the chicken broth and melted butter or margarine. Using a fork so you won't pack down the meat and bread, stir in the ground chicken, eggs, a heavy sprinkling of salt and pepper and 2 tablespoons of the dill weed. Mix well. This will be a soft mixture. Refrigerate 3 hours so it can be handled more easily. Form plump, oblong patties, 2 by 3 inches. Dredge them with flour. In a skillet on a conventional stove, or in a browning skillet, heat 2 tablespoons of the butter or margarine and one of the oil. Brown the *côtelettes* evenly on both sides, several at a time, adding more butter or margarine and oil as you need it. If you can, place them in one layer in a large shallow glass casserole or, if necessary, overlap them. Cover with the heavy cream and sprinkle with the remaining dill weed. Cook in the center of the oven, uncovered, for 10 minutes. Rotate the casserole half a turn. Cook 5 minutes. Let set, covered, 10 minutes. *Serves 6.*

ROSEMARY CHICKEN OR RABBIT

Speed-cook; 12 minutes

If you want a new taste treat, substitute rabbit for chicken in this recipe. Delicate, white-fleshed rabbits are sold in supermarkets, have less fat than chicken, and, many people (including us) believe, more flavor.

3 garlic cloves
5 sprigs fresh rosemary or 1
  teaspoon dried rosemary
Pinch of hot chili powder
¼ cup dry white wine
¼ cup olive oil

3 tablespoons lemon juice
1 teaspoon salt (optional)
½ teaspoon pepper
One 3½-pound chicken, cut up, or
  3 pounds rabbit

In a glass casserole, blend the garlic, rosemary, chili powder, wine, olive oil, lemon juice, salt, and pepper. Add the chicken or rabbit, turning to coat with the mixture. Marinate at least 3 hours, turning the pieces several times. Remove the chicken or rabbit. In the center of the oven, bring the marinade to a simmer. Add the chicken or rabbit pieces, skin side down, in one layer, with the thicker parts near the edge of the dish. Cook, covered, 4 minutes. Turn the chicken or rabbit over. Cook 4 minutes. Rotate dish half a turn. Cook 4 minutes. Let set, covered, 15 minutes. Test for tenderness. *Serves 4.*

CHICKEN OR PHEASANT WITH SHALLOTS AND CHABLIS

Speed-cook; 20 minutes

You can get as fancy as you want with microwaves. If you can afford it, make this dish with pheasant rather than chicken. This is a delicately flavored dish.

One 3½-pound chicken or
   pheasant, cut up
24 medium shallots, peeled

1 cup Chablis
½ teaspoon dried savory
Salt and pepper to taste

In a skillet on a conventional stove or in a preheated browning skillet, brown the chicken or pheasant pieces. Place them in a glass casserole, skin side down, in one layer, thicker parts near the edge of the dish. Arrange the shallots among the chicken or pheasant pieces. Pour in the wine. Sprinkle with the savory, salt, and pepper. Cook in the center of the oven, uncovered, 8 minutes. Turn the chicken or pheasant over. Cook 8 minutes. Rotate dish half a turn. Cover. Cook 4 minutes. Let set, covered, 10 minutes. Test for tenderness. Serve the shallots with the chicken or pheasant. *Serves 4.*

PO VALLEY FARMER'S CHICKEN

Speed-cook; 27 minutes

3 tablespoons butter or margarine
1 tablespoon olive oil
4 small chicken thighs
2 small whole chicken breasts, cut
   into halves
Salt and pepper to taste
4 anchovy fillets, cut into pieces
2 garlic cloves, minced

One 16-ounce can plum tomatoes,
   put through a food mill
4 black olives, sliced
4 green olives, sliced
1 teaspoon dried basil
¼ teaspoon hot red pepper flakes
1 teaspoon capers, rinsed and
   drained

In a glass casserole, in the center of the oven, heat the butter or margarine and the oil. Add the chicken and cook 3 minutes. Sprinkle lightly with salt and pepper, then remove from the casserole. In the same dish, cook the anchovies 1 minute or until they can be stirred into a paste. Stir in the garlic, tomatoes, olives, basil, red pepper flakes, and capers, blending well. Cook 5 minutes. Stir. Add the chicken pieces, skin side down, in one layer, thicker parts near the edge of the dish. Spoon the sauce over the chicken. Cook in the center of the oven, covered with waxed paper, 7 minutes. Rotate casserole half a turn. Cook 5 minutes. Turn the chicken pieces over. Spoon the sauce over them. Cook 3 minutes. Let set, covered, 10 minutes. Test for tenderness. Serve the chicken with the spicy sauce spooned atop. *Serves 6.*

CHICKEN WITH SWEET AND HOT SAUSAGES

Speed-cook; 40 minutes

One 16-ounce can Italian plum
 tomatoes, broken up
One 3½-pound chicken, cut up
Salt and pepper to taste
2 small sweet Italian sausages, cut
 into halves
2 small hot Italian sausages, cut
 into halves
2 tablespoons olive oil

2 small white onions, chopped
2 garlic cloves, minced
1 medium green pepper, cored,
 seeded, and cut into 1-inch
 cubes
½ teaspoon dried oregano
¼ cup chicken broth
¼ cup dry white wine

In a glass bowl, in the center of the oven, cook the tomatoes for 10 minutes, stirring once or twice; set aside. Lightly sprinkle the chicken pieces with salt and pepper. Prick the sausages in several places with the point of a knife. In a large glass casserole, in the center of the oven, heat the olive oil. Arrange the chicken skin side down, thicker parts near the edge of the dish, and the sausages in the casserole in one layer. Cover the dish with waxed paper to prevent splattering. Cook 5 minutes. Turn the chicken and sausages over; cook 5 minutes. Remove from the casserole. Pour off all but 1 tablespoon of the liquid. Stir in the onions, garlic, and green pepper. Cook 5 minutes, or until soft. Stir in the tomatoes, chicken, and sausages, and sprinkle with the oregano; pour in the broth and wine and stir well. Cover and cook 10 minutes. Rotate dish half a turn. Cook 5 minutes. Let set, covered, 15 minutes. Test for tenderness. *Serves 4.*

PERUVIAN CHICKEN

Speed-cook; 27 minutes

2 slices bacon, diced
One 3½-pound chicken, cut up
Salt and pepper to taste
1 medium-size white onion,
  chopped
2 medium-size ripe tomatoes,
  peeled, seeded, and coarsely
  chopped

4 pork link sausages, cut into
  ¼-inch-thick slices
1 cup rice
2 cups chicken broth
2 tablespoons chopped chives
⅛ teaspoon hot red pepper flakes

In a skillet on a conventional stove or in a preheated browning skillet, cook bacon 2 minutes. Sprinkle the chicken pieces with salt and pepper and brown in the bacon fat. Remove the chicken. Stir into the skillet the onion, tomatoes, sausage, rice, broth, chives, and red pepper flakes. Cook 5 minutes. Transfer this mixture to a glass casserole and add the chicken, skin side down, in one layer, thicker parts near the edge of the dish. Cover with waxed paper. Cook in the center of the oven 10 minutes. Rotate the dish half a turn at 5 minutes, and turn the chicken pieces over at 10 minutes. Cook another 10 minutes, rotating the dish half a turn at 5 minutes. Almost all of the broth should be absorbed, and the rice should be moist, not dry. Let set, covered, 5 minutes. Test for tenderness and seasoning. *Serves 4.*

VIRGINIA CHICKEN STEW

Speed-cook; 20 minutes

One 10½-ounce can condensed
  chicken gumbo soup
2 ounces brandy
2 tablespoons lemon juice
1 celery rib, scraped and sliced
1 small bay leaf
1 teaspoon salt (optional)
¼ teaspoon pepper

¼ teaspoon poultry seasoning
2 small whole chicken breasts, cut
  in halves
4 small chicken thighs
8 small white onions, root ends
  scored
2 medium potatoes, peeled and cut
  into 1-inch cubes

In a glass casserole, stir in the soup, brandy, lemon juice, celery, bay leaf, salt, pepper, and poultry seasoning. Place in the center of the oven and cook 5 minutes. Stir well into a smooth sauce. Add the chicken pieces, skin side down, in one layer, thicker parts near the edge of the dish. Cook, covered, 4 minutes. Turn the chicken. Cook 4 minutes. Arrange the onions around the outer edge, and the cubed potatoes around the chicken pieces, near the center. Cover. Cook 7 minutes. Let set, covered, 10 minutes. Test chicken and vegetables for tenderness. *Serves 4.*

THYME CHICKEN IN TOMATO SAUCE

Speed-cook; 14 minutes

2 large whole chicken breasts, cut in halves and boned
1 small green pepper, cored, seeded, and cut into thin strips
1 medium-size white onion, thinly sliced

Salt and pepper to taste
¼ teaspoon dried thyme
One 10½-ounce can condensed tomato soup
2 tablespoons red wine vinegar

Place the chicken breasts in a glass casserole, skin side down, in one layer, thicker parts near the edge of the dish. Arrange the pepper strips and onion slices around the chicken. Sprinkle lightly with salt and pepper and the thyme. Blend the tomato soup and vinegar and pour over the chicken. Cover with waxed paper. Cook in the center of the oven 7 minutes, rotating the dish half a turn at 4 minutes. Turn the chicken over. Cook 7 minutes, rotating the dish half a turn at 4 minutes. Let set, covered, 5 minutes. Test for tenderness and seasoning. *Serves 4.*

YUCATÁN CHICKEN IN PAPER

Speed-cook; 20 minutes

In Yucatán this tasty boned chicken would be cooked wrapped in banana leaves. But parchment paper works well.

1 cup olive oil
½ cup lemon juice
1½ teaspoons salt (optional)
½ teaspoon black pepper
⅛ teaspoon hot red pepper flakes
¼ teaspoon dried oregano
¼ teaspoon ground cumin

4 garlic cloves, crushed
2 whole chicken breasts, cut in halves and boned
4 chicken thighs, boned
8 sheets parchment cooking paper, each large enough to completely encase a chicken piece

In a large bowl, blend the olive oil, lemon juice, salt, black pepper, red pepper flakes, oregano, cumin, and garlic. Marinate the chicken pieces in this mixture 8 hours, turning several times. Do not drain the chicken, but remove from the dish well coated with the marinade. Wrap each piece in a sheet of the cooking paper, envelope fashion, completely encasing it. Arrange the wrapped chicken pieces in a glass casserole in one layer. Cover and cook 10 minutes. Turn the chicken over. Cook 10 minutes. Let set, covered, 10 minutes. Serve in the paper for guests to unwrap. *Serves 4.*

CORNISH GAME HENS IN SAUERKRAUT AND WHITE WINE

Speed-cook; 35 minutes

This is a famous Alsatian recipe. Partridge or pheasant is usually used, but Cornish game hens are excellent for a fraction of the cost.

Four ¾-pound Cornish game hens, trussed	2 garlic cloves, chopped
Salt and pepper to taste	1 quart well-drained sauerkraut
3 tablespoons butter or margarine	1½ teaspoons caraway seeds
1 tablespoon cooking oil	1 cup Chablis
5 small shallots or 2 small white onions, chopped	

Sprinkle the game hens lightly with salt and pepper. On a conventional stove or in a preheated browning skillet, brown the game hens in the butter or margarine and oil, being careful not to tear the skins. Remove. Add the shallots or onions and garlic and cook until soft. Transfer the contents of the skillet to a glass casserole. Stir in the sauerkraut, caraway seeds, and wine, mixing them well with the shallots and garlic. Cook in the center of the oven 10 minutes, stirring well after 5 minutes. Stir well and bury the birds on their sides in the sauerkraut. Cover the casserole. Cook 10 minutes. Rotate casserole half a turn. Cook 5 minutes. Stir the sauerkraut well and turn the birds on their other sides. Bury them again in the sauerkraut. Cook 10 minutes. Let set, covered, 15 minutes. Test for tenderness and seasoning. *Serves 4.*

Variations: After you have accomplished this dish, try interesting variations using the same technique (increase the cooking time 5 minutes), substituting pork hocks, pork chops, or boned loin of pork.

Note: Freeze some of the sauerkraut after the dish has cooked to serve with hot dogs. See Super Hot Dog I and II, page 157.

ROAST TURKEY WITH RICE AND SAUSAGE STUFFING

Speed-cook, 48 minutes; slo-cook, 96 minutes

We suggest a stuffing that will be a welcome change from the bread-and-sage type that everybody uses. Do this your own way, using microwaves to save both your own energy and cooking energy, adjusting amounts according to the size of the turkey. We cook poultry 6 minutes to the pound, allowing for carry-over cooking while the bird is setting, covered, after removing it from the microwaves.

Rice and Sausage Stuffing

3 cups cooked rice
½ pound sweet Italian sausage
 meat, cooked and drained
2 tablespoons each of chopped
 onion and chopped celery,
 sautéed until soft in butter or
 margarine

½ cup spinach, cooked, drained,
 and chopped
⅛ teaspoon dried oregano
⅛ teaspoon dried tarragon
Salt and pepper to taste

In a large bowl mix all stuffing ingredients well.

One 8-pound turkey
1 large garlic clove, mashed

2 tablespoons cooking oil
1 teaspoon pepper

Fill the turkey with the stuffing. Truss. If you French-truss with a needle as we suggest (pages 86–87), it won't be necessary to skewer the cavity closed to keep the stuffing inside. If you don't, use a crust of bread, and/or skewers (not metal), or sew the opening closed. Dry the bird, rub it well with the garlic then the oil, and sprinkle with pepper. With small strips of aluminum foil, cover the ends of the legs and wings, and the breast tip adjacent to the cavity so that small portion of the breast will not dry out and harden. Make certain that no foil touches the sides of the oven; it could cause pitting. Place the turkey on its side on an inverted plate in a large glass baking dish in the center of the oven. Cover the turkey loosely with waxed paper to prevent the sides of the oven from being splattered.

To speed-cook: Cook 12 minutes. Turn the turkey breast down. Baste the bird, then remove all of the liquid. Cook 12 minutes. Rotate the dish half a turn at 6 minutes. Turn the turkey on the other side. Remove the liquid in the bottom of the dish, reserving some if you are making gravy. Cook 12 minutes, rotating dish half a turn at 6 minutes. Place the turkey on its back.

Baste. Remove liquid. Cook 12 minutes, rotating dish half a turn at 6 minutes.

If you are using a meat thermometer (only when the bird is out of the oven!), the turkey should be removed when it reads 180°. It is properly cooked at 190°, but letting it set, covered with aluminum foil, for 20 minutes will finish the cooking. The proper time to test for tenderness is after the setting period. We prefer the old sharp-fork test rather than the meat-thermometer test. Pierce the thickest part of the thigh. If the juices run clear, it is done. If yellowish-pink, it isn't ready and probably will need another 5 minutes under microwaves. Besides finishing the cooking, it is also advantageous to let the bird set, covered, to give the juices time to settle, making it more moist and easier to carve. This turkey will be golden brown from the microwaves. If you like it darker, place it under a conventional broiler, or under the browning unit on your microwave oven, if you are lucky enough to have one.

To slo-cook, or simmer: Start off as with speed-cook, with the bird on its side, but change the position after cooking 24 minutes, and change the position again after each 24 minutes. Rotate the dish half a turn after each 12 minutes. *Serves 8 to 10.*

BONELESS TURKEY BREAST

Speed-cook; 22 minutes

Popular today are offerings of boned turkey in varying sizes: breasts, white and dark meat rolls, also whole legs and thighs. It is no longer necessary to buy an entire turkey. You can have the parts of the bird that you like best. The breast leads in popularity.

One 4-pound boned turkey breast
3 tablespoons *unsalted* butter or
  margarine
1 tablespoon cooking oil
½ teaspoon pepper
1 tablespoon lemon juice
¼ teaspoon dried tarragon
Salt to taste

Place the breast on an inverted saucer in a glass casserole. Heat the butter and oil in a measuring cup under microwaves until the butter or margarine melts. Remove. Blend in the pepper, lemon juice, and tarragon. Brush the breast lightly with this sauce. Cover with waxed paper. In the center of the oven, cook the breast 6 minutes. Rotate the dish half a turn. Baste with the sauce. Cook 6 minutes. Turn the breast over. Baste with the sauce. Cook 5 minutes. Baste. Turn breast over. Cook 5 minutes. Baste. Let set, covered, 10 minutes. Test for tenderness. *Serves 4 to 6.*

ROAST DUCKLING TARRAGON

Speed-cook; 28 minutes

It is surprising how few of us eat duckling. It could be that the cooking mystifies. These delicious dark-fleshed birds do well under the micro-waves.

One 4½- to 5-pound duckling
Salt and pepper to taste
1 tablespoon chopped fresh
    tarragon or ½ teaspoon dried
    tarragon

2 small garlic cloves
Grated rind of 1 small lemon
1 small apple, sliced
2 small carrots, sliced
3 small white onions, sliced

Cut off the tips of the wings. Sprinkle the cavity of the bird with salt, pepper, and the tarragon. Place the garlic, lemon rind, and apple inside the cavity. Truss the bird. Prick the thighs, back, and breast. With small strips of aluminum foil, cover the ends of the legs and wings, and the breast tip adjacent to the cavity. Place an inverted saucer in a glass casserole. Lay the duckling on its side on the saucer. Arrange the carrots and onions around it. Cook in the center of the oven, covered, 10 minutes. Turn the duckling on the other side. Baste the bird, then siphon off all liquid. Cook 10 minutes. Rotate the dish half a turn. Turn the duckling breast up. Baste. Cook 8 minutes. Let set, covered, 15 minutes. Test for tenderness. If the bird is more duck than duckling, it may need another 5 minutes under microwaves. Duckling is medium rare (at its best) if the juices that run from the thick part of the thigh are pink (not red!) when pricked; well done if the juice is yellow. If you want the duckling dark brown and crusty, place it under the broiler of a conventional stove for a few minutes. *Serves 4.*

ROAST DUCKLING WITH PARSNIPS

Speed-cook; 25 minutes

The French often pair parsnips with duckling. It seems an odd couple, but is a winning combination.

One 4½- to 5-pound duckling
Salt and pepper to taste
⅛ teaspoon dried thyme

2 tablespoons butter or margarine
1 tablespoon cooking oil

1 herb bouquet (2 sprigs each of parsley and thyme, 1 sprig of tarragon, 1 bay leaf tied in a cheesecloth bag. You can use dried herbs, but not ground ones.)

1 pound scraped firm parsnips
½ cup hot chicken broth

Cut off the tips of the wings. Season the cavity with salt, pepper, and the dried thyme. Truss the bird. Prick the thighs, back, and breast. With small strips of aluminum foil, cover the ends of the legs and wings, and the breast tip adjacent to the cavity. In a skillet on a conventional stove, or in a preheated browning skillet, heat the butter or margarine and oil. Using a wooden spoon and fork, being careful not to break the skin, brown the duckling evenly. Place the bird on its side on an inverted saucer in a glass casserole. Add the herb bouquet. Cook in the center of the oven, covered, 10 minutes. Siphon off the liquid. Turn the duckling on the other side. Cook 5 minutes. Siphon off all liquid. Rotate the dish half a turn. Place the bird breast side down. Arrange the parsnips around the duckling and pour in the hot chicken broth. Cook 5 minutes. Place the bird on its back. Cook 5 minutes. Baste the duckling and parsnips. Let set, covered, 15 minutes. Test parsnips and bird for tenderness. If the bird is more duck than duckling, it may need another 5 minutes under microwaves. Duckling is medium rare (at its best) if juices that run from the thick part of the thigh are pink (not red!) when pierced with a knife or fork; well done, if yellow. If you want the duckling dark brown and crusty, place it under the broiler of a conventional stove for a few minutes. *Serves 4.*

10

~~~~~~~~~~

MEATS

Now we come to the heart of the matter: meat and microwaves. Microwaves do magical things, cooking a meat loaf in 10 to 15 minutes, a hamburger in a minute or two, a hot dog in 25 seconds. As stated elsewhere, they will cook all meats in a quarter of the time of conventional cooking, some in less time.

Finicky guests, who threaten to take the bloom off that beautiful rare roast of beef by wanting it well done, can be pleased in seconds. Simply slice off their portions and cook them to their preference under microwaves. Fifteen seconds will make a juicy piece of rare beef medium; in 25 seconds it will be well done.

There are other benefits of cooking meat under microwaves, many of which you will discover for yourself by trial. For example, you will discover that while cooking, meat shrinks only 10 to 12 percent, not the 25 to 35 percent of conventional cooking. The speed is responsible for this saving.

Microwaves, however, do not have the magic to tenderize the less tender cuts of meat such as chuck and stewing beef. Thus, as in conventional cookery, it pays dividends in the long run to use the better cuts. If you use stewing meats or bargain cuts, they should be tenderized first according to the directions on the tenderizer package. A meat hammer for steaks, and marinating in tomato juice and wine, etc., also help.

If you have a slo-cook, or simmer, setting on your microwave oven, it is possible to cook a savory, reasonably tender stew, using ordinary stew meat. Even so, stews may end up on the chewy side. Much depends upon the condition of the meat, the cut, its age, what you cook it in, and other factors in this mysterious chemistry of cooking. We use good aged sirloin in our stews, and always cut up a nice small leg of lamb for stews, skipping the tougher cuts. Usually our stews are tender; however, not always. If you overcook for even 2 minutes, the meat can become chewy.

It is simple common sense to reason that larger pieces of meat in a stew will take longer to cook than the smaller pieces. Thus, it is important to try to cube them all the same size, so that some are not overdone and chewy and others undercooked.

Be advised that rib or sirloin cook quickly, and that round and chuck do not.

Smaller cuts, 3 to 3½ pounds, do better than larger cuts.

Any piece of meat that cooks in less than 15 minutes will not brown under microwaves. But steaks, chops, and hamburgers can be beautifully cooked and browned in minutes, using the effective microwave browning skillet. We will use the skillet often in this chapter. It is a marvel for the small, tender cuts.

Ground meat does better than any other meat under microwaves. Grinding, of course, tenderizes it and the extremely fast cooking results with it seem almost magical.

Do not salt large pieces of meat before cooking, even with seasoned salt. Salt will toughen the outer layer of meat. Pepper, spices, herbs, and soy sauce are fine to use. Season to taste with salt after the cooking is completed.

Microwave cookery is similar to the Chinese method, which also is fast, requires that pieces of meat be small and of uniform size, and is stirred often to change the cooking position of the meat and/or vegetables.

It is more effective to cook a dinner for eight in two batches. Also, when doubling a recipe, add two-thirds of the original cooking time.

Begin cooking roasts with the fat side down. Place the roast on a baking or roasting dish on a special microwave trivet or on an inverted saucer to keep it out of its juices. Cover loosely with waxed paper or a paper towel to prevent splattering. Baste the meat with the juices and, using a large spoon or a bulb baster, remove all liquid periodically, saving some for gravy if you wish, discarding the rest. This is important. Liquid absorbs microwave energy, stealing it from the meat, slowing and altering the cooking period, throwing your timing off.

Halfway through the cooking time, turn the roast over. In order to ensure even cooking, it is also a good idea to rotate the dish half a turn each fourth of the cooking time.

After the meat is removed from the oven it will continue to cook, heat flowing to the center. Allow for this in your timing. If you want it rare at 6 minutes per pound, cook it only 5 per pound. Then let it set, covered, 20 minutes before testing for tenderness or using the meat thermometer.

Try to select uniformly shaped roasts. If they taper, the slender end will cook faster, drying out. This can be averted by covering the end with a small piece of aluminum foil. Do not use large pieces of foil. And do not let them touch the sides of the oven. They can pit them.

Cooking times that follow are based on meat at room temperature. Do *not* take meat from the refrigerator and immediately cook it. Let it stand at least 1 hour, though not more than 2 hours, depending upon the size of the meat.

Because they are more uniform, rolled roasts do better than bone-in roasts. Bones also prevent microwaves from penetrating properly. Cover any protruding bones with small strips of aluminum foil. Do the same with a leg of lamb or veal.

Pot roasts, and all roasts from less tender cuts, need a setting period of at least 20 minutes, covered, after the cooking time has been completed.

If you are going to cook meat that you have defrosted, let large pieces set at room temperature for 1½ hours after defrosting, smaller pieces 45 minutes to an hour.

Some tips about roasts: If cooking a standing rib roast, turn it over 3 times during the cooking period, side to side and then fat side up. If the boned, rolled roast is thicker than 5 inches, turn it over 4 times during cooking period, top to bottom, then end to end. This balances the cooking, assisting the waves in cooking the meat evenly.

And undercook! Even though we are cautious and undercook, do not even trust our directions. Take a minute from our cooking time, or even more, until you are certain that the meat is cooked to your taste. You can always let it set for 10 minutes or so and test a piece to see if it is cooked as you like it.

The danger and confusion in all meat cookery is the astounding speed of the microwaves. Even after you have used a microwave oven for months, you'll find that you are tempted, because of the years at the conventional stove, to "put it back for just a few more minutes." Don't. That's the way to disaster.

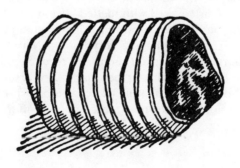

BEEF

Hamburgers and the Browning Skillet: A Discussion

Why open this chapter with hamburger recipes? Two reasons: They are every-body's favorite, and ground meat cooks very easily and well under micro-waves. The browning skillet is not needed to cook hamburgers—or anything. As noted, you can even place a hamburger on a paper plate and cook it. But do *not* ever cook a hamburger on a bun, as some books suggest. The juices from the meat will make the bun a soggy mess.

Back to the browning skillet. Follow the simple directions that come with it and it will not only produce a superior hamburger (without the use of cook-ing fat or oil) but also will brown, sear, grill, fry, and sauté everything from steak, chicken, and lamb chops to mushrooms in butter.

You will have to experiment with the skillet, using your own taste as the test, whether you want your hamburgers (or steaks or chops) rare, medium, or well done, taking into consideration the thickness of the hamburger. We like rare hamburgers; we cook our half-pound patties in the browning skillet 45 seconds on one side and 30 seconds on the other, and let them set on hot, toasted, buttered buns for 30 seconds before we add mustard, relish, ketchup, or chili sauce.

If you do not want to use the browning skillet, you can time one quarter-pound hamburger at 1 minute on one side and 30 seconds on the other for medium rare. Cook two quarter-pounders 2½ minutes for medium rare, and four for 4 minutes, 2 minutes on one side, 2 on the other. If you are not using the browning skillet, brush the hamburgers when you turn them with whatever drippings have collected. If you want the hamburgers to look brown, dilute a dark liquid seasoning with a little water and brush it over them.

We point out that no one knows the color of a hamburger once it has been doused with ketchup, or covered with melted cheese.

But we also point out that the browning skillet is a unique utensil that does more than brown. It sears, and cooks very hot and very fast, thus retaining the juices in hamburgers, steaks, and chops. We recommend using the brown-ing skillet on some of our favorite recipes that follow. A tip for better brown-ing: If liquid has collected in the skillet after you have browned one side of the meat, the other side will brown better if you pour off that liquid and cook with a dry pan.

BLUE-CHEESE BURGERS

Speed-cook; 3 minutes

All ground meats need the addition of some liquid to keep them moist throughout cooking, helping prevent the dry flavor of too many so-called "hamburgers."

1½ pounds ground top or bottom
   round
1 teaspoon seasoned salt

¼ cup beef broth
Four ½-inch cubes blue cheese,
   chilled

In a bowl, blend well the beef, seasoned salt, and broth. Form into four 1½-inch-thick patties. Bury a cube of the blue cheese in the center of each, molding the beef around it. Preheat the 9½-inch browning skillet 4½ minutes. Add the patties and cook 1½ minutes on each side. These will be on the rare side. Let them set, covered, 35 seconds to continue to melt the cheese. *Serves 4.*

BURGUNDY BURGERS

Speed-cook; 3 minutes

As we've said, one of the many advantages of microwave cooking is that it can do away with cooking oils and fats—if you will let it. Steaks, chops, and hamburgers can all be grilled to perfection on the browning skillet without cooking oils or fats. This also gives the meat a much better flavor, as it is prepared, so to speak, with its own personality. Here is a recipe that will surprise you with its flavor.

1½ pounds good ground chuck
2 ounces dry red wine

1 teaspoon seasoned salt

In a bowl blend well all ingredients. Shape into four 1½-inch-thick patties. Preheat the 9½-inch browning skillet 4½ minutes. Add the beef patties. Cook 1½ minutes on each side. These will be on the rare side. If you like yours cooked a bit more, add another 25 seconds to each side. Careful, though! Almost before you can say "medium rare," the microwaves will have prepared a well-done patty. *Serves 4.*

ITALIAN CHEESEBURGERS

Speed-cook; 3 minutes

"Hamburger" is a catchall word for chopped meat that isn't always of the highest grade. We call ours "ground meat" and always grind our own. We suggest that you do, too, thereby being certain of what you are getting. In Italy, beef isn't of the quality it is here. Often the Italians grind it and couple it with imagination to produce a simple but exceptional dish.

1½ pounds ground beef, preferably sirloin
½ small white onion, minced
1 teaspoon Dijon mustard

Salt and pepper to taste
¼ pound Gorgonzola cheese, crumbled into small pieces

In a bowl, place the ground beef, onion, mustard, salt, and pepper, blending well. Shape into 1½-inch-thick patties, oblong rather than the usual round form. Preheat the 9½-inch browning skillet 4½ minutes. Add the meat patties. Cook 1½ minutes on each side. Sprinkle the cheese evenly over each patty. Cook just until melted. These will be rare. If you like yours cooked a bit more, add another 25 seconds to each side before sprinkling with the cheese. *Serves 4.*

HAMBURGER SHELL PIE

Speed-cook; 11 minutes

1½ pounds ground chuck
1 egg, beaten
1 teaspoon salt (optional)
½ teaspoon pepper
One 10½-ounce can condensed vegetable soup

1 garlic clove, minced
¼ teaspoon dried oregano
½ cup grated sharp cheese

Mix together the ground chuck, egg, salt, and pepper. Line the sides and bottom of a 9-inch glass pie plate with the meat mixture, making a shell. In a glass measuring cup, blend the soup, garlic, and oregano and cook in the center of the oven 3 minutes. Pour the warm soup mixture into the meat pie shell. Cook in the center of the oven 4 minutes. Rotate the plate half a turn. Cook 4 minutes. Sprinkle with the cheese; place under the broiler of a conventional stove until the cheese is melted. *Serves 4.*

MILANO MEAT LOAF

Speed-cook; 15 minutes

Meat loaf may seem mundane to many, but not this one, which will have your guests asking for the recipe.

½ pound bulk pork sausage
½ pound ground chuck
½ pound ground pork
½ pound ground veal
One 8-ounce can tomato sauce
  with spices and green pepper
2 eggs, beaten
¾ cup bread crumbs

2 white onions, finely chopped and
  sautéed in butter until soft
½ cup grated Parmesan cheese
2 tablespoons minced white raisins
2 tablespoons minced fresh Italian
  parsley
2 teaspoons salt (optional)
1 teaspoon pepper

Place all the ingredients in a large bowl and blend well. Lightly butter a 2-quart glass loaf dish. Spoon the meat mixture evenly into the dish but do not pack it down. Do not let the ends taper down as they will dry out. Place, uncovered, in the center of the oven. Cook 15 minutes, rotating half a turn every 5 minutes. Let set, covered, 10 minutes. *Serves 6.*

LOW-COST MINUTE MEAT LOAF

Speed-cook; 10 minutes

2 pounds ground chuck
One 10-ounce can condensed
  chicken gumbo soup
1 egg, beaten
½ cup bread crumbs
1 medium onion, chopped

2 tablespoons chopped fresh
  parsley
1 tablespoon Worcestershire sauce
1 teaspoon salt (optional)
½ teaspoon pepper
Pinch of nutmeg

In a bowl, combine all the ingredients and mix well. Butter a glass loaf pan and spoon the mixture evenly into it. Do not pack it. Cook in the center of the oven 5 minutes. Rotate the pan half a turn. Cook 5 minutes. Let set, covered, 5 minutes. *Serves 6.*

FAST-MIX MICROWAVE MEATBALLS

Speed-cook; 14 minutes

This is excellent with rice, barley, or couscous (page 168).

1 pound ground chuck
½ cup bread crumbs
1 medium onion, chopped
1 egg, beaten
½ teaspoon seasoned salt
¼ teaspoon pepper

2 tablespoons butter
One 10½-ounce can condensed
   cheddar cheese soup
⅓ cup milk
2 tablespoons chopped fresh
   parsley

In a bowl, blend the ground meat, bread crumbs, onion, egg, seasoned salt, and pepper. Shape into small meatballs. In a glass casserole, in the center of the oven, melt the butter, add the meatballs, and cook 4 minutes, turning them at 2 minutes to cook evenly. Blend the soup, milk, and parsley and pour over the meatballs. Cover with waxed paper. Cook 5 minutes. Stir. Cook 5 minutes. Stir. Let set, covered, 5 minutes. *Serves 4.*

MEATBALLS STROGANOFF

Speed-cook; 8½ minutes

1 pound ground sirloin or other
   cut of beef
1 egg, beaten
⅓ cup bread crumbs
¼ cup light cream
1 teaspoon salt (optional)
½ teaspoon pepper
⅛ teaspoon ground mace
2 tablespoons Hungarian paprika

3 tablespoons butter or margarine
1 tablespoon olive oil
4 medium mushrooms, thinly
   sliced
4 shallots, chopped
2 tablespoons Madeira
¼ cup canned beef gravy
¼ cup heavy cream
½ cup sour cream

In a bowl, blend well the ground beef, egg, bread crumbs, light cream, salt, pepper, and mace. Shape into balls about 1 to 1½ inches in diameter. Sprinkle the paprika on a sheet of waxed paper. Roll the meatballs in it, covering them evenly. Heat the butter or margarine and oil in a glass casserole and cook the meatballs in the center of the oven 2 minutes. Turn them; cook 1 minute. Add the mushrooms and shallots. Cook 1 minute. Stir in the wine, beef gravy, and heavy cream. Cover with waxed paper and cook 2 minutes. Stir. Cook 2 minutes. Stir in the sour cream. Cook 30 seconds. Stir. This should be hot but not boiling. Excellent with rice, couscous (page 168), or fine noodles. *Serves 4.*

HUNGARIAN BEEF GOULASH WITH MEATBALLS

Speed-cook; 19 minutes

A real goulash is mainly meat, usually served with noodles. This is an authentic goulash, modified for the microwaves, using ground beef instead of the usual cubes, which often end up chewy. The flavor secret is using Hungarian paprika. Try to get it, for it can make all the taste difference. We like this with green noodles that have been tossed with butter and cheese.

2 pounds ground chuck
2 large eggs, beaten
2 tablespoons beef broth
1 medium onion, minced
⅓ cup bread crumbs
1½ teaspoons salt (optional)
½ teaspoon pepper
½ cup flour
2 tablespoons butter or margarine

1 tablespoon cooking oil
5 medium onions, chopped
2 small green peppers, cored, seeded, and chopped
One 16-ounce can heavy tomato puree
⅓ cup dry red wine
2 tablespoons Hungarian paprika

In a bowl, blend the ground beef, egg, beef broth, minced onion, bread crumbs, 1 teaspoon salt, and the pepper. Form the meatballs into the size you prefer and roll them in the flour. In a glass casserole, in the center of the oven, heat the butter or margarine and oil. Cook the meatballs 3 minutes. Turn them. Cook for 3 minutes. Remove the meatballs. To the same casserole, add the chopped onions and green peppers. Cook 3 minutes, or until soft. Stir in the tomato puree, wine, ½ teaspoon salt, and the paprika. Cook 5 minutes. Stir. Add the meatballs. Cover with waxed paper. Cook 2½ minutes. Stir. Cook 2½ minutes. Stir. Let set, covered, 10 minutes. *Serves 4 to 6.*

CORNY BEEF

Speed-cook; 14 minutes

1 pound ground round steak
2 tablespoons butter or margarine

1 small sweet red pepper, cored, seeded, and chopped

1 small green pepper, cored, seeded, and chopped
2 medium-size white onions, finely chopped
Salt and pepper to taste

One 16-ounce can cream-style corn
2 medium-size ripe tomatoes, sliced
½ cup buttered bread crumbs

In a glass casserole, in the center of the oven, cook the beef in the butter or margarine for 5 minutes, stirring after 2½ minutes. Pour off the liquid. Stir in the peppers and onions. Season with salt and pepper. Cook 5 minutes, stirring after each 2½ minutes. In another glass casserole, alternate layers of the meat mixture with the corn. Place the sliced tomatoes atop. Sprinkle lightly with salt and pepper. Sprinkle with the bread crumbs. Cook 4 minutes, rotating the dish half a turn at 2 minutes. Place the casserole under the broiler of a conventional oven until the bread crumbs are browned. *Serves 4.*

"HOT" CHINESE BEEF SHREDS

Speed-cook; 3 minutes 10 seconds

1 pound flank steak, shredded (see note)
1½ tablespoons dry sherry
¼ cup soy sauce
½ cup peanut oil
¾ cup shredded carrots

1½ tablespoons finely shredded gingerroot
½ teaspoon hot red pepper flakes
1½ cups shredded celery ribs
Salt to taste

Place the beef in a bowl and mix well with the sherry and soy sauce. Preheat a 9½-inch browning skillet 4½ minutes. Remove from the microwave oven. Add half the oil, carefully, as it may splatter. Add the beef to the skillet, also carefully. Place in the center of the oven and cook 2 minutes, stirring every 30 seconds. The edges of the beef should be brown. Remove the beef with a slotted spoon and place in a strainer over a bowl. Pour off the liquid and preheat the skillet 2½ minutes. Add the remaining oil. Stir in the carrot shreds. Cook 30 seconds, stirring after 15 seconds. Stir in the gingerroot, red pepper flakes, and celery. Cook 20 seconds, stirring at 10 seconds. Return the beef to the skillet, mixing it well with the other ingredients. Cook 20 seconds. Test for seasoning, adding salt if necessary. If vegetables are too crunchy for your taste, put the skillet under the microwaves until they are soft enough, remembering that both beef and vegetables can be overcooked in seconds. *Serves 4.*

Note: Modern Chinese cooks make shredding an easy operation by putting the meat in the freezer until it is firm enough to shred quickly, but is not solidly frozen. Hold at room temperature 1 hour before cooking.

TEXAS CHILI CON CARNE

Speed-cook; 29 minutes

2 small white onions, chopped
½ green pepper, cored, seeded and
   chopped
1 garlic clove, minced
1 tablespoon olive oil
1½ pounds ground beef chuck
1 small dried red chili pepper,
   minced
1 tablespoon chili powder

½ teaspoon ground cumin
½ teaspoon salt (optional)
1 small bay leaf, crumbled
One 16-ounce can plum tomatoes,
   broken up
3 tablespoons tomato paste
Two 16-ounce cans dark red
   kidney beans (undrained)

In a deep glass casserole, in the center of the oven, cook the onions, green pepper, and garlic in the olive oil 3 minutes, or until soft, stirring after 1½ minutes. Stir in the ground beef. Cook 5 minutes, stirring at 2½ minutes. Stir in the chili pepper, chili powder, cumin, salt, bay leaf, tomatoes, and tomato paste. Mix well. Cover and cook in the center of the oven 7 minutes. Stir. Rotate casserole half a turn. Cook 7 minutes. Stir in the beans and their liquid. Cover. Cook 4 minutes. Stir. Cook 3 minutes. Let set, covered, 10 minutes. This is delicious served with nothing but a spoon, but it can become a fast and savory supper spooned over buttered noodles. *Serves 6 to 8.*

BEAUMONT BEEF AND RICE

Speed-cook; 20 minutes

Here's a tasty one-dish meal that is simple and savory.

1½ pounds ground chuck
2 medium onions, chopped
1 garlic clove, chopped
1 celery rib, scraped and chopped
1 small sweet red pepper, cored,
   seeded, and chopped

One 10-ounce package frozen
   okra, defrosted
½ cup rice
One 16-ounce can plum tomatoes,
   broken up
½ cup dry red wine

Salt and black pepper to taste

3 teaspoons chili powder

¼ teaspoon cayenne pepper

In a glass casserole, in the center of the oven, cook the beef 3 minutes. Stir in the onions, garlic, celery, red pepper, okra, and rice. Cook 2 minutes. Stir in the tomatoes, wine, salt, black pepper, chili powder, and cayenne pepper. Blend well. Cover. Cook 10 minutes, rotating the dish half a turn after 5 minutes. Uncover. Cook 5 minutes. Stir well. Let set, covered, 10 minutes. *Serves 4 to 6.*

CHINESE CURRIED BEEF TENDERLOIN

Speed-cook; 4½ minutes

2 tablespoons peanut oil

5 whole scallions, thinly sliced

3 thin slices fresh gingerroot, shredded

1 tablespoon curry powder

1½ pounds beef tenderloin, cut into ¼-inch slices, then into strips

Salt to taste

2 tablespoons dry sherry

½ cup beef broth mixed with 1 teaspoon sugar

1 tablespoon cornstarch dissolved in 2 tablespoons water

In a glass casserole, in the center of the oven, heat the peanut oil. Add the scallions and cook 1 minute. Stir in the gingerroot and curry powder. Cook 1 minute. Stir. Lightly salt the beef and stir it into the casserole with the other ingredients. Cook 1 minute, stirring well after 30 seconds. Stir in the sherry and the sweetened beef broth. Cover the casserole. Cook 45 seconds. Stir in the cornstarch, blending well with the beef and onions. Cook 45 seconds. Stir. Let set, covered, 5 minutes. Test for tenderness and seasoning. *Serves 4.*

SIMPLE STROGANOFF

Speed-cook; 12½ minutes

2 tablespoons butter or margarine

1 medium onion, chopped

1 garlic clove, minced

1 pound round steak, cut in narrow, 1-inch-thick strips and tenderized (if you feel wealthy, use fillet of beef)

Salt and pepper to taste

One 10½-ounce can condensed mushroom soup

Pinch of nutmeg

One 4-ounce can sliced mushrooms, drained

1 cup sour cream

In a glass casserole, in the center of the oven, heat the butter or margarine and cook the onions and garlic 2 minutes, or until soft. Stir in the beef, seasoning lightly with salt and pepper. Cook 4 minutes. Turn the beef. Stir in the mushroom soup and nutmeg. Cook 4 minutes, stirring after 2 minutes. Stir in the mushrooms. Cook 2 minutes. Let set, covered, 5 minutes. Test for tenderness. Stir in the sour cream. Cook 30 seconds, or until just hot but not boiling. Serve with buttered noodles. *Serves 4.*

FLEMISH BEEF STEW

Slo-cook; 48 minutes

2 tablespoons butter or margarine
2 garlic cloves, cut into halves
2 pounds top sirloin, cut into 1½-inch cubes or pieces
⅛ teaspoon dried thyme
1 teaspoon pepper
2 tablespoons flour

12 ounces beer at room temperature
1 teaspoon salt (optional)
8 small white onions, root ends scored
4 medium carrots, scraped and halved

In a glass casserole, in the center of the oven, melt the butter or margarine, add the garlic, and cook 1 minute. Add the beef, sprinkle with thyme and pepper, and cook 1 minute. Sprinkle with the flour. Stir. Cook 1 minute. Pour in the beer and sprinkle with the salt. Stir. Cover and slo-cook in the center of the oven 10 minutes. Rotate the casserole half a turn. Cook 10 minutes. Stir. Cook 10 minutes. Let set, covered, 10 minutes. Arrange the onions and carrots in a circle around the side of the casserole, surrounding the beef. Cover. Cook 10 minutes. Rotate casserole half a turn. Cook 5 minutes. Let set, covered, 10 minutes. Test the meat and vegetables for tenderness. Serve with lavishly buttered warm bread and, of course, beer. *Serves 4 to 6.*

QUICK TOMATO BEEF STEW

Speed-cook; 28 minutes

2 tablespoons butter or margarine
1 pound stewing beef, cut into cubes and tenderized
Salt and pepper to taste

One 10½-ounce can condensed tomato soup
½ cup beef broth
¼ teaspoon dried thyme

4 medium-size white onions, root
    ends scored
4 medium carrots, cut into halves

3 potatoes, peeled and cut into
    quarters

In a glass casserole, in the center of the oven, melt the butter or margarine, and cook the beef 4 minutes, stirring, seasoning lightly with salt and pepper. Blend the soup and beef broth; pour into the casserole. Sprinkle in the thyme. Cover and cook 8 minutes. Stir. Rotate the casserole half a turn. Cook 8 minutes. Stir. Rotate the casserole half a turn. Arrange the vegetables in an outside circle around the beef. Cook 8 minutes. Let set, covered, 15 minutes. Test meat and vegetables for tenderness. *Serves 4.*

BOEUF À LA MODE (POT ROAST)

Speed-cook, 38 minutes; slo-cook, 1 hour 16 minutes

Select a piece of beef that is evenly shaped. If one end is narrower it will cook more quickly and be dryer than the rest of the roast. Remember, too, that the meat will cook while it is setting, so work that into your cooking computations. For example, with this recipe, in a conventional stove, we cook the beef 3 hours at 300°. Thus, a quarter of that time at speed-cooking would be 45 minutes. Slo-cooking would be half that time, or 1½ hours. But allowing for the carry-over cooking while the meat is setting, we have adjusted the times to 38 minutes for speed-cook, and 1 hour 16 minutes for slo-cooking. We prefer to slo-cook pot roasts and stews. The meat is more tender.

    Cut against *the grain when you are slicing pot roasts and braised meats. The meat will not break up and shred.*

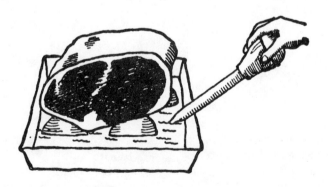

½ cup flour
1 teaspoon salt (optional)
½ teaspoon pepper
One 3½-pound bottom round roast
2 tablespoons butter or margarine
1 tablespoon cooking oil
One 8-ounce can seasoned tomato
   sauce

¼ cup red wine
¼ cup water
3 medium-size white onions,
   quartered
2 garlic cloves, cut into quarters

Blend the flour, salt, and pepper and dredge the beef. On a conventional stove or in a preheated browning skillet, heat the butter or margarine and oil and brown the beef evenly. Transfer the beef to a glass casserole with a tight-fitting lid. Blend the tomato sauce, wine, and water and, in a 2-cup glass measuring cup, bring to a boil in the microwave oven. Pour it over the meat and surround the meat with the onions and garlic. Place the casserole, covered, in the center of the oven.

To speed-cook: Cook 9 minutes. Rotate the dish half a turn. Cook 9 minutes. Rotate the dish half a turn. Cook 9 minutes. Turn the roast over. Cook 9 minutes. Rotate the dish half a turn. Cook 2 minutes. Baste. Let set, covered, 15 minutes. Test for tenderness.

To slo-cook: Cook 15 minutes. Rotate the dish half a turn. Cook 15 minutes; rotate half a turn. Cook 15 minutes. Turn the roast over. Cook 15 minutes. Rotate dish half a turn. Turn the roast over. Cook 16 minutes. Let set, covered, 15 minutes. Test for tenderness.

Strain the sauce. Heat to simmering and pass it *au naturel* in a gravy boat at the table, for guests to spoon over their sliced beef. *Serves 6.*

SAUERBRATEN

Speed-cook; 45 minutes

We've proven to ourselves often that microwaves can master many classic dishes. Here is a German offering that will have family and friends purring. Don't let the list of ingredients put you off. It's easy. Since this dish marinates 2 days in your refrigerator, we'll balance the time by speed-cooking it. In the regular oven, this dish ordinarily cooks about 3 hours; it can be slo-cooked under microwaves in half that time. Please yourself!

1 cup dry red wine
1 cup red wine vinegar
1 cup water

1 large onion, sliced
2 medium carrots, sliced
2 celery ribs, sliced

3 small bay leaves
8 whole black peppercorns,
   crushed
1 teaspoon salt (optional)
One 3- to 3½-pound rolled, tied
   beef rump, bottom or top

round (select a uniformly solid,
   fat-free chunk)
½ cup gingersnap cookie crumbs

Two days before you wish to cook this dish, place all the ingredients except the beef and the gingersnaps in a large glass casserole. Mix them thoroughly, then add the beef; cover the casserole and marinate the beef in the refrigerator for two days, turning the beef several times. Remove the beef and strain the marinade. Bring the strained marinade to a boil on the conventional stove. Return the beef to the glass casserole and pour the hot marinade over it. Cook in the center of the oven 20 minutes. Turn the beef over. Cook 20 minutes. Let set, covered, 20 minutes. Test for tenderness. Set the meat aside on a warm serving platter and make the sauce: In a glass bowl, mix the gingersnap cookie crumbs with 2 cups of the marinade in which the beef cooked. Cook 5 minutes, stirring, until the cookie crumbs are dissolved and sauce is simmering, and has been sufficiently thickened with the gingersnaps. If not thick enough, add more gingersnap crumbs. Cut the warm beef into ⅛-inch-thick slices, against the grain, and arrange overlapping slices on the platter. Mask each slice with a thin film of the hot sauce. Pass the remaining sauce at the table. *Serves 4 to 6.*

CLASSIC SWISS STEAK

Speed-cook; 33 minutes

½ cup flour
1 teaspoon salt (optional)
½ teaspoon pepper
½ teaspoon allspice
Four ½-inch-thick bottom round
   steaks (each about 4 ounces)
5 tablespoons butter or margarine

4 small white onions, thinly sliced
2 garlic cloves, minced
6 medium mushrooms, sliced
1 cup canned tomatoes, put
   through a food mill
3 tablespoons tomato paste
½ cup beef broth

Blend the flour, salt, pepper, and allspice. Dredge the steaks well with the seasoned flour. With the edge of a heavy saucer, pound the flour into the steaks. This will tenderize and somewhat flatten them. In a skillet on a conventional stove, or in a 9½-inch browning skillet, brown 2 steaks in 1½ tablespoons butter or margarine 1 minute on each side. Repeat for other 2 steaks. If using a browning skillet, wipe the skillet with a paper towel before browning the last two steaks. Transfer the steaks to a glass casserole just large enough to hold them in one layer. In a small glass casserole, heat 2 table-spoons butter or margarine and cook the onions and garlic 2 minutes, or until soft. Stir in the mushrooms, tomatoes, tomato paste, and beef broth and cook 3 minutes, or until simmering, stirring after 2 minutes. Pour this vegetable sauce over the steaks. Cover the casserole and cook in the center of the oven 8 minutes. Rotate the casserole half a turn. Cook 8 minutes. Turn the steaks over, spooning the sauce over them, and cook 8 minutes. Let set, covered, 10 minutes. Test for tenderness and seasoning. *Serves 4.*

PALMINA THOMPSON'S BAKED STEAK

Speed-cook; 18 minutes

We have three points to make before we describe this simple but delicious dish: (1) You can cook the steaks without prebrowning, adding about 6 minutes to the cooking time, but the dish won't be as tasty. (2) You can use the conventional stove for browning. But we use the 9½-inch brown-ing skillet, as we do with most steaks, chops, and hamburgers, and this recipe follows that technique. (3) It isn't necessary to partially precook the potatoes, but we found that this made them more mealy and flavorful.

2 medium potatoes of equal size   ⅔ cup flour
   (unpeeled)   3 tablespoons butter or margarine
3 medium onions, thinly sliced   1½ cups beef broth
Salt and pepper to taste
4 top or bottom round steaks (each
   about 4 ounces)

Pierce the potatoes in several places with the sharp point of a knife. Cook in the center of the oven 2 minutes, turning them at 1 minute. Let cool, then peel and cut into ¼-inch-thick slices. In a glass baking dish, arrange the onions in one layer, seasoning lightly with salt and pepper. Arrange the potatoes in one layer on the onions. Lightly season the steaks with salt and pepper and dredge with the flour. With the edge of a heavy saucer, pound the flour well into both sides of the steaks. Preheat a 9½-inch browning skillet 4½ minutes. Remove from the oven and add half the butter or margarine. When melted add two steaks and cook in the center of the oven 2 minutes on each side. Repeat process with remaining steaks, first wiping the skillet with a paper towel and preheating 2½ minutes. Arrange the steaks on top of the potatoes in the baking dish. Pour the beef broth into the browning skillet. Cook 2 minutes, stirring after each minute. Pour the broth over the steak. Cover the dish. Cook in the center of the oven 3 minutes. Turn the steaks. Cook 3 min-utes. Let set, covered, 10 minutes. Test for tenderness. *Serves 4.*

GREEN PEPPER STEAK

Speed-cook; 31 minutes

½ cup flour
1 teaspoon salt (optional)
¼ teaspoon pepper
¼ teaspoon dried marjoram
Four ½-inch-thick slices round
    steak (each about 4 ounces)
One 10½-ounce can condensed
    tomato soup

¼ cup water
2 medium green peppers, cored,
    seeded, and cut into 8 strips
2 small white onions, sliced
1 garlic clove, minced
2 tablespoons lemon juice

Blend the flour, salt, pepper, and marjoram and pound into both sides of the steaks with the edge of a heavy saucer. This will also tenderize and somewhat flatten them. On a conventional stove or in a preheated browning skillet, brown the steaks evenly on both sides 2 at a time. In a large glass casserole, blend well the soup, water, peppers, onions, garlic, and lemon juice. Cook 4 minutes, stirring at 2. Add the steaks. Cover them well with the sauce. Cover the casserole and cook in the center of the oven 8 minutes. Rotate the dish half a turn. Cook 7 minutes. Turn the steaks over, spooning the sauce over them. Cook 7 minutes, uncovered; rotate dish half a turn. Cook 5 minutes. Let set, covered, 10 minutes. Test for tenderness and seasoning. *Serves 4.*

EASY SWISS STEAK WITH VEGETABLES

Speed-cook; 21 minutes

One 1-pound round steak ½ inch
    thick
Salt and pepper to taste
4 medium carrots, scraped and cut
    into 2-inch pieces

2 medium potatoes, each cut into
    equal-size quarters
One 10½-ounce can condensed
    onion soup
¼ cup beef broth

With a meat mallet or the edge of a heavy saucer, pound the steak well to tenderize it. Season lightly with salt and pepper and cut into 4 serving pieces. Place the steaks in a glass casserole and arrange the vegetables in a circle around them. Blend the soup and beef broth. Pour over the steaks and the vegetables. Cook, covered, in the center of the oven 7 minutes. Rotate the dish half a turn. Cook 7 minutes. Turn the steak and vegetables over. Cook 7 minutes. Let set, covered, 10 minutes. Test for tenderness. *Serves 4.*

SIRLOIN STEAK AU POIVRE

Speed-cook; 6½ minutes

For this dish you must use the 9½-inch browning skillet. This delicious steak with its unique flavor is famed in Europe, but seldom served here. Oddly enough, we discovered it in Hong Kong.

2½ tablespoons whole black peppercorns
4 strip sirloin or shell steaks (each about 7 ounces)
2 tablespoons butter or margarine
2 teaspoons olive oil

2 tablespoons brandy
¼ cup beef gravy (canned or your own)
½ teaspoon Dijon mustard
¼ teaspoon Worcestershire sauce
Salt to taste

Place the peppercorns between sheets of waxed paper and crush them, using a rolling pin. Spread the crushed peppercorns on a large piece of waxed paper. Press both sides of the steaks firmly into the peppercorns until they are almost completely coated. Using your fingers and the heel of your hand, press the peppercorns into the steaks. For steaks on the rare side, follow our cooking time; or cook to your preference, adjusting the time accordingly. Preheat a 9½-inch browning skillet 4½ minutes. Remove from microwaves. Add half the butter or margarine and oil. Place 2 steaks in the skillet and cook in the center of the oven 75 seconds on each side. Transfer the steaks to a hot serving platter and keep warm. Wipe the skillet with a paper towel and preheat 2½ minutes. Add the remaining butter or margarine and oil and cook the other two steaks 75 seconds on each side. Transfer to the serving platter. To the juices in the browning skillet add the brandy, beef gravy, mustard, Worcestershire sauce, and salt, stirring until well blended. Place under microwaves for 1½ minutes, or until the sauce is simmering. Stir well, then spoon the hot sauce over the steaks. *Serves 4.*

CHINESE-STYLE SIRLOIN STEAK

Speed-cook; 10 minutes

Yes, the Chinese cook steak. Their problem is getting it, for in China it is very expensive. We had it this way in Hong Kong. If you are tired of serving steak the same old way, here's a tasty change of pace.

One 2-pound sirloin steak, about 1 inch thick

3 whole scallions, chopped
1 garlic clove, minced

2 thin slices fresh ginger
¼ cup dry sherry
¼ cup soy sauce

¼ teaspoon salt (optional)
2 tablespoons peanut oil

Trim half the fat from the steak, then cut in half to make two small steaks. In a bowl, blend the scallions, garlic, ginger, sherry, soy sauce, and salt. Place the steaks in a flat-bottomed dish. Pour the marinade over them and let set ½ hour at room temperature. Turn the steaks, spooning the marinade over them, and let set ½ hour. Drain and reserve the marinade. Dry the steaks, brush on both sides with the oil. Preheat a 9½-inch browning skillet for 4½ minutes. Cook one of the steaks in the skillet for 2 minutes, covered with waxed paper. Turn and cook 1 minute. Brush the steak with marinade. Cook the steak 1 minute. Turn. Brush with the marinade. Cook 1 minute. Transfer to a warm platter and cook the other steak after wiping the skillet with a paper towel and preheating it 2½ minutes. Test the steaks. They should be tender and pink. *Serves 4.*

GARLIC STEAK ROMANO

Speed-cook; 6 minutes

Here is a Roman specialty combining beef and cheese, giving steaks a new personality for a main course. The recipe is also excellent for hamburgers.

3 garlic cloves, minced
½ cup grated Romano cheese
3 tablespoons butter or margarine,
    softened
1 tablespoon Marsala
1 tablespoon brandy

1 teaspoon tomato sauce
¼ teaspoon salt (optional)
½ teaspoon pepper
4 strip sirloin or shell steaks (each
    about 7 ounces)

In a bowl combine all ingredients except the steaks and blend into a paste. Preheat a 9½-inch browning skillet 4½ minutes. Cook two steaks in the center of the oven 75 seconds on each side. Remove steaks and keep warm. Wipe the skillet with a paper towel, preheat it 2½ minutes and cook the remaining two steaks 75 seconds on each side. Test the steaks to see if they are done to your taste. Spread the seasoning paste over the steaks. Place all 4 steaks under microwaves for 1 minute or until the mixture bubbles. *Serves 4.*

FILLET OF BEEF WITH HERB BUTTER

Speed-cook; 5½ minutes, cooking 2 fillets at a time

This is the tenderest of all beef. If some say that it is tasteless, then they do not know how to cook it. Most people overcook these nuggets. A browning skillet plus microwaves handle them beautifully, leaving them moist, pink, and full of flavor—if you time correctly. Herb Butter also enhances their flavor.

Four ½-inch-thick slices beef fillets   4 tablespoons Herb Butter (below)
   (each 6 to 8 ounces)   2 teaspoons olive oil
Pepper to taste   Salt to taste

Sprinkle the fillets with pepper. Preheat the 9½-inch browning skillet 4½ minutes. Add 1 tablespoon of the Herb Butter and half the oil, distributing it evenly in the hot skillet. Add two fillets. Cook in the center of the oven 1½ minutes on each side. Remove the fillets and keep warm. Pour off any liquid in the skillet and heat it 2½ minutes. Add 1 tablespoon of the Herb Butter and the remaining oil. Cook the remaining fillets 1½ minutes on each side. Sprinkle the fillets lightly with salt. Serve with the remaining Herb Butter spread over them. The fillets will be rare. Increase the cooking time according to your preference. *Serves 4.*

Herb Butter

1 cup (½ pound) chilled unsalted   1 tablespoon chopped fresh
   butter or margarine   parsley
1 teaspoon lemon juice   ½ teaspoon pepper
½ teaspoon soy sauce   ¼ teaspoon dried tarragon
½ teaspoon Worcestershire sauce   ¼ teaspoon dried thyme
1 teaspoon Dijon mustard

Take the butter or margarine from the refrigerator and place in a glass measuring cup. Heat under microwaves in the center of the oven 10 seconds. It should be just slightly softened. Blend in remaining ingredients, working into a smooth mixture. Shape into two sticks. Wrap in plastic wrap, then in aluminum foil and freeze. To use, take right from the freezer and slice off pieces as you need them. Let come to room temperature before you place a slice or two atop steak. Herb Butter is also excellent on fish.

Makes 1 cup (½ pound), enough for 16 steaks.

FILLET MIGNON ROSSINI

Speed-cook; 8 minutes, including the sauce

This is a special recipe for those times when you want to celebrate. It's expensive. It's memorable. It's perfect for the browning skillet and microwaves.

Four 1½-inch-thick slices beef
   fillets (each 6 to 8 ounces)
3 tablespoons butter or margarine
2 tablespoons flour
1 cup beef broth
½ cup dry red wine

Salt and pepper to taste
Four ¼-inch-thick slices pâté de
   foie gras
Four ½-inch-thick slices bread fried
   in butter (optional)

Preheat the 9½-inch browning skillet 4½ minutes. Do not add any butter or fat. Grill the 4 fillets for 1½ minutes. Turn them. Grill 1½ minutes. These will be rare. Increase the cooking time according to your preference. Transfer the fillets to a warm platter and cover with aluminum foil to keep warm. Pour off liquid from the skillet. Add the butter or margarine and flour to the skillet, stirring into a smooth paste. Gradually stir in the beef broth. Place in the center of the oven 2 minutes, stirring every 30 seconds. Remove. Stir into a smooth sauce. Heat 1 minute, stirring after 30 seconds. Gradually stir in the wine. Heat 1 minute, stirring after 30 seconds. Stir in salt and pepper. Cook 1 minute, or until the sauce is smooth and thickened, stirring every 30 seconds. Place one slice of pâté atop each warm fillet. Make sure that the sauce is piping hot, and spoon some over the pâté. Serve immediately. You also may serve each fillet on a ½-inch-thick slice of bread fried in butter; top with the pâté and sauce, as above. *Serves 4.*

ROAST BEEF SIRLOIN WITH QUICK SAUCE BORDELAISE

Speed-cook; 15 minutes

Save this one for guests who truly appreciate elegant beef accompanied by your best burgundy. Talk to your butcher; get his best. You need a fine piece of boneless sirloin strip, the meat from which superb steaks are cut.

One 3-pound piece boneless sirloin
   strip
Pepper to taste

Quick Sauce Bordelaise (recipe
   follows)

Sprinkle the beef lightly with pepper. On a conventional stove, or in a pre-heated browning skillet, brown the beef evenly. Transfer it to a glass casserole, on an inverted saucer. Cover with waxed paper. Cook in the center of the oven 4 minutes. Rotate the casserole half a turn. Cook 4 minutes. Pour or siphon off any liquid in the casserole, reserving 1 tablespoon for the sauce. Turn the meat over. Cook 4 minutes. Rotate half a turn. Cook 3 minutes. Transfer the roast to a warm platter. Let set, covered with aluminum foil, 10 minutes while you prepare Quick Sauce Bordelaise. When ready to serve, slice the beef and pass the sauce at the table. *Serves 4 to 6.*

Quick Sauce Bordelaise

Speed-cook; 3 minutes

1 tablespoon reserved liquid from Roast Beef Sirloin casserole (above)
3 medium-size white onions, minced
½ cup dry red wine
½ cup beef gravy (canned or your own)

½ teaspoon salt (optional)
1 teaspoon cornstarch blended with 2 tablespoons water
2 tablespoons butter or margarine, softened

In the casserole you cooked the sirloin roast in, combine reserved liquid, the onions, wine, gravy, and salt. Cook 2 minutes, or until the onions are soft, stirring after 1 minute. Stir in the cornstarch. Cook for 1 minute, stirring each 30 seconds. Remove from the oven and stir in the softened butter or margarine.

VEAL

VEAL-RICE LOAF

Speed-cook; 14 minutes

The less expensive cuts of veal can be used for this. The loaf is also excellent cold for a summer supper.

1 small sweet red pepper, cored, seeded, and chopped
1 medium-size white onion, chopped

1 garlic clove, minced
2 tablespoons butter or margarine
1½ pounds ground veal

3 slices bacon, cooked until crisp,
   drained, and finely chopped
1½ cups cooked rice
2 eggs, beaten
¼ teaspoon Worcestershire sauce
½ cup heavy cream

2 tablespoons dry vermouth
2½ tablespoons chopped fresh
   parsley
1½ teaspoons salt (optional)
½ teaspoon pepper
½ teaspoon dried tarragon

Cook the first three ingredients together in the butter or margarine until soft. In a bowl, combine with the remaining ingredients, blending well. Butter a glass loaf dish. Spoon the meat mixture into it evenly, but do not pack it down. Do not let the ends taper down or they will dry out. Cook, uncovered, in the center of the oven 14 minutes, rotating the pan half a turn at 7 minutes. Let set, covered, 10 minutes before slicing. *Serves 4 to 6.*

VEAL CHOPS MILANESE

Speed-cook; 15 minutes

This is a classic dish, its name derived from its sauce.

½ cup flour
1 teaspoon salt
½ teaspoon pepper
4 boned loin veal chops (each
   about 8 ounces), pounded until
   ¼ inch thick
2 eggs
2 teaspoons water
1 tablespoon olive oil
1 cup bread crumbs (approximately)

7 tablespoons butter or margarine
1 tablespoon flour
4 medium mushrooms, thinly
   sliced
2 ounces boiled calf tongue (not
   pickled), cut into very thin strips
   (optional)
1 cup tomato sauce
Salt and pepper to taste

Blend the first three ingredients and dredge the chops with the seasoned flour. Beat together the eggs, water, and olive oil and dip the chops into the mixture, then dredge with the bread crumbs, pressing the crumbs into the meat with your fingers until they are well coated. In a skillet on a conventional stove, or in a preheated browning skillet, melt 2 tablespoons of butter or margarine. Cook 2 chops, 1 minute on each side, or until brown. Place them in a glass baking dish just large enough to hold 4 chops in one layer. If using the browning skillet, dry with paper towels, preheat, then add 2 tablespoons of butter or margarine. Cook the remaining 2 chops as you did the others and add them to the baking dish. Place the dish in the center of the oven and cook 3 minutes. Turn the chops over. Cook 3 minutes. Let set, covered, 10 minutes. Test for tenderness and seasoning. Meanwhile, blend 1 tablespoon each of butter or margarine and flour and reserve.

While the chops are setting, heat 2 tablespoons of butter or margarine in a glass casserole and cook the mushrooms 1 minute. Stir in the tongue and tomato sauce. Cook 3 minutes, stirring every minute. Stir in the blended butter or margarine and flour. Cook 1 minute. Stir well. Add salt and pepper to taste. Spoon the sauce over the chops and serve. *Serves 4.*

VEAL SCALLOPS PARMESAN

Speed-cook; 12 minutes

This is an Italian classic, adapted a bit for the microwaves.

½ cup flour
1 teaspoon salt (optional)
½ teaspoon pepper
Four ½-inch-thick veal slices from the leg (each about 6 ounces), flattened slightly
2 eggs beaten with 2 tablespoons heavy cream
1 cup bread crumbs (approximately)
⅓ cup grated Parmesan cheese

1 tablespoon butter or margarine
2 medium-size white onions, chopped
2 small garlic cloves, chopped
One 6-ounce can tomato paste
3 tablespoons dry white wine
⅓ cup water
¼ teaspoon dried basil
¼ teaspoon dried oregano
4 thin slices mozzarella cheese

Blend the first three ingredients and dredge the veal slices with the mixture. Dip them into the eggs, then dredge with bread crumbs. In a skillet on a conventional stove or in a preheated browning skillet, brown the veal in oil or butter or margarine lightly on both sides. Arrange the veal in a glass casserole in one layer and sprinkle with the Parmesan cheese. In a small glass casserole, melt the butter or margarine and cook the onions and garlic about 2 minutes, or until soft, stirring after 1 minute. Stir in the tomato paste, wine, water, basil, and oregano. Cook uncovered 3 minutes, stirring after each minute. Spoon the sauce over the veal. Cover. Cook the veal 6 minutes, rotating the dish half a turn at 3 minutes. Let set, covered, 5 minutes. Test for tenderness. Top each piece of veal with a slice of mozzarella cheese. Cook 1 minute, or until the cheese melts. *Serves 4.*

STUFFED VEAL ROLLS

Speed-cook; 5 minutes

12 slices veal, each 3 inches by 1
    inch and ½ inch thick, flattened
    very thinly between sheets of
    waxed paper
12 very thin slices prosciutto or
    ham, each 3 inches by 1 inch
12 very thin slices mozzarella
    cheese, each 2 inches by 1 inch,
    chilled

½ cup flour
1 teaspoon salt (optional)
½ teaspoon pepper
2 tablespoons butter or margarine
1 tablespoon olive oil
2 garlic cloves, cut into halves
⅓ cup Marsala

On each slice of veal place a slice of ham, then top with a slice of mozzarella. Roll up, like a miniature jelly roll. Pinion with toothpicks to keep the ham and cheese firmly encased. Blend the flour, salt, and pepper and dredge the veal rolls in the mixture; shake off any excess flour. In a glass casserole, in the center of the oven, heat the butter or margarine and oil, and cook the garlic 1 minute. Add the veal rolls, arranging them in a circular pattern. Cook 2 minutes, turning the veal over at 1 minute. Pour in the wine. Cover. Cook 2 minutes, turning the rolls at 1 minute. Let set, covered, 5 minutes. Test for tenderness. These are delicate little morsels that should not be overcooked. *Serves 4.*

SWISS VEAL

Speed-cook; 7 minutes

This delicious offering may well be the national dish of Switzerland. It's a great party dish that few of your guests will ever have eaten.

4 tablespoons butter or margarine
2 tablespoons cooking oil
2½ pounds veal from the leg, cut
    into strips 2 inches by 1 inch
    and ¼ inch thick
2 small white onions, finely
    chopped

⅓ cup dry white wine
1 cup heavy cream
1 tablespoon cornstarch dissolved
    in 2 tablespoons water
Juice of ½ lemon
Salt and pepper to taste

In a skillet on a conventional stove or in a preheated browning skillet, heat half the butter or margarine and oil and brown the veal. In a glass casserole, cook the onions in the remaining butter or margarine and oil under microwaves 2 minutes, or until soft. Stir in the wine. Cook 2 minutes. Stir in the cream. Cook 2 minutes. Stir in the veal strips, cornstarch, lemon juice, salt, and pepper. Cook 1 minute. Stir. Let set, covered, 10 minutes. Test for tenderness and seasoning. *Serves 4 to 6.*

RAGOUT OF VEAL

Speed-cook; 14 minutes

1½ pounds veal shoulder, cut into 1½-inch cubes
Salt and pepper to taste
3 tablespoons butter or margarine
1 tablespoon cooking oil
8 small white onions, root ends scored

One 10½-ounce can condensed cream of mushroom soup
Pinch of rosemary
8 medium mushrooms, cut into quarters
1 cup sour cream

Lightly season the veal with salt and pepper. In a glass casserole, in the center of the oven, heat the butter or margarine and oil. Add the veal. Cook 3 minutes, turning the meat at 1½ minutes. Add the onions. Cook 2 minutes. Stir in the soup and rosemary. Cover. Cook 3 minutes. Rotate casserole half a turn. Cook 3 minutes. Stir in the mushrooms. Cook, uncovered, 2 minutes. Stir in the sour cream. Cook 1 minute. Stir. Let set, covered, 10 minutes. Test for tenderness and seasoning. *Serves 4.*

LAMB

LESBOS LAMB MEATBALLS

Speed-cook; 14 minutes

We spent two pleasant months on this little-known Greek island of Lesbos, dining on little known lamb dishes and literally nothing else. This was a favorite and served over rice.

2 pounds lean lamb shoulder, ground

½ cup bread crumbs
2 eggs, beaten

3 tablespoons coarsely chopped
  pine nuts
3 tablespoons finely chopped fresh
  parsley
¾ cup dry red wine
1½ teaspoons salt (optional)
½ teaspoon pepper
¼ teaspoon ground cumin

2 tablespoons butter or margarine
1 tablespoon cooking oil
3 small white onions, finely
  chopped
1 small cucumber, peeled, seeded,
  and diced
3 tablespoons chili sauce

In a bowl thoroughly mix the lamb, bread crumbs, eggs, pine nuts, parsley, ¼ cup wine, salt, pepper, and cumin. Shape into firm meatballs no more than 1½ inches in diameter. In a skillet on a conventional stove or in a preheated browning skillet, brown the meatballs. Set aside. In a glass casserole heat the butter or margarine and oil and cook the onions 2 minutes, or until soft. Add the meatballs, any liquid in their skillet, the cucumber, chili sauce, and ½ cup wine. Stir well. Cook, uncovered, 6 minutes. Turn the meatballs. Cook 6 minutes. Let set, covered, 5 minutes. *Serves 4 to 6.*

MIDDLE-EASTERN MEAT LOAF

Speed-cook; 15 minutes

1½ pounds ground lamb
½ cup bread crumbs
1 egg, beaten
4 whole scallions, finely chopped
2 large pimientos, coarsely
  chopped
¼ cup minced Italian parsley
1 small navel orange, peeled and
  seeded, membranes removed,
  and diced

Juice of ½ small lemon
1 teaspoon salt (optional)
½ teaspoon pepper
¼ teaspoon ground cumin
Pinch of cinnamon

Place all the ingredients in a large bowl and mix well. Butter a glass loaf dish. Spoon in the lamb mixture evenly; do not pack it down. Do not let ends taper down, or they will cook faster and dry out. Cook, uncovered, in the center of the oven 15 minutes. Rotate half a turn every 5 minutes. Let set, covered, 10 minutes. *Serves 4.*

LAMB CHOPS IN MUSHROOM SAUCE

Speed-cook; 16 minutes

Four 1½-inch-thick loin lamb chops
Salt and pepper to taste
1 teaspoon dried oregano
2 tablespoons butter or margarine
¾ pound fresh mushrooms,
   coarsely chopped

1 tablespoon flour
3 tablespoons dry red wine
½ cup beef gravy (canned or your
   own)
2 tablespoons finely chopped
   roasted unsalted peanuts

Sprinkle the chops lightly with salt and pepper. Sprinkle the oregano over them. In a glass casserole, in the center of the oven, melt the butter or margarine, add the mushrooms, and cook 1 minute. Sprinkle the mushrooms with the flour and stir. Stir in the wine and gravy. Cook 3 minutes, stirring after each minute. Arrange the chops in the casserole in one layer, with thicker parts near the edge of the dish. Spoon the mushroom sauce over them. Cook 4 minutes. Rotate the casserole half a turn. Cook 4 minutes. Turn the chops over and spoon the sauce over them. Sprinkle with the chopped peanuts. Cook, covered, 4 minutes. Let set, covered, 5 minutes. Test for tenderness and seasoning. *Serves 4.*

LAMB CAKE WITH CURRANT JELLY SAUCE

Speed-cook; 15 minutes

1½ pounds ground lean lamb
2 tablespoons chopped bacon
1 cup bread crumbs
1 large onion, chopped
2 small eggs, beaten
2 tablespoons coarsely chopped
   pine nuts
1 tablespoon chopped fresh
   parsley

1½ teaspoons salt (optional)
½ teaspoon poultry seasoning
2 tablespoons dry red wine
½ cup currant jelly
2 tablespoons water
1 teaspoon Dijon mustard

In a bowl mix well the lamb, bacon, bread crumbs, onion, eggs, pine nuts, parsley, salt, poultry seasoning, and wine. Butter a glass loaf dish. Spoon the mixture into it evenly. Do not pack it down. Don't let the ends taper down, or they will cook faster and dry out. Cook in the center of the oven 15 minutes, rotating the dish half a turn every 5 minutes. Let set, covered, 15 minutes. Place the currant jelly, water, and mustard in a small glass bowl or measuring cup. Bring to a boil. Stir well. Pass the hot sauce at the table with the sliced lamb loaf. *Serves 4 to 6.*

LAMB BLANQUETTE

Speed-cook; 28 minutes

This is a simple country dish, usually served once a week in French homes. Don't let the list of ingredients discourage you. It is a simple dish to prepare, and a dazzler. Few Americans know it. It can also be prepared with veal, pork, or breast of chicken. We like the delicate flavor of lamb.

2 pounds boneless leg of lamb, cut into 1-inch cubes
2 cups boiling water
2 small white onions, each stuck with a whole clove
1 carrot, cut into ½-inch slices
1 celery rib, cut into ½-inch slices
1 small bay leaf
½ teaspoon caraway seeds
¼ teaspoon dried thyme
¼ teaspoon dried marjoram

2 cups boiling beef broth
1 teaspoon salt
12 small fresh mushroom caps
12 small white onions, root ends scored
¼ cup butter or margarine
¼ cup flour
⅓ cup heavy cream
2 ounces Madeira
Juice of ½ lemon
Salt and pepper to taste

Place the lamb in a deep glass casserole. Pour the boiling water over it and cook in the center of the oven 2 minutes. Drain the lamb and rinse it with warm water, then return it to the casserole along with the 2 onions stuck with cloves, carrot, celery, bay leaf, caraway seeds, thyme, marjoram, beef broth, and salt. Cover the casserole and cook 15 minutes, rotating the casserole half a turn every 5 minutes. Remove the lamb and strain the liquid. Return lamb to the casserole. In a glass bowl, in ¼ cup of the liquid the lamb cooked in, cook the mushrooms 2 minutes. Remove them with a slotted spoon and add them to the casserole. Using the liquid that you cooked the mushrooms in, cook the 12 small onions 5 minutes. Remove with a slotted spoon, adding them to the casserole. In a separate glass casserole, melt the butter or margarine, stir in the flour and blend into a smooth paste. Using the liquid the vegetables cooked in plus about 2 cups of the remaining liquid, make a medium-thick sauce, cooking about 2 minutes, stirring every 30 seconds. Stir in the cream, wine, and lemon juice. Blend well. Season with salt and pepper. Add the lamb cubes, mushrooms, and onions. Stir. Cook 2 minutes, or until simmering. Stir gently and serve with rice or noodles. *Serves 4 to 6.*

LAMB SHANKS IN WINE

Speed-cook, 30 minutes; slo-cook, 60 minutes

These are meaty, tasty, inexpensive cuts of lamb favored in the Middle Eastern countries, but mainly overlooked here.

4 lamb shanks, each large enough
    for 1 serving
Salt and pepper to taste
Flour for dredging
2 tablespoons butter or margarine
2 tablespoons cooking oil
2 garlic cloves

4 small carrots, scraped and diced
3 celery ribs, scraped and diced
2 medium-size white onions,
    chopped
1 cup dry red wine
1 cup fresh or defrosted frozen
    peas

Season the lamb shanks with salt and pepper and dredge them with flour. Heat the butter or margarine and oil in a glass casserole. Add the lamb shanks and garlic, the thicker parts of the shanks near the edge of the dish. To speed-cook, cook in the center of the oven 3 minutes. Turn the shanks. Cook 3 minutes. Cover the casserole. Cook 5 minutes. Turn the shanks. Stir in the carrots, celery, and onions; cook 5 minutes. Turn the shanks. Stir in the wine and cook 5 minutes. Rotate the casserole half a turn. Cook 4 minutes. Stir in the peas. Remove the lid and cook 5 minutes. Let set, covered, 15 minutes. Test for tenderness and seasoning. If these are shanks from a sheep, not a lamb, you may have to finish under microwaves for another 4 minutes. Stir the sauce and spoon it over the lamb when serving. To slo-cook, rotate the dish half a turn every 10 minutes, turning the shanks in the middle of the cooking time. *Serves 4.*

FARIKAL LAMB AND CABBAGE

Speed-cook, 25 minutes; slo-cook, 50 minutes

This is a favorite Norwegian dish we first had while sailing along that country's coast on the way to the fjord country. It is heavy on pepper and personality.

1½ pounds lean lamb from the
    shoulder or leg, cut into ¾-inch
    cubes
1 large head cabbage (Savoy is
    best), cut into 1-inch cubes
1½ teaspoons caraway seeds

1 teaspoon salt (optional)
1½ teaspoons pepper
¼ cup flour
¾ cup water
¾ cup dry white wine

In a glass casserole, arrange alternating layers of lamb cubes and cabbage, sprinkling the caraway seeds, salt, pepper, and flour over each layer, and finishing with a layer of cabbage. Place the water and wine in a glass bowl or cup. Bring to a boil under the microwaves. Pour over the cabbage and lamb. Cover the casserole tightly. Speed-cook in the center of the oven 25 minutes, rotating the casserole a fourth of a turn every 5 minutes. If you slo-cook, rotate a fourth of a turn every 10 minutes. Let set, covered, 20 minutes. Test for tenderness. *Serves 4 to 6.*

QUICK THICK LAMB CHOPS

Speed-cook; 4 minutes

Lamb chops such as these are a luxury. The browning skillet plus the microwave oven ensure that they will be cooked to perfection. Nearly everyone overcooks these meaty masterpieces. Classically, they should be pink when served.

Four 2-inch-thick loin lamb chops,
  trimmed of most fat, at room
  temperature
Pepper to taste

1 tablespoon cooking oil
3 garlic cloves, cut in halves
Salt to taste

Sprinkle the lamb chops with pepper. Preheat the 9½-inch browning skillet 4½ minutes. Add the cooking oil and garlic. Cook the chops 2 minutes. Pour off any liquid in the skillet. Turn the chops. Cook 2 minutes. Let set, covered, 5 minutes. Test for tenderness. Sprinkle lightly with salt. If you want them less pink, give them another 15 seconds on each side. Careful, however, as these chops can be overcooked almost at the blink of an eye. *Serves 4.*

DUBLIN LAMB STEW

Speed-cook, 30 minutes; slo-cook, I hour

6 medium potatoes, cut into ½-
  inch-thick slices
6 medium-size white onions, cut
  into ¼-inch-thick slices
2 pounds lean lamb, preferably
  from the leg, cut into ¾-inch
  cubes

Salt and pepper to taste
1½ cups beef broth
2 tablespoons chopped fresh
  parsley

In a large glass casserole, place alternating layers of potatoes, onions, and lamb, seasoning each layer lightly with salt and pepper, and finishing with a layer of potatoes. In a glass bowl, bring the beef broth to a simmer. Pour it over the lamb and vegetables, then sprinkle with parsley. Cover the casserole tightly. To speed-cook: Cook in the center of the oven 10 minutes. Rotate the dish half a turn. Cook 10 minutes. Rotate half a turn. Cook, uncovered, 10 minutes. Let set, covered, 10 minutes. Test for tenderness and seasoning. To slo-cook: Rotate a fourth of a turn every 15 minutes. *Serves 6.*

SIMPLE CALCUTTA LAMB CURRY

Speed-cook, 30 minutes; slo-cook, 1 hour

Most of us don't do enough with curried dishes. Why? Stage fright at the last moment, afraid that they may be too "hot," worried that guests won't like them? Curry is pleasing and isn't difficult. We find that mixing our own curry powder, as we learned in India, gives a much more sparkling flavor. By using microwaves, you'll save at least an hour in cooking time on this dish. Use part of that saved time to make your own curry powder. You'll never go back to the commercial mixtures.

3 pounds boneless leg of lamb, cut
   into 1-inch cubes
Salt to taste
2 tablespoons butter or margarine
2 tablespoons cooking oil
1 cup chopped onions
2 garlic cloves, minced
1 medium apple, peeled, cored,
   and chopped

2 tablespoons flour
2 tablespoons Curry Powder
   (following)
1 cup chicken broth
⅓ cup dry white wine
2 medium tomatoes, peeled,
   seeded, and chopped
2 tablespoons heavy cream

Lightly sprinkle the lamb cubes with salt. In a glass casserole, in the center of the oven, heat the butter or margarine and oil. Add the lamb. To speed-cook: Cook 2 minutes, turning the lamb. Add the onions and garlic. Cook 3 minutes, or until onions are soft. Stir in the apple and sprinkle in the flour and curry powder, mixing well with the lamb and onions. Cook 5 minutes, stirring in the chicken broth at 2½ minutes. Stir in the wine and tomatoes. Bring to a simmer. Stir well. Cover the casserole and cook 10 minutes. Rotate half a turn. Cook 10 minutes. Stir. Let set, covered, 20 minutes. To slo-cook: Rotate a fourth of a turn every 10 minutes, stirring each time. Test for tenderness and seasoning. Stir in the heavy cream just before serving. If not hot enough, place under the microwaves until just simmering. Serve immediately. Rice is a must. *Serves 4 to 6.*

Curry Powder

2 teaspoons ground coriander
2 teaspoons ground cumin
1 teaspoon ground cardamom
1 teaspoon ground turmeric

½ teaspoon ground ginger
¼ teaspoon ground black pepper
Pinch of ground hot red pepper

In a bowl, blend all the ingredients thoroughly.

STUFFED LAMB SHOULDER, ITALIAN STYLE

Speed-cook; 24 minutes

2 small white onions, chopped
1 celery rib, scraped and chopped
2 garlic cloves, minced
2 tablespoons butter or margarine
One 3½-pound boned shoulder of
  lean lamb
6 slices dry crustless bread,
  crumbled
1 tablespoon chopped currants
1 tablespoon chopped fresh
  parsley

3 tablespoons grated Parmesan
  cheese
1 large egg, beaten
½ teaspoon salt (optional)
½ teaspoon pepper
1 garlic clove put through a garlic
  press and mixed with 1
  tablespoon olive oil

Sauté the first three ingredients in the butter or margarine until soft. Spread the boned lamb flat, skin side down. In a bowl, blend the bread, sautéed vegetables, currants, parsley, cheese, egg, salt, and pepper. Spoon the stuffing onto the lamb, spreading it evenly. Carefully roll up into a compact package; tie well with string to contain the stuffing. Try to do this evenly, so that the ends are not narrow or tapering; microwaves will dry them out. Rub the stuffed shoulder well with the garlic-and-oil mixture. Sprinkle with more pepper. Place on an inverted saucer in a large glass casserole. Cook in the center of the oven, uncovered, 12 minutes, rotating the casserole a fourth of a turn every 4 minutes. Turn the lamb shoulder over. Baste the lamb and spoon or siphon off all liquid. Cook 12 minutes, rotating a fourth of a turn every 4 minutes. Let set, covered, 15 minutes. Test for tenderness. *Serves 4 to 6.*

ROAST MARINATED LEG OF LAMB

Speed-cook; 25 minutes

Tired of the old way of serving leg of lamb? Here's a tastebud treat that will sharpen your respect for that old reliable main course.

One 4-pound leg of lamb	2 whole garlic cloves
2 garlic cloves, each cut into 4 slivers	1 clove
	1 small bay leaf
2 cups dry red wine	1 tablespoon salt (optional)
½ cup olive oil	½ teaspoon pepper
2 small carrots, sliced	1½ teaspoons dried oregano
1 celery rib, sliced	⅛ teaspoon ground cumin
1 large onion, sliced	

About 6 to 7 hours before you wish to serve the lamb, cut 8 small slits in it with a sharp knife and insert the garlic slivers. In a large bowl, blend the remaining ingredients. Add the lamb, turning it several times. Cover the bowl and marinate the lamb in the refrigerator 5 hours, turning it four times. Remove from the refrigerator and continue to marinate at room temperature 1 hour. Drain and dry the lamb. Cover the bone end with a small piece of aluminum foil. Place the lamb, fat side down, on an inverted plate or saucer in a glass casserole. Cook, uncovered, in the center of the oven 10 minutes. Turn the lamb over and baste it with the pan juices. Spoon or siphon off with a bulb baster all of the liquid in the casserole. Cook the lamb 10 minutes, turn it over, baste with the juices and spoon or baste off all remaining liquid. Cook 5 minutes. Let set, covered, 15 minutes. Test for tenderness. This lamb should be slightly pink, which is classic. If you like it less rare, adjust the cooking time to your taste. *Serves 6 to 8.*

PORK AND HAM

BERLIN CARAWAY MEATBALLS

Speed-cook; 13 minutes

These meatballs, with a Germanic flavor all their own, could be a family or company main-dish hit.

1 cup sour cream	2 teaspoons caraway seeds
3 tablespoons flour	2 pounds lean pork, ground

1 cup bread crumbs
2 eggs, beaten
½ cup milk
1½ tablespoons chopped fresh
  parsley
1½ teaspoons salt (optional)

½ teaspoon pepper
¼ teaspoon poultry seasoning
1 medium onion, chopped
2 tablespoons butter or margarine
6 medium mushrooms, sliced
½ cup beef broth

Blend the first three ingredients in a bowl and set aside. In a separate bowl, mix well the pork, bread crumbs, eggs, milk, parsley, salt, pepper, and poultry seasoning. Shape into 1½-inch meatballs. In a skillet on a conventional stove or in a preheated browning skillet, brown the meatballs evenly. In a deep glass casserole, in the center of the oven, cook the onion in the butter or margarine 1 minute, or until soft, stirring after 45 seconds. Stir in the mushrooms, cook 1 minute, stirring after 30 seconds. Stir in the beef broth and meatballs. Cover the casserole and cook 10 minutes, stirring; rotate the dish half a turn after 5 minutes. Stir in the sour cream mixture and cook 1 minute, or until simmering. Stir and let set, covered, 10 minutes. Serve the meatballs in their sauce. *Serves 6.*

FRICADELLE FLAMANDE

Speed-cook; 20 minutes

Here's a novel pork-meatball dish from our cooking mentor, the great French chef Antoine Gilly, proving that chefs are not always complicated.

3 small white onions, chopped
2 garlic cloves, minced
1 tablespoon butter or margarine
  for sautéing
2 eggs, separated
2 pounds lean pork, ground
1 cup bread crumbs
⅛ teaspoon nutmeg
1½ teaspoons salt (optional)
½ teaspoon pepper

3 tablespoons butter or margarine
24 small white onions, root ends
  scored
6 medium potatoes, peeled and
  trimmed into the size and shape
  of eggs
1½ cups chicken broth
½ cup dry white wine
½ cup chopped fresh parsley

Sauté the chopped onions and garlic in butter or margarine until soft. Beat the egg yolks; beat the egg whites separately until stiff. In a large bowl mix well the pork, bread crumbs, egg yolks, sautéed onions and garlic, nutmeg, salt, and pepper. Mix in the beaten egg whites. Form meatballs the size and shape of an egg. On a conventional stove or in a preheated browning skillet, brown the meatballs in the 3 tablespoons of butter or margarine. Transfer to a deep glass casserole and arrange the whole onions and the potatoes around them. Pour in the chicken broth and wine. The liquid should only half cover the meatballs and vegetables. Cover. Cook in the center of the oven 10 minutes, rotating the casserole half a turn after 5 minutes. Turn the meatballs and vegetables over. Cook, uncovered, 5 minutes. Rotate half a turn. Cook 5 minutes, or until the vegetables are tender. Let set, covered, 15 minutes. Drain off the cooking liquid before serving. Sprinkle the meatballs with the parsley and serve with the vegetables. Pass a good, sharp mustard. *Serves 6.*

BRAISED PORK CHOPS

Speed-cook; 14 minutes

1 white onion, minced
1 small garlic clove, minced
½ cup chicken broth
3 tablespoons lemon juice
3 tablespoons chili sauce

1 tablespoon Worcestershire sauce
1 teaspoon Dijon mustard
½ teaspoon salt (optional)
½ teaspoon pepper
Four ¾-inch-thick pork chops

Eight hours before you plan to cook the pork chops, mix thoroughly all ingredients except the pork chops in a flat-bottomed dish. Add the chops, turning to coat both sides with the marinade. Marinate in the refrigerator 6 hours, then at room temperature 1 hour, turning several times. Remove the chops and drain, scraping off the onion and garlic, and dry. Reserve the marinade. In a skillet on a conventional stove or in a browning skillet, brown the chops evenly on both sides. Arrange in a glass casserole just large enough to hold them in one layer, the thicker parts of the chops near the edge of the dish. Pour the marinade into a glass bowl. Bring to a simmer in the oven. Pour over the chops. Cook in the center of the oven, tightly covered, 7 minutes. Turn the chops. Rotate the casserole half a turn. Cook 7 minutes. Turn the chops. Let set, covered, 15 minutes. Test for tenderness. *Serves 4.*

PORK CHOPS À LA BOULANGÈRE

Speed-cook, 15 minutes; slo-cook, 30 minutes

This unusually tasty dish, named for the local baker's wife, is served weekly in many French villages. In France, bread is baked twice a day, morning and late afternoon. When the afternoon baking is finished and the wood-burning stove is still hot, the housewives arrive at the bakery with their covered casseroles. For a small fee, the baker's wife slides them into her husband's idle oven on the wooden paddle. Microwaves do the job almost as well.

A trick from the French housewife: Leaving the bone in for flavor, pound the chops lightly around the bone with the edge of a heavy saucer or a meat mallet. This somewhat tenderizes and flattens the chops, which will return to near their original thickness while cooking.

Four 1-inch-thick loin pork chops	1½ cups hot chicken broth
4 small potatoes, cut in halves	1 teaspoon salt (optional)
8 small white onions, root ends scored	½ teaspoon pepper
	⅛ teaspoon dried thyme
2 garlic cloves, cut in halves	

Pound the pork chops lightly. In a skillet on a conventional stove or in a preheated browning skillet, brown the chops evenly. In a glass casserole, place the browned chops in one layer, the thicker parts near the edge of the dish. Arrange the potatoes, onions, and garlic in an outer circle around the chops. Pour in the chicken broth and sprinkle with the salt, pepper, and thyme. To speed-cook: Cook in the center of the oven, covered, 5 minutes. Rotate the dish half a turn. Cook 5 minutes. Turn the chops and vegetables over. Cook, uncovered, 5 minutes, rotating half a turn at 2½ minutes. Let set, covered, 10 minutes. To slo-cook: Rotate the dish half a turn every 5 minutes. Turn the chops and vegetables at 15 minutes, and let set, covered, 10 minutes. Test for tenderness. *Serves 4.*

Variations: This dish can be interestingly varied by substituting veal chops, chicken pieces, or Italian sausage for the pork chops.

PORK CHOPS IN SOUR CREAM

Speed-cook; 18 minutes

1 cup bread crumbs	1 cup chicken broth
1 teaspoon salt (optional)	2 tablespoons wine vinegar
½ teaspoon pepper	1½ teaspoons sugar
⅛ teaspoon dried thyme	1 small bay leaf
Four 1-inch-thick pork chops	½ cup sour cream
Flour for dredging	
2 eggs beaten with 2 tablespoons cream	

Blend the first four ingredients. Coat the chops with flour, dip into the eggs, then dredge with the seasoned bread crumbs. In a skillet on a conventional stove or in a browning skillet, brown the chops evenly. Place them in a large glass casserole in one layer, thicker parts near the edge of the dish. In a glass bowl, blend the chicken broth, wine vinegar, and sugar. Add the bay leaf and bring to a simmer in the oven. Stir and pour over the chops in the casserole. Cover the casserole tightly. Cook in the center of the oven 10 minutes. Turn the chops over and rotate the dish half a turn. Cover and cook 7 minutes. Transfer the chops to a warm serving platter. Cover and let set 10 minutes. Test for tenderness. Remove the bay leaf from the casserole, stir in the sour cream, and cook 1 minute, or until hot. Do not boil. Serve over the chops. *Serves 4.*

CANTON PORK CHOPS

Speed-cook; 10 minutes

4 whole scallions, chopped
2 garlic cloves, minced
1½ teaspoons brown sugar
⅓ cup soy sauce
2 tablespoons dry sherry

⅛ teaspoon hot sauce
Four ¾-inch-thick loin pork chops,
    trimmed of most fat
2 tablespoons peanut oil

In a flat-bottomed dish, mix the scallions, garlic, brown sugar, soy sauce, sherry, and hot sauce. Place the chops in the marinade, turning to coat both sides. Let them stand at room temperature 1 hour, turning several times during that time. Remove the chops from the marinade. Reserve the marinade. Dry the chops. Preheat the 9½-inch browning skillet 4½ minutes. Add the peanut oil. Place the chops in the skillet in one layer, the thicker parts near the edge of the pan, and cook 3 minutes. Pour off any liquid in the pan; turn the chops over and cook 3 minutes. Pour the marinade over the browned chops. Cover the skillet. Cook 4 minutes. Let set, covered, 10 minutes. Test for tenderness. *Serves 4.*

BROCCOLI AND SLICED PORK, CHINESE STYLE

Speed-cook; 8 minutes

½ cup light brown sugar
⅓ cup dry sherry
⅛ cup soy sauce
1 bunch (about 1½ pounds) fresh
    broccoli
⅓ cup peanut oil

½ teaspoon salt
3 thin slices fresh ginger, shredded
2 garlic cloves, minced
1 pound pork loin, cut into strips
    2 by ½ by ¼ inches

In a bowl, blend the first three ingredients and set aside. Cut the florets off the broccoli and cut in half if large. Peel the stems and cut them into ⅛-inch diagonal slices. In a glass casserole, pour the peanut oil. Sprinkle in the salt. Add the ginger and garlic. Cook 1 minute, stirring after each 30 seconds. Stir in the pork. Cook 1½ minutes. Turn the pork. Cook 1½ minutes. Stir in the broccoli. Cook 1½ minutes, stirring after each 45 seconds. Add the brown sugar/sherry/soy sauce mixture. Stir well. Cook 2½ minutes to heat the sauce through, stirring at 1 minute. Let set, covered, 10 minutes. Test for tenderness. The meat should be tender; the broccoli crunchy. *Serves 4.*

STUFFED PORK CHOPS

Speed-cook; 10 minutes

The object here is to get nice loin chops and fill them with an interesting stuffing. You can use prepared stuffings; some of them are good, but your own will be better.

1 small white onion, minced	½ teaspoon salt (optional)
1 celery rib, minced	¼ teaspoon pepper
1 tablespoon butter or margarine	¼ teaspoon dried basil
1 cup bread crumbs	½ teaspoon poultry seasoning
2 prunes, finely chopped	9 tablespoons chicken broth
1 tablespoon chopped fresh parsley	Four 1-inch-thick boned loin pork chops

Sauté the onion and celery in the butter or margarine until soft. Combine in a bowl with the remaining ingredients except the chicken broth and pork chops and mix well. Gradually add 5 tablespoons of the broth. Divide the stuffing into four portions. With a sharp knife, cut a deep pocket into the side of each chop and fill with the stuffing. Close the cavity with toothpicks. Lightly sprinkle both sides of the chops with salt and pepper. In a skillet on a conventional stove or in a preheated browning skillet, brown the chops on both sides. Place them in a large glass casserole in a single layer, thicker parts near the edge of the casserole. Pour in the remaining chicken broth. Cover tightly. Cook in the center of the oven 5 minutes. Turn the chops. Cook, uncovered, 5 minutes. Let set, covered, 10 minutes. Test for tenderness. Baste well with the sauce in the casserole, spooning it over the chops just before serving. *Serves 4.*

PORK FROM HEAVEN

Speed-cook; 17 minutes

In Germany's Silesia this is called "heavenly pork" or "pork from heaven," depending upon the translation. You can be sure of one thing: It is a unique dish.

1 pound mixed dried fruit (apples, pears, pitted apricots, prunes, etc.)
Port wine (optional)
1½ pounds pork shoulder, cut into 1-inch cubes

Salt and pepper to taste
2 tablespoons butter or margarine
1 tablespoon cooking oil
2 tablespoons cornstarch
1 clove
1 teaspoon brown sugar

Soak the fruit in water as suggested on the package. (If you want to get fancy and give yourself and your guests a new taste delight, soak the fruit in a mixture of half water and half port wine.) Drain the fruit, reserving 1 cup of the liquid. Sprinkle the pork lightly with salt and pepper. In a skillet on a conventional stove or in a preheated browning skillet, brown the pork cubes evenly in the butter or margarine and oil. Transfer the pork to a glass casserole. Arrange the drained fruit around the meat. In a glass dish or bowl, blend the cornstarch with the reserved cup of liquid the fruit soaked in and cook in the center of the oven 2 minutes, stirring every 30 seconds. Stir in the clove and brown sugar. Bring to a simmer. Pour the sauce over the pork and fruit. Cover the casserole tightly. Cook in the center of the oven 5 minutes. Stir. Cook 5 minutes. Stir. Cook 5 minutes. Let set, covered, 15 minutes. Test for tenderness and seasoning. *Serves 4.*

DANISH PORK TENDERLOIN

Speed-cook; 16 minutes

Beef fillets, or tenderloins, are popular, but few of us experiment with those tender nuggets of pork also called tenderloins. We prefer them to beef. So do the Scandinavians, who have a masterful hand with them. We cook these tender slices in the browning skillet.

½ cup flour
1 teaspoon salt (optional)
½ teaspoon pepper
Pinch of rosemary

1½ pounds pork tenderloin, cut into ½-inch-thick slices (allow at least 2 slices for each serving)
2 tablespoons butter or margarine

1 tablespoon cooking oil
1 medium-size white onion, thinly
   sliced
½ cup dry white wine

8 medium mushrooms, thinly
   sliced
4 large stuffed green olives, sliced
2 tablespoons lemon juice

Blend the first four ingredients and use to dredge the pork slices. Preheat a 9½-inch browning skillet 4½ minutes. Heat half the butter or margarine and oil and cook half the pork slices 1 minute on each side, or until brown. Pour off any liquid or fat in the skillet, dry with a paper towel and preheat 2½ minutes. Brown the remaining pork slices in the remaining butter or margarine and oil. Remove the pork. Add the onion to the skillet and cook 1 minute, or until soft. Pour in the wine. Cook 3 minutes, or just until it simmers. Add the mushrooms and the browned pork slices. Cover the skillet. Cook 3 minutes. Turn the pork slices. Cook 3 minutes. Stir in the olives and lemon juice. Cook 2 minutes. Let set, covered, 10 minutes. Test for tenderness and seasoning. *Serves 4.*

POACHED PORK LOIN

Speed-cook; 21 minutes

We'll bet that few of your guests (or even you!) ever have eaten this. Fried, roasted, stewed, broiled—but rarely do we find poached pork in any home or on any menu. This may well be the tastiest of all.

One 3-pound boned loin of pork,
   tied
1 white onion, cut into halves
2 garlic cloves, cut into halves
2 small carrots, cut into quarters
2 celery ribs, cut into quarters
2 whole cloves

1 small bay leaf
⅛ teaspoon dried thyme
1½ teaspoons salt (optional)
½ teaspoon pepper
⅛ cup dry white wine
1 cup boiling chicken broth

In a deep glass casserole just wide enough to hold the pork loin, place the pork, vegetables, herbs, seasonings, and wine. Pour in enough boiling chicken broth to reach halfway up the loin. Cook, covered, in the center of the oven 7 minutes, rotating the dish half a turn. Cook 7 minutes. Turn the pork over. Cook 7 minutes. Let set, covered, 20 minutes. Test for tenderness. Serve either hot or cold, cut into thin slices. *Serves 4 to 6.*

DEVILED HAM

Speed-cook; 8 minutes

½ cup light brown sugar
½ cup butter or margarine,
   softened
1½ teaspoons dry mustard

¼ cup hot water
One 2-pound, 1-inch-thick
   precooked center-cut ham steak
½ cup milk

In a bowl, blend the brown sugar, butter or margarine, mustard, and water. Place the ham in a glass casserole just large enough to hold it. Spread the brown-sugar mixture over the ham. Pour the milk around it. Cook in the center of the oven 4 minutes. Rotate the dish half a turn. Cook 4 minutes. Let set, covered, 10 minutes. Test for tenderness. Yams or sweet potatoes baked in the microwave oven are excellent with this. They can be cooked while the ham is "setting." *Serves 4 to 6.*

HAM LOAF WITH MUSTARD SAUCE

Speed-cook; 16 minutes

2 medium onions, minced
1 garlic clove, minced
2 tablespoons butter or margarine
2½ pounds lean precooked ham,
   ground
Pepper to taste

2 eggs, beaten
1 cup bread crumbs
½ cup light cream
Brown sugar
1 teaspoon dry mustard
Mustard Sauce (below)

In a glass dish, in the center of the oven, cook the onions and garlic in the butter or margarine 2 minutes, or until they are soft. In that dish, mix the onions and garlic in their butter or margarine with the remaining ingredients except the brown sugar and dry mustard. Spoon the mixture evenly into a buttered glass loaf pan, making certain that the ends do not taper down, as they could dry out. Cover the loaf with a light layer of brown sugar and sprinkle with the dry mustard. Cook in the center of the oven 7 minutes. Rotate the dish half a turn. Cook 7 minutes. Let set, covered, 10 minutes. Make the Mustard Sauce while the ham is setting, and pass it at the table with the ham loaf. *Serves 6 to 8.*

Mustard Sauce

1 cup heavy cream, whipped
¼ cup Dijon mustard

Pinch of dry mustard
½ cup mayonnaise

Blend the ingredients into a smooth sauce.

RED HAM LOAF WITH HORSERADISH SAUCE

Speed-cook; 15 minutes

1 medium onion, finely chopped
1 celery rib, scraped and finely
   chopped
2 tablespoons butter or margarine
1 pound lean ham, ground
½ pound lean pork, ground
½ cup bread crumbs

½ teaspoon dry mustard
⅛ teaspoon pepper
1 egg, beaten
One 10½-ounce can condensed
   tomato soup
2 teaspoons prepared horseradish

In a glass dish, in the center of the oven, cook the onion and celery in the butter or margarine 2 minutes, or until they are soft. In a bowl, mix thoroughly the onion, celery, ham, pork, bread crumbs, mustard, pepper, egg, and half the tomato soup. Spoon the mixture evenly into a buttered glass loaf pan, making certain that the ends do not taper down, as they could dry out. Cook in the center of the oven 8 minutes. Rotate the pan half a turn. Cook 5 minutes. Let set, covered, 10 minutes. Meanwhile, make a simple horseradish sauce: In a glass measuring cup mix the remaining soup with the horseradish. Cook until hot. Pass with the ham. *Serves 4 to 6.*

HAM MEDALLIONS WITH MADEIRA SAUCE

Speed-cook; 6 minutes

8 medallions precooked ham, 3
   inches in diameter and ¼ inch
   thick
5 tablespoons butter or margarine
2 tablespoons flour

1 teaspoon Dijon mustard
¼ cup Madeira
¼ cup chicken broth
Pepper to taste
¼ cup heavy cream

In a preheated 9½-inch browning skillet, cook half the ham medallions in 1 tablespoon of the butter or margarine, 30 seconds on each side. Dry the skillet with a paper towel and cook the remaining ham slices in 1 tablespoon of the butter or margarine 30 seconds on each side. Transfer the ham to a serving dish and keep warm. In a glass bowl or large measuring cup, heat 2 tablespoons of the butter or margarine 1 minute, or until melted. Blend in the flour and mustard, stirring until you have a smooth paste. Stir in the wine and chicken broth and cook 2 minutes, stirring every 30 seconds, until you have a smooth sauce. Stir in the pepper, cream, and remaining tablespoon of butter or margarine. Taste for seasoning. Spoon enough sauce over the ham in its serving dish to mask it well. Heat in the oven 1 minute, rotating the dish half a turn at 30 seconds. It should be just heated through. It is also effective to place the sauced ham under a conventional broiler until the sauce is golden. *Serves 4.*

SCALLOPED HAM WITH POTATOES

Speed-cook; 20 minutes

4 medium potatoes, peeled and
   sliced
¼ cup water
2 medium onions, finely chopped
3 tablespoons butter or margarine
3 tablespoons flour

2 cups milk
½ teaspoon pepper
3 cups diced ham
⅓ cup grated sharp cheddar cheese
1 tablespoon chopped fresh
   parsley

In a glass casserole, cook the potatoes in the water 8 minutes or until they are tender but crisp. Carefully stir at 4 minutes. Let set 5 minutes, then drain. In a glass bowl, cook the onions in the butter or margarine 3 minutes or until soft. Stir in the flour and blend well. Stir in the milk and pepper. Stirring after 2 minutes, cook in the center of the oven 4 minutes, or until you have a smooth sauce. In the casserole you cooked the potatoes in, arrange alternating layers of potatoes and ham, spooning the milk sauce over each layer. Sprinkle the cheese and parsley on top and cook in the oven 5 minutes, or until the cheese has melted and the sauce is bubbling. Let set, covered, 3 minutes. *Serves 4 to 6.*

HAM IN BEER

Speed-cook; 16 minutes

One 4-pound canned precooked
   ham (the Polish hams are
   excellent)
⅓ cup beer

¼ cup molasses
2 teaspoons dry mustard
12 whole cloves

Score the ham on both sides and place it on an inverted saucer in a glass casserole just large enough to hold it. Blend the beer, molasses, and mustard and brush the ham with the mixture. Cover loosely with waxed paper and cook in the center of the oven 8 minutes, rotating the casserole half a turn at 4 minutes. Siphon off any liquid in the casserole. Turn the ham over, brush with the sauce and stud with the cloves. Cover with waxed paper and cook 8 minutes, rotating half a turn at 4 minutes. Let set, covered, 20 minutes. *Serves 6 to 8.*

COOKING BACON

When we first saw a microwave oven demonstrated (and bought one) over a decade ago, a friend went along as a spectator. As is usual, and spectacular, the demonstrator cooked a slice of bacon on a piece of paper towel in 1 minute. Our friend, a bacon devotee of long standing, watched open-mouthed. To shorten the anecdote, he bought a microwave oven for the sole purpose of cooking bacon, and even today uses it for little else. Cooked conventionally, bacon can be a messy business, with the cooked result often disappointing.

Of the special utensils for cooking bacon in the microwave oven, the one we like best is a glass tray with a trivet that keeps the bacon out of its own grease. All you need do is place the bacon on it and cover it with a piece of paper towel. When the cooking is finished, pour the grease from the bottom of the tray.

A couple of other points about bacon: There are dishes such as quiches that call for quite a lot of bacon. It must be cooked, drained of fat, then broken up. Microwaves do everything except break it up. The bacon is crisp in mere minutes. And there is no splattered stove to clean up.

Because the fat flows off the bacon onto the paper towel while the bacon is cooking, the cooked bacon is virtually fat-free. You merely have to blot it with a piece of paper towel. Thus, from a health standpoint (if you can use this criterion at all where bacon is concerned), the fat is cooked out of the bacon and you consume very little. And let's not forget the cleanup: You simply throw the paper towel away. How often have we cooked bacon, forgotten to discard the grease, then had the dickens of a job getting that cold bacon grease out of the pan.

Use a triple layer of paper towels in a glass dish. Place from one to four strips on the towels (we've found it more effective to cook no more than four strips at a time), then cover with a paper towel. If you must cook, perhaps, a half pound of bacon at one time, cut the strips in half and make layers, covering each with a paper towel.

Bacon cooked according to the following timing will be crisp; if you like it less crisp, time it according to your own taste.

1 strip: 1 minute 15 seconds
2 strips: 2 minutes 20 seconds
4 strips: 4 minutes
24 half-slices: 6½ minutes

KIELBASA SAUSAGE WITH RED CABBAGE

Speed-cook; 15 minutes

This Polish sausage, three-fourths pork, one-fourth beef, and lightly flavored with garlic, has become very popular. (See a tasty cocktail treat, Kielbasa Sausage Canapés, page 52). Called Duszone w Czerwonej Kapuscie, *this recipe from Polish friends is a favorite of ours and a unique party dish, as you can increase amounts (and cooking time) without problems.*

1 small head red cabbage, shredded, blanched, and drained (see note)
1 tablespoon white vinegar
2 tablespoons butter or margarine
2 tablespoons flour
1 cup dry red wine
½ teaspoon sugar
1 tablespoon lemon juice
Salt and pepper to taste
One 1-pound ring kielbasa sausage

Sprinkle the blanched cabbage with the vinegar. In a suitable glass casserole, in the center of the oven, melt the butter or margarine. Blend in the flour and slowly stir in the wine. Stirring every 30 seconds, cook 2 minutes or until you have a smooth sauce. Stir in the cabbage, sugar, and lemon juice, blending well. Season with salt and pepper. Cover the casserole and cook 4 minutes. Rotate the casserole half a turn and stir. Cook 4 minutes. Prick the sausage in several places with the sharp point of a knife. Push the cabbage aside, making a well and center the coiled sausage in the casserole. Cover and cook 5 minutes, rotating the dish half a turn at 2½ minutes and turning the sausage over. Let set, covered, 10 minutes. Test for tenderness. *Serves 4.*

Note: This main dish can be speeded up by using commercial precooked red cabbage, therely eliminating the seasoning and cooking of the raw cabbage.

Variation: This recipe can be tastefully varied by substituting potatoes and small white onions for the cabbage and its seasonings, and chicken broth for the red wine. Eliminate the flour. Cook the sausage and vegetables together 10 minutes, rotating the dish half a turn at 5 minutes and turning the sausage over at that point. This should also set, covered, 10 minutes.

LENTILS AND SAUSAGE SUPPER

Speed-cook; 35 minutes 20 seconds

This one, Lenticchie e Cotechino, *we found in Italy, in the Abruzzi. It could be the tastiest lentil dish ever created. This can be prepared ahead and reheated when ready to serve. Preparation on a conventional stove would take about 2 hours.*

2 cups dried lentils
1½ pounds cotechino sausage (a
   fine, garlicky Italian sausage) or
   a sausage of your choice
2 cups chicken broth
1 celery rib, scraped and chopped
2 small carrots, scraped and
   chopped

2 small white onions, minced
2 tablespoons olive oil
2 garlic cloves, chopped
2 sprigs fresh thyme or ¼ teaspoon
   dried
Salt and pepper to taste
1 teaspoon sweet Hungarian
   paprika

Wash lentils well and soak them in cold water 2½ hours. Pierce the sausage in several places and place in a deep glass casserole, just large enough to hold it. Half cover with boiling water. Cover the casserole and cook in the center of the oven 5 minutes. Turn the sausage over and cook 5 minutes. Let the sausage set, covered, 10 minutes. Remove from the water and let cool. When cool enough to handle, peel off the skin and cut the sausage into ½-inch-thick slices.

Drain the lentils and place them in a deep casserole. Add the chicken broth, celery, carrots, half the onions, 1 tablespoon of the olive oil, the garlic, thyme, salt, pepper, and sausage slices. Cover the casserole and cook in the center of the oven 20 minutes, rotating the dish half a turn every 5 minutes.

In a glass pie plate, cook the remaining onions in the remaining oil 2 minutes, or until soft. Stir in the paprika and cook 20 seconds—no longer. If overcooked, paprika becomes bitter. Stir the onions and paprika into the lentil casserole, cover, and let set 1 hour.

When ready to serve, return the lentil casserole to the center of the oven and cook 3 minutes, or until it is simmering. Stir well. This is not a soup, but is thick and should be eaten with a spoon. Serve it in warm soup bowls with plenty of warm, crusty bread. *Serves 4 to 6.*

SAUSAGE ALLA PIZZAIOLA

Speed-cook; 27 minutes

4 medium-size hot Italian sausages
4 medium-size sweet Italian
  sausages
3 tablespoons olive oil
3 garlic cloves, cut into halves
One 29-ounce can heavy tomato
  puree

½ teaspoon sugar
1 teaspoon salt (optional)
½ teaspoon pepper
½ teaspoon dried oregano
1 tablespoon chopped Italian
  parsley

With the sharp point of a knife, prick the sausages in several places. In a glass casserole, in the center of the oven, cook the garlic in the oil 1 minute. Add the sausages. Cook 3 minutes. Turn the sausages. Cook 3 minutes. Pour off all but 1½ tablespoons of the liquid and oil. Add the tomato puree, sugar, salt, pepper, oregano, and parsley. Stir. Cover the casserole with waxed paper to prevent splattering. Cook in the center of the oven 10 minutes. Stir. Turn the sausages. Cook 5 minutes. Rotate casserole half a turn. Cook 5 minutes. Let set, covered, 15 minutes. Test for tenderness. This is excellent with small boiled potatoes, or a pasta such as rigatoni. *Serves 4.*

HOT DOGS

You will probably have been told in microwave instructional booklets that all you have to do is place the frankfurter in a bun, wrap it in a paper napkin or paper towel, slip it into the oven, and, almost before you can say "mustard and relish," the hot dog is ready. True. But by using part of the leftovers from another dish (Cornish Game Hens in Sauerkraut and White Wine, page 104), you can prepare a hot dog that will be your all-time favorite sandwich—if you like sauerkraut. What you must do is save the leftover sauerkraut from that Cornish hen dinner and freeze it in 2-tablespoon portions in plastic wrap. Then you're in business for the super dogs. Here are two ways to serve them.

SUPER HOT DOG # 1

Speed-cook; 25 to 28 seconds for 1 hot dog, 40 seconds for 2 hot dogs

This will taste much like those hot dogs sold from the carts that steam the franks and the rolls. If those are a favorite, then this recipe won't dis-

appoint you. Also try the next one (our creation) and see what you've been missing.

1 frankfurter
1 hot dog roll
2 tablespoons wine sauerkraut
   (page 104)

Place the frankfurter in the roll. Spread defrosted sauerkraut on it. Close the roll as tightly as possible. Wrap it in a paper napkin. Tuck in the ends. Cook in the oven 25 to 28 seconds. This sandwich will be quite soft, even though the napkin will absorb part of the moisture. *Serves 1.*

SUPER HOT DOG # 2

Speed-cook; hot dog and sauerkraut, 45 seconds; toasting bun, about 30 seconds

Butter or margarine
1 hot dog roll
1 frankfurter
2 tablespoons wine sauerkraut
   (page 104)

Butter the bun lavishly and toast it. Keep it warm. If the sauerkraut is frozen, defrost it 20 seconds in the oven. Remove when hot. Cook the hot dog 25 seconds. Place it on the toasted bun. Spread on the hot sauerkraut. Super! *Serves 1.*

11

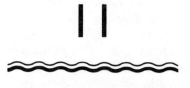

PASTA, RICE, AND SOME UNUSUAL GRAINS

PASTA

WE FIND it more effective, and the pasta better, if we limit the servings to four for each cooking period, allowing about 2 ounces of pasta for each serving. Also, it is best to have the water boiling first, rather than waiting for it to boil under microwaves. In fact, the conventional stove brings water to a boil faster than the microwaves. We will describe here the pasta microwave cooking technique and, in most cases, the recipes in this chapter will call for cooked pasta rather than repeat the cooking procedure.

COOKED PASTA

Speed-cook; 6 minutes

8 ounces pasta   ½ tablespoon salt (optional)
6 cups boiling water

Place the pasta in a 3-quart glass casserole. Pour in the boiling water and add the salt. Cook in the center of the oven, uncovered, 3 minutes. Stir. Cook 3 minutes. Let set, covered, 10 minutes.

All pasta should be cooked *al dente,* "to the tooth," a bit chewy, with a little core remaining, especially the string or rod types, such as spaghetti, vermicelli, linguine, and ziti. If you are going to cook the larger kinds, such as rigatoni, tufoli, and lasagne, add 1 tablespoon of olive oil to the water to prevent the pasta from sticking together. Also, as in all microwave cooking, you are going to have to be alert and test. Common sense will tell you that the method of cooking pasta described here is relative. If you are going to cook a very thin and delicate type of pasta, such as vermicelli, it will cook faster than a thicker spaghetti. Thus, you reduce the cooking time by 2 minutes, and the setting time by 5 minutes. Then test. You will have to experiment, always leaning to less time rather than more.

As delicious and versatile as pasta is, it becomes gummy and soft, almost unpalatable, if overcooked, losing all of its personality. The Italians, the most skilled pasta cooks, test the pasta while it is cooking, forking out a string and judging "by the tooth." This is an excellent idea that prevents overcooking.

The professionals, the pasta chefs in Italy, have a procedure that produces a superior pasta every time. We offer it here for your consideration. It is certainly worth the little extra effort.

When the pasta is cooked *al dente,* if it is a string or rod type, remove it from the water with pasta tongs, or with a fork. Shake off the excess water. This will leave a little coating of water on each strand of pasta that will help prevent the strands from sticking together. If you drain it, it brings it all together, and almost surely will produce a slightly gummy pasta, even if it is cooked to perfection. "Togetherness" is not recommended for pasta. Of course, if you are cooking elbow macaroni, rigatoni, etc., you cannot remove it with a fork. Use a slotted spoon, or, as a last resort, drain it, but do it quickly.

In the meantime, have a large bowl with 3 tablespoons of butter (for 8 ounces of pasta) in the warmer of your conventional stove. At hand have a cup of grated cheese and some black pepper; a pepper mill is preferred.

As you fork the pasta out of the water and shake off the excess moisture, place it in the warm bowl with the butter. When all the pasta is in the bowl, use a wooden spoon and fork to toss it with the butter. This will coat each strand and further protect it from becoming gummy. Add a couple of good grinds of black pepper and 2 tablespoons of the grated cheese. Toss again. Now is the time to also add 3 tablespoons of the sauce you are going to cover it with. Toss it. Serve the pasta in warm bowls or plates, with more sauce and cheese atop. Serve it quickly. Pasta should not wait for the guests. The guests should wait for the pasta.

There it is, the professionals' way. Do it any way that pleases you. But be warned: Too long under the microwaves and pasta will return almost to its natural state. Even though this is a microwave book there is no objection to cooking the pasta on the conventional stove—your own way. Most recipes here call for cooked pasta.

PASTA BOLOGNESE

Speed-cook; 13 minutes

This, possibly the most famous of all the many pasta dishes, usually requires 22 ingredients and more than an hour to cook. By utilizing the prepared filetto *sauce in this chapter you can complete the dish in minutes.*

1 garlic clove, minced
1 tablespoon olive oil
1 pound ground beef of your choice (preferably top sirloin)
Salt and pepper to taste
2½ cups Filetto di Pomodoro (below)
3 medium mushrooms, thinly sliced, sautéed in butter under

microwaves 2 minutes, and drained
4 large chicken livers, coarsely chopped
⅓ cup heavy cream
½ cup grated Parmesan cheese
1 pound spaghettini, cooked and drained

In a glass casserole, in the center of the oven, cook the garlic in the oil 30 seconds. Add the ground beef, seasoning with salt and pepper. Cook 2 minutes. Stir. Cook 2 minutes. Drain the oil from the beef. In the center of the oven, in a large glass measuring cup, heat the *filetto* sauce 3 minutes, or until it bubbles. Pour the hot sauce into the casserole with the beef. Stir well. Add the sautéed mushrooms and the chicken livers. Cook 2½ minutes. Stir in the heavy cream. Cook about 3 minutes, stirring after each 1½ minutes. The mixture should be bubbling. Stir. Toss half the meat sauce with the hot cooked spaghettini. Add half the cheese and toss again. Transfer to warm soup plates. Spoon the remaining sauce atop, sprinkle with the remaining cheese and serve. *Serves 4 to 6.*

FILETTO DI POMODORO

Speed-cook; 17 minutes

This is an elegant, light tomato sauce that restaurant owners in Italy often prepare and serve to themselves and their staff on Sundays. It freezes well, so it pays dividends to make a batch and put it in the freezer for emergencies—or for the famous Pasta Bolognese (above).

Use this sauce on any of your favorites: spaghetti, linguine, noodles. One cup of sauce will serve 2; allow 2 or 3 ounces of pasta for each serving.

1½ tablespoons olive oil
1 tablespoon butter or margarine
¼ cup minced ham or bacon fat
3 medium-size white onions,
  chopped
6 large fresh basil leaves, minced,
  or 1½ tablespoons dried basil

1 teaspoon dried oregano
Two 1-pound cans Italian plum
  tomatoes, put through a food
  mill
½ teaspoon sugar
Salt and pepper to taste

In a glass casserole, heat the oil and butter or margarine. Add the ham fat and cook in the center of the oven 2½ minutes. Stir. Cook 2½ minutes. Stir in the onions, basil, and oregano. Cook 2 minutes, or until onion is soft. Add the tomatoes and sugar. Season with salt and pepper. Stir well.

   Cook, uncovered, 5 minutes. Stir. Cook 5 minutes. Stir. Let set, covered, 10 minutes. The sauce is ready when you can run a wooden spoon through it without leaving a watery trail. *Yields about 7 cups of sauce.*

LINGUINE ALLA CARBONARA

Speed-cook; 13 minutes

This is the famous Roman dish that combines pasta with bacon and eggs.

8 slices bacon
2 eggs
1 cup grated Parmesan cheese
2 tablespoons chopped fresh
  parsley

2 tablespoons pepper
8 ounces linguine

Have four rimmed soup bowls warming in the oven of your conventional stove (200°) or in a special warmer.

   Spread a double layer of paper towels on a 12-inch glass pie plate or cake dish, or on a microwave oven bacon cooker. Arrange the bacon strips on the paper, side by side, not overlapping. Cover with a paper towel. Cook in the center of the oven 3 minutes. Rotate dish half a turn. Cook 4 minutes. Remove the bacon from the paper towels. Pat any remaining fat off with fresh paper towels. Cut the bacon into pieces about half the size of a thumbnail and keep them warm. Place the eggs, cheese, parsley, and pepper in a large bowl and beat with a whisk or an electric beater until well blended. Mix 1 tablespoon of bacon pieces into the cheese and eggs. Cook the linguine as directed on page 159 (or on the conventional stove) and, working quickly, take it directly from the hot water, shake off the excess water, and add the pasta to the cheese-egg mixture. The pasta must be hot to slightly set the eggs as you toss it. Using a wooden spoon and fork, toss the linguine gently, but well, with the cheese and eggs. Serve immediately in the warm soup bowls topped with the remaining crisp bacon pieces. *Serves 4.*

CLASSIC FETTUCCINE

Speed-cook; 7 minutes 40 seconds

For the really classic version, thinly sliced white truffles should garnish the fettuccine, but who can afford them?

1 stick butter
8 ounces fettuccine noodles,
   cooked *al dente* and drained
   (takes 6 minutes)

½ cup heavy cream, warmed
½ cup grated Parmesan cheese
Pepper to taste
1 large egg yolk

In a large glass casserole, in the center of the oven, melt the butter (it will take about 1 minute). Stir in the hot cooked noodles. Toss. Add half the cream and cheese. Toss. Cook 20 seconds. Add the remaining cream and cheese. Toss. Add a liberal amount of pepper. Toss. Cook 20 seconds. Add the egg yolk and toss quickly, blending it with the pasta. Serve immediately in hot bowls or plates. *Serves 4.*

WILLIAM BAUSERMAN'S MACARONI— WITH FOUR VARIATIONS ON A THEME

Speed-cook; 15½ minutes

2 cups elbow macaroni
4 tablespoons butter or margarine
2 tablespoons flour
2 cups light cream

Salt and white pepper to taste
1 cup crushed saltine crackers
12 slices sharp cheddar cheese

Cook the macaroni *al dente,* as directed on page 159 (or on the conventional stove). Drain and rinse quickly with cold water. Add 2 tablespoons of the butter or margarine and toss. Heat the remaining butter or margarine in a glass bowl for 30 seconds, or until melted. Stir in the flour and blend into a smooth paste. Gradually add the cream, stirring until you have a smooth sauce. Cook 2 minutes. Add salt and pepper. Stir, and cook 1 minute, or until thickened. Butter a deep glass casserole and sprinkle in a light layer of crushed crackers. Add a layer of macaroni. Sprinkle in another light layer of crackers, then a layer of the cheese. Lightly sprinkle with salt and pepper. Add the remaining macaroni and repeat the layering procedure, ending with cheese on top. Pour the cream sauce over the contents, filling to about one-third from the top of the casserole (you may not need all of the sauce). Cook in the center of the oven 3 minutes. Rotate casserole half a turn. Cook 3 minutes. Place under the broiler of a conventional stove until the top is golden and crusty. Serve with a side dish of well-chilled stewed tomatoes. *Serves 4.*

Variation I: Add one 7-ounce can of drained, flaked, water-pack tuna to the macaroni and toss, then layer in the casserole as directed and cook.

Variation II: Cook the macaroni and toss with the butter as directed, then place in an ungreased casserole. Do not make the cream sauce. Shape a well in the center of the macaroni and fill with sour cream. Sprinkle generously with shredded, very sharp cheddar cheese, and cook as directed.

Variation III: Instead of serving tomatoes separately as suggested, add one 16-ounce can drained, coarsely chopped tomatoes mixed with ½ teaspoon dried oregano and/or basil to the mixture. Cook as directed. If you use the tomatoes then eliminate the cream sauce.

Variation IV: Cook the basic recipe in a low-sided, flat-bottomed baking dish in a single layer, using half the cream sauce and as much cheese as you like. (It cannot be too cheesy, as cheese and macaroni are boon companions.)

POLISH-STYLE NOODLES

Speed-cook; 13 minutes

½ pound hot Italian sausage meat
¼ cup hot water
½ small head of cabbage, shredded

Salt and pepper to taste
8 ounces egg noodles, cooked and drained

In a large glass pie plate, in the center of the oven, cook the sausage meat 2½ minutes. Stir. Cook 2½ minutes. Drain the sausage, reserving 1½ tablespoons of the fat. Place that fat in a glass casserole, add the cooked sausage, the hot water, cabbage, salt to taste, and much pepper. Cover with plastic wrap, puncturing the center to permit steam to escape. Cook in the center of the oven 4 minutes. Rotate the dish half a turn. Cook 4 minutes. Let set, covered,

10 minutes. Stir in the hot noodles. Toss with the cabbage and sausage. If not hot enough, place under the microwaves 1½ minutes, or until suitably heated. *Serves 4.*

JARRATT'S RIGATONI

Speed-cook; 1½ minutes

This recipe comes from our friend Vernon Jarratt, who formerly owned George's, one of Rome's most famous restaurants. It is a house specialty that has held the place of honor on the menu for many years.

4 tablespoons butter or margarine
½ pound thinly sliced prosciutto or
   other ham, cut into julienne
   strips
8 ounces rigatoni (large tubes),
   cooked and drained (keep hot)

2 egg yolks
½ cup heavy cream
Pinch of nutmeg
½ cup grated Parmesan cheese

In a large glass pie plate, in the center of the oven, melt half the butter or margarine and cook the ham 30 seconds. Add the rigatoni, mixing well with the ham. In a bowl, beat the egg yolks with the cream and nutmeg just enough to mix well, not until frothy. Pour it over the pasta-ham mixture. Stir it in gently, so that the pasta tubes are not broken. Stir in the remaining butter or margarine. Cook 30 seconds. Stir gently. Cook 30 seconds, or until very hot. Stir gently. Serve with the cheese sprinkled atop. *Serves 4.*

RICE

Four tips to make rice tastier:

(1) Before cooking rice in liquid, sauté it in butter or margarine with chopped onions. Use 2 tablespoons of butter or margarine and 2 small chopped white onions for 1 cup of rice. In a glass pie or cake plate, melt the butter or margarine and cook the onions about 2 minutes, or until soft. Stir in the rice, turning it and making certain that it is coated with the butter or margarine and well mixed with the onions. Cook 20 seconds. Then add the rice, onions, and butter or margarine to 2½ cups boiling liquid. If the liquid is cold, it will take about 6 minutes to bring it to a boil under microwaves.

(2) Cook the rice in chicken broth.

(3) After the rice is cooked, do not stir it. Fluff it with a fork. This separates the grains and prevents it from massing and becoming gummy.

(4) If you are serving plain rice as a side dish, it is a good idea to blend in 2 tablespoons of melted butter or margarine and 1 tablespoon of chopped parsley, then fluff the rice. It improves the flavor and gives the rice interesting color.

Precooked rice, the minute variety, needs only to be brought to the boil, then let set, covered, 5 minutes. Note: We avoid the minute variety—it mushes too quickly.

COOKING LONG-GRAIN RICE

Speed-cook; 9 minutes 20 seconds

2 small white onions, chopped
2 tablespoons butter or margarine
½ teaspoon salt (optional)

1 cup long-grain rice
2½ cups boiling chicken broth

You'll need a 2-quart casserole to make certain that you won't have a boil-over.

Cook the onions in butter or margarine 2 minutes, add the salt and rice and cook 20 seconds. Mix well, then stir all into the boiling chicken broth. Cook, covered, in the center of the oven 7 minutes. Let set, covered, 10 minutes. Remember not to stir but to fluff the rice with a fork before serving. *Makes 3¼ cups rice, serving 6.*

RISOTTO MILANESE

Speed-cook; 9 minutes

This is a famous rice dish that will go well with any lamb, veal, or poultry dish and is a table-talk combination. We are incorporating the rice cooking technique described earlier, not only as a reminder, but to demonstrate that this simple mixing of flavors can raise rice to epicurean status.

1 medium-size white onion, finely
   chopped
1 garlic clove, minced
2 tablespoons butter or margarine
1 cup long-grain rice

2½ cups boiling chicken broth
Salt and pepper to taste
¼ teaspoon ground saffron
½ cup grated Parmesan cheese

In a glass casserole, in the center of the oven, cook the onion and garlic in the butter or margarine 2 minutes, or until soft. Stir in the rice, coating it well with the butter or margarine. Stir in the broth, salt, pepper, and saffron. Cover the casserole and cook 4 minutes. Stir. Cook 3 minutes. Let set, covered, 10 minutes. Fluff with a fork, mixing in the cheese. Serve hot. *Serves 4 to 6.*

RICE WITH TUNA

Speed-cook; 9 minutes

1 cup long-grain rice
One 10½-ounce can condensed
    cream of mushroom soup,
    stirred until smooth
2 cups boiling chicken broth
2 white onions, chopped

½ teaspoon salt (optional)
One 10-ounce package frozen
    "petite" peas, thawed
One 7-ounce can fancy solid white
    tuna, drained and flaked

In a casserole, blend the rice, soup, broth, onions, and salt. Stir well. Cook, covered, in a large casserole in the center of the oven 3 minutes. Rotate casserole half a turn. Cook 3 minutes. Stir in the peas and tuna. Cook 3 minutes, until simmering. Let set, covered, 10 minutes. *Serves 4 to 6.*

SPEEDY SPANISH RICE SUPPER

Speed-cook; 11 minutes

2 medium onions, chopped
1 small green pepper, cored,
    seeded, and chopped
2 tablespoons butter or margarine
1 pound ground beef chuck
One 10½-ounce can condensed
    tomato soup

¼ cup water
2 teaspoons red wine vinegar
½ teaspoon salt (optional)
Pinch of dried basil
Pinch of dried oregano
2 cups hot cooked rice
1 canned pimiento, cut up

In a glass casserole, in the center of the oven, cook the onions and pepper in the butter or margarine about 3 minutes, or until soft, stirring after 1½ minutes. Add the beef and cook 2 minutes. Stir. Cook 2 minutes. Stir in the tomato soup, water, vinegar, salt, basil, and oregano, blending well. Cook 1 minute. Stir. Cook 1 minute. Stir in the cooked rice and pimiento. Cook 2 minutes. Stir. Let set, covered, 5 minutes. *Serves 4 to 6.*

COUSCOUS

Speed-cook; 5½ minutes

This traditional Moroccan dish of steamed semolina is usually served with various vegetables and meats, especially lamb. It has a unique nutlike flavor, and offered instead of rice will mark you as a host or hostess with imagination. You can add to its personality by lightly browning chopped walnuts (or pine nuts) and raisins (or currants) and stirring them in just before serving.

2 cups beef broth
1 cup couscous
1 medium-size white onion,
   chopped

2 tablespoons butter or margarine
½ teaspoon salt (optional)
½ teaspoon ground cumin

In a glass casserole, heat the broth 4 minutes, or until it boils. Gradually stir in the couscous. Add the onion, butter or margarine, salt, and cumin. Stir. Cook 1 minute. Stir. Cook 30 seconds. Let set, covered, 15 minutes, or until all the liquid is absorbed. Fluff with a fork. *Serves 4 to 6.*

BULGUR WHEAT PILAF

Speed-cook; 10 minutes

Long before man learned to grind wheat into flour, he parboiled it in open kettles and spread it in the sun to dry. It is crunchy, chewy, nutritious, having a delicious nutlike flavor—and few of your guests will know what it is. If you are interested in cooking one-upmanship, this is your dish. It is excellent with chicken, pork, lamb, and even the stew-type dishes.

1 cup water
1 cup chicken broth
1 cup bulgur wheat
2 tablespoons butter or margarine
½ teaspoon salt (optional)

¼ teaspoon pepper
¼ cup chopped scallions
1 teaspoon chopped fresh mint
Juice of ½ lemon

In a deep glass casserole, heat the water and broth 4 minutes, or until boiling. Stir in the bulgur wheat, butter or margarine, salt, and pepper. Cover and cook 3 minutes. Stir. Cook 3 minutes. Let set, covered, 10 minutes, or until the liquid is absorbed. Just before serving, stir in the scallions, mint, and lemon juice.

BARLEY IN BEEF BROTH

Speed-cook; 15 minutes

Barley is a cereal grass, bearing bearded flower spikes with edible seeds. These are versatile seeds, used not only for food, but to make beer, ale, and whisky. If you haven't tried barley except as a drink, or in a soup such as Scotch Broth, try it as a delicious, nut-flavored change from rice, pasta, or potatoes. It is also excellent with stew-type dishes, mating well with the gravy.

3 cups boiling beef broth
1 cup barley
1½ teaspoons salt (optional)

2 tablespoons butter or margarine
¼ cup grated sharp cheddar cheese

Pour the boiling broth into a deep glass casserole (it must be deep enough to prevent a boil-over) and stir in the barley and salt. Cover and cook in the center of the oven 5 minutes. Stir. Cook 5 minutes. Stir. Cook 5 minutes. Stir. Let set, covered, 15 minutes. Drain. Stir in the butter or margarine and cheese with a fork. The barley should be slightly chewy. *Serves 4 to 6.*

12

LEFTOVERS

IF WE were asked point-blank which one facet or function of the microwave oven was the best, which one accomplished what no other cooking medium could, we wouldn't hestitate to answer, even though microwaves have numerous advantages over conventional cookery: Leftovers.

Whether you are just warming them up, or creating new dishes from leftovers, nothing—we repeat, nothing—can put life back into yesterday's dishes the way microwaves can. They reheat food without loss of flavor or quality. No other method can match this, or even come close to accomplishing it.

We offer an incident to illustrate. Pasta lovers of the fanatic type, we never throw out leftover pasta. But before the advent of microwaves it had to be heated in a double boiler. It was pretty good, but not great. This twice-heated pasta was apt to be gummy, and along the way it lost much of its flavor. Shortly after we acquired our first microwave oven and were still experimenting, with little confidence in ourselves or the space machine, we had an excellent dinner of linguine with white clam sauce, cooked the conventional way. As usual, eyes larger than stomachs, we overcooked by a considerable amount and ended up with a large bowl of leftover pasta. Pushed into the back of the refrigerator, it was forgotten, then accidentally discovered a week later. As suggested in the literature received with the new oven, we covered it with plastic wrap, placed the bowl of pasta in the center of the oven and heated it one minute. We stirred it and heated it another 30 seconds. The microwaves brought that week-old pasta back, tasting exactly as good as it did the night it was cooked. It seemed the impossible, made possible.

Here are two more pluses of the microwave oven: (1) double-duty from food, and (2) economy. All leftovers take on a fresh personality. If you combine leftover meats, seafood, poultry, and vegetables with either cooked or uncooked combinations, you'll have a taste treat that not only will surprise you but give you a new respect for leftover food.

And with the microwave oven you do not have to rush to eat those leftovers. Put them in containers that can go directly from the freezer to the oven, and have them when you please. It isn't necessary to eat turkey for a week, even though the leftovers can be planned with imagination.

Although this was mentioned previously, it is worth repeating in this section. If you are making a stew or other casserole dish, plan ahead for "leftovers" and double the amounts. After cooking, place half in a casserole and pop it into the freezer. These precooked dishes can then become a "just-cooked" main dish in minutes.

The magic of microwaves also permits you to use nonfrozen cooked foods by varying them in another meal, thus making all your cookery "two in one," if you prefer. A good example of this is the utilization of roast leg of lamb slices (or any roast) in Leftover Lamb or Beef with Vegetables, page 177.

Do not discard leftover mashed potatoes or any leftover pureed vegetables that in the past you would not have reheated. They can be frozen, heated in the microwave oven and will taste freshly cooked.

An epicure and friend recently ran a taste test. He microwave-cooked, then froze, mashed parsnips. He then cooked another fresh batch on a conventional stove. He served them both, the freshly cooked ones and the microwave-heated frozen batch, and defied anyone to tell the difference. His food-knowledgeable friends could detect no difference, although two of them did think the frozen offering from the microwave oven was moister and tasted fresher.

Points to remember about leftovers:

Cover tightly with plastic wrap all food to be stored, or place it in containers with covers. This will preserve moisture and that is important.

Try to slice meats thinly and uniformly. Keep in mind that the larger the portions, the longer the cooking time. Twelve servings are more effectively cooked in two batches; heating is faster and more evenly distributed.

If the food in large portions can be stirred, or rearranged in the casserole, it will heat, or cook, more quickly and more evenly. If it can't be stirred or have its position in the dish changed, rotate the dish half a turn after each 2 minutes.

After the cooking period, large casseroles of food should always be allowed to set, covered, at least 5 minutes.

As with all microwave cookery, watch the timing. If you are heating leftover pasta, don't let your attention wander and cook it 10 minutes or you will have rope. Also, leftover rice will become lead pellets if heated too long under microwaves. However, if prepared with other foods, cooked pasta and rice can stand more than mere heating.

If you are defrosting, pay attention. If uncertain, check the defrosting guide that came with your oven. Give the defrosted food the proper resting time, then just reheat the defrosted leftovers; do not cook. Start with 2 minutes, then check to see if the food is hot enough. This is important, for pieces of meat or poultry that have already been cooked can toughen if you leave them too long under the microwaves. Vegetables will dry out; seafood will suffer; rolls will harden.

Time: Watch it! This is quick and easy cookery, but it is not casual.

CREAMED BEEF AND PEAS WITH NOODLES

Speed-cook; 7½ minutes

1 large onion, chopped	2 cups diced cooked beef
2 tablespoons butter or margarine	½ cup cooked peas
One 10½-ounce can condensed cream of mushroom soup	Salt and pepper to taste
⅛ cup light cream	2 cups cooked noodles

In a glass casserole, in the center of the oven, cook the onion in half the butter or margarine 2 minutes, or until soft. Blend in the soup and cream and stir until smooth. Stir in the beef and peas. Season with salt and pepper. Cook 2 minutes. Stir. Cook 2 minutes. Cover. Heat the noodles with the remaining butter or margarine 1 minute. Toss. Heat 30 seconds. Serve the creamed beef and peas over the hot noodles. *Serves 4.*

CHICKEN AND SPINACH

Speed-cook; 6½ minutes

This simple offering is a favorite Viennese dish. If you have the will-power, save the breast when you broil or roast a whole large chicken, as that is generally used. This also is an excellent way to revive tired turkey.

3 tablespoons butter or margarine	1½ cups chicken broth
3 tablespoons flour	½ cup heavy cream

1 teaspoon lemon juice
Salt and pepper to taste
2 cups cooked rice

2 cups cooked leaf spinach
2 cups cooked chicken, cut into
   bite-size slices

In a glass bowl, in the center of the oven, melt the butter or margarine. Stir in the flour and cook about 30 seconds, stirring until you have a smooth paste. Gradually pour in ½ cup of the chicken broth, stirring as it is added. Cook 30 seconds. Stir in the remaining broth; cook 1 minute, stirring after 30 seconds. Stir in the cream and lemon juice, season with salt and pepper, and cook 1½ minutes, stirring every 30 seconds, or until you have a smooth, medium-thick sauce.

In a glass casserole, arrange the rice in an even layer. Spoon 3 or 4 table-spoons of the sauce over it. Layer the spinach evenly on top of the rice, spooning 3 or 4 tablespoons of sauce over it. Cover the spinach with the chicken slices and spoon on the remaining sauce. Cover with plastic wrap. Cook 1½ minutes. Rotate the dish half a turn. Cook 1½ minutes. Test to see if it is hot enough. *Serves 4.*

CHICKEN À LA KING

Speed-cook; 8½ minutes

Here's an old favorite, given a new flavor with the microwave magic.

1 medium-size white onion,
   chopped
2 tablespoons chopped green
   pepper
2 tablespoons butter or margarine
Salt and pepper to taste
1 tablespoon flour
One 10½-ounce can condensed
   cream of chicken soup

¼ cup heavy cream
2 tablespoons dry sherry
1 cup cooked sliced mushrooms
2 cups cubed cooked chicken
2 tablespoons diced pimiento
Pinch of nutmeg
4 slices toasted bread or 4 biscuits

In a glass casserole, in the center of the oven, cook the onion and green pep-per in the butter or margarine 3 minutes, or until soft. Season with salt and pepper and stir in the flour. Blend the soup, cream, and sherry; stir into the casserole with the onion and pepper. Cook 1½ minutes. Stir. Add the mush-rooms, chicken, pimiento, and nutmeg. Stir well. Cover loosely with waxed paper and cook in the center of the oven 2 minutes. Rotate the dish half a turn. Stir. Cook 2 minutes. Test to see if hot enough. Serve over the toast or biscuits. *Serves 4.*

CORNED BEEF AND CABBAGE

Speed-cook; 7 minutes

Here's a dinner that will taste as if hours instead of minutes were spent on it.

One 10½-ounce can condensed
  cream of celery soup
1 medium onion, chopped
4 cups shredded cabbage
1 teaspoon dry mustard

½ teaspoon salt (optional)
½ teaspoon pepper
¼ teaspoon caraway seeds
1½ cups diced cooked corned beef

Place all the ingredients except the corned beef in a glass casserole. Mix well. Cover with plastic wrap and cook in the center of the oven 3 minutes. Stir. Cook 2 minutes. Let set, covered, 5 minutes. Test the cabbage for tenderness. Add the corned beef, stir, and cook 2 minutes. *Serves 4.*

COUSCOUS AND CHICKEN

Speed-cook; 6 minutes

This dish, called moghrabiye *in Lebanon, converts leftover chicken or lamb into an exotic dinner.*

1 large onion, chopped
1 tablespoon butter or margarine
2½ cups hot chicken broth
1 can chick-peas, drained
1 cup couscous

2 cups cooked chicken or lamb,
  cut into bite-size pieces
Salt and pepper to taste
½ teaspoon turmeric
Good pinch of cinnamon

In a glass casserole, in the center of the oven, cook the onion in the butter or margarine 2 minutes, or until soft. Stir in the hot chicken broth and the chick-peas. Cook 2 minutes. Stir in the couscous, chicken, salt, pepper, turmeric, and cinnamon. Cook 2 minutes. Stir. Let set, covered, 10 minutes. *Serves 4.*

HURRY-UP BEEF HASH

Speed-cook; 6 minutes

One 10½-ounce can condensed
   cream of celery soup
⅓ cup chopped fresh parsley
1 medium onion, minced
1½ teaspoons Worcestershire sauce
1 teaspoon salt (optional)

¼ teaspoon pepper
2 cups diced cooked beef
2 cups diced cooked potatoes
2 tablespoons butter or margarine
2 tablespoons milk

In a bowl, mix half the soup with the parsley, onion, one teaspoon of the
Worcestershire sauce, the salt, pepper, beef, and potatoes. In an ovenproof
glass casserole, in the center of the oven, melt the butter or margarine. Stir
in the beef-potato mixture. Cook 2 minutes. Stir. Cook 2 minutes. Place
under the broiler of a conventional stove until brown and crisp. In a glass
measuring cup, mix the remaining soup with the remaining Worcestershire
sauce and the milk. Cook 2 minutes, or until bubbling. Serve as a sauce to
pour over the hash. *Serves 4.*

HASTY HAM AND RICE

Speed-cook; 4 minutes

*A baked ham hangs around quite a while and tends to get as boring as
any visitor who stays too long. Here's a refreshing change for it.*

2 cups ground cooked ham
2 cups cooked rice
2 small ripe tomatoes, peeled,
   seeded, chopped, and drained
   in a strainer
1 small green pepper, cored,
   seeded, and diced
1 small white onion, minced

⅓ cup mayonnaise
2 tablespoons Madeira wine
1 teaspoon Dijon mustard
2 tablespoons butter or margarine
½ cup bread crumbs
3 tablespoons grated sharp
   cheddar cheese

In a bowl, thoroughly mix the ham, rice, tomatoes, green pepper, onion, mayonnaise, Madeira, and mustard. Spoon evenly into a glass casserole and cook
in the center of the oven 2 minutes. Rotate casserole half a turn. Cook 2
minutes. In a small glass measuring cup, melt the butter or margarine and
stir in the bread crumbs, coating them well. Sprinkle the bread crumbs and
cheese over the ham mixture. Place under the broiler of a conventional stove
until the cheese melts and the bread crumbs are brown. *Serves 4.*

LEFTOVER LAMB WITH VEGETABLES IN THE FRENCH MANNER

Speed-cook; 8 minutes

Traditionally, the appeal of this dish is the contrast of the crunchy vegetables with the well-cooked lamb. The vegetables should be just tender but quite firm. Microwaves are the perfect medium for this dish.

2 tablespoons olive oil
Juice of 1 small lemon
1 garlic clove, minced
1 small white onion, finely
   chopped
1 sweet red pepper, cored, seeded,
   and thinly sliced
4 small leeks (white part only),
   sliced

2 small zucchini (unpeeled), cut
   into ¾-inch slices
One 3-inch strip lemon peel, no
   white portion
1 teaspoon salt (optional)
½ teaspoon pepper
3 small ripe tomatoes, cut into
   quarters
2 cups cubed cooked lamb

In a glass casserole, combine the oil, lemon juice, garlic, and onion and cook in the center of the oven 2 minutes. Stir. Add the sweet pepper, leeks, zucchini, lemon peel, salt, and pepper. Cover. Cook 2 minutes. Rotate casserole half a turn. Cook 2 minutes. Add the tomatoes and the lamb. Cover. Cook 2 minutes. Let set, covered, 5 minutes. *Serves 4.*

NEXT-DAY HAM WITH NOODLES

Speed-cook; 5½ minutes

4 tablespoons butter or margarine
1 medium onion, chopped
⅛ teaspoon dried tarragon
Pepper to taste
One 10½-ounce can condensed
   cream of chicken soup

⅓ cup medium cream
2 cups cooked noodles
½ cup cut-up cooked string beans
2 cups diced cooked ham
1 garlic clove, minced
½ cup bread crumbs

In a glass casserole, in the center of the oven, melt half the butter or margarine and cook the onion and tarragon 2 minutes, or until the onion is soft. Season with the pepper. Blend the soup with the cream and stir into the onion in the casserole. Stir in the noodles, beans, and ham. Cover loosely with waxed paper. Cook 1½ minutes. Rotate casserole half a turn. Cook 1½ minutes. In a small glass measuring cup, cook the garlic in the remaining butter or margarine 30 seconds. Stir in the bread crumbs. Sprinkle the crumbs over the ham mixture and place under the broiler of a conventional stove until the crumbs are brown and crisp. *Serves 4.*

LEFTOVER LAMB OR BEEF WITH VEGETABLES

Speed-cook; 6 minutes

We were always glad when Joe Auer, a friend noted in the food field, roasted a leg of lamb. And we didn't care whether we were invited for that beautifully pink leg of lamb. It was the next day we were interested in, for that was when Joe served a leftover dish that he had concocted. It is memorable, especially when accompanied by plenty of lavishly buttered, crusty warm bread and washed down with a velvety red burgundy. Bravo Joe Auer!

3 medium-size potatoes, peeled, cooked, and cut into ¼-inch-thick slices
1 pound broccoli, cooked
2 medium onions, thinly sliced
2 cups bite-size slices cooked lamb (see note)

Salt and pepper to taste
¼ teaspoon dried oregano
1½ cups tomato sauce
4 tablespoons butter or margarine

In a large glass casserole, alternate layers of potatoes, broccoli, onions, and lamb, lightly sprinkling each layer with salt, pepper, and oregano. Spoon tomato sauce over each layer and dot with butter or margarine. The top layer should be potatoes covered with tomato sauce and dotted with butter or margarine. Cover tightly and cook 3 minutes. Rotate the casserole half a turn and cook 3 minutes, or until very hot. The onions should be slightly crunchy. *Serves 4.*

Note: This dish is always best if the roast lamb was cooked in the French style, the meat pink.

SHEPHERD'S PIE

Speed-cook; 7½ minutes

Classically, leftover lamb is used in this simple but surprisingly tasty dish, but any meat—beef, veal, or pork—will do.

1 medium onion, minced
3 tablespoons butter or margarine
2 tablespoons flour
¾ cup beef broth
2 tablespoons minced fresh parsley
3 cups cubed cooked lamb

Salt and pepper to taste
Pinch of mace
3 cups mashed cooked potatoes
3 tablespoons grated cheese of
  your choice

In a glass dish or bowl, in the center of the oven, cook the onion in the butter or margarine 2 minutes, or until soft. Stir in the flour, then, in small amounts, the beef broth, cooking 30 seconds at a time and stirring until you have a smooth sauce. This will take about 1½ minutes. Stir in the parsley, lamb, salt, pepper, and mace. Cover the bottom of a glass casserole with half the mashed potatoes. Spoon the meat mixture over the potatoes, then cover with the remaining mashed potatoes. Dot with butter or margarine. Cook in the center of the oven 2 minutes. Rotate the casserole half a turn. Cook 2 minutes or until hot. Sprinkle the cheese atop and place under the broiler of a conventional stove until brown and crusty on top. *Serves 4 to 6.*

PORK FRIED RICE

Speed-cook; 6 minutes

Here is a fast, Chinese-style method for creating an exotic dish from left-over pork.

2 tablespoons peanut oil
2 cups cooked rice
2 cups coarsely shredded cooked
  pork
Salt and pepper to taste

1½ tablespoons soy sauce
2 eggs, lightly beaten
4 whole scallions, cut into halves
  lengthwise, then into ½-inch
  pieces

Pour the oil into a glass dish or a deep pie plate, and stir in the rice well, to coat the grains. Cook in the center of the oven 1 minute. Stir. Cook 1 minute. Stir in the pork. Season with salt and pepper. Cook 1 minute. Stir in the soy sauce. Cook 1 minute. Pour the eggs over the pork and rice. Stir well. Cook

1 minute. Stir. Cook 1 minute. Stir. The dish should not be dry, but if it is
too moist for your taste, cook another minute or two. Before serving, garnish
with the cut-up scallions. *Serves 4.*

SWIFT STEW WITH DUMPLINGS

Speed-cook; 13 minutes

One 16-ounce can whole white
  onions, drained (reserve the
  liquid)
Beef broth
1 tablespoon cornstarch
One 10½-ounce can condensed
  vegetable soup

2 cups diced cooked beef, veal, or
  lamb
Salt and pepper to taste
1 cup prepared buttermilk biscuit
  mix
⅓ cup milk

Measure the onion liquid and combine with enough beef broth to make 1
cup. Blend in the cornstarch. In a glass casserole, mix the broth mixture,
soup, onions, meat, salt, and pepper. Cover and cook in the center of the
oven 8 minutes, or until the edges bubble. Blend the biscuit mix and the milk,
to make about 8 dumplings. Drop the dough, a tablespoon at a time, onto
the bubbling stew. Cover and cook 2½ minutes. Rotate the casserole half a
turn. Cook 2½ minutes. *Serves 4.*

SACHENHAUSEN STEW

Speed-cook; 11 minutes

Here is a German Topf, *or stew, that uses a variety of leftover meats.
Use any kind that you have.*

1 medium onion, chopped
1 garlic clove, chopped
2 medium potatoes, peeled and
  diced
3 tablespoons butter or margarine
1 cup cubed cooked beef
1 cup cubed cooked veal
1 cup cubed cooked pork
1 ripe tomato, peeled, seeded and
  chopped

Salt and pepper to taste
One 11-ounce can beef gravy
⅓ cup cider or red wine
1 teaspoon lemon juice
One 4-ounce can mushroom
  pieces, drained
1 cup cooked peas
2 tablespoons chopped fresh
  parsley

In a large glass casserole, in the center of the oven, cook the onion, garlic, and potatoes in the butter or margarine 3 minutes. Stir in the meats and tomato and season with salt and pepper. Cook 2 minutes. Stir in the beef gravy, cider, and lemon juice. Cover. Cook 2 minutes. Stir. Cook 2 minutes. Add the mushroom pieces and peas. Cook 2 minutes. Stir. Test to see that the potatoes are tender and the stew is hot enough. Sprinkle with the parsley before serving. *Serves 4 to 6.*

THIRD-DAY TURKEY LOAF

Speed-cook; 9 minutes

Have your turkey for dinner, skip two days, then have it again on the third day in this luscious loaf that will make everyone happy that you had the turkey that first day.

½ cup chopped sweet red pepper
½ cup chopped onion
1 tablespoon butter
6 cups chopped cooked turkey
1 cup bread crumbs
1 egg, beaten

⅓ cup chili sauce
⅓ cup mayonnaise
½ teaspoon salt (optional)
¼ teaspoon pepper
½ teaspoon seasoned salt
⅛ teaspoon dried thyme

In a glass bowl, in the center of the oven, cook the sweet pepper and onion in the butter 2 minutes, then combine with the remaining ingredients in a large bowl and mix thoroughly. Spoon the turkey mixture evenly into a buttered glass loaf pan. Do not let the ends taper or they will dry out. Cook 3½ minutes in the center of the oven. Rotate dish half a turn and cook 3½ minutes. Let set, covered, 5 minutes. This is delicious either hot or cold. *Serves 6 to 8.*

TURKEY DIVAN

Speed-cook; 4 minutes

Here is a fast, tasty way to revive that tired holiday turkey.

One 10-ounce package frozen asparagus spears, cooked and drained
4 large slices cooked turkey breast
Salt and pepper to taste

One 10½-ounce can condensed vegetable soup
⅓ cup heavy cream
½ cup grated Romano or Parmesan cheese

Arrange the asparagus spears in a single layer in a shallow glass casserole. Cover them with the turkey slices and sprinkle lightly with salt and pepper. Blend the soup and cream into a smooth sauce and pour it over the turkey. Cover loosely with waxed paper. Cook in the center of the oven 2 minutes. Rotate casserole half a turn. Cook 2 minutes. Sprinkle with the cheese. Place under the broiler of a conventional stove until the cheese and sauce are bubbling and brown. *Serves 4.*

VEAL PAPRIKASH

Speed-cook; 7½ minutes

> *Leftover veal is worth doing something special with, especially when you have microwaves as a helpmate.*

1 medium-size white onion, finely chopped
1 small green pepper, cored, seeded, and cut into thin slivers
3 tablespoons butter or margarine
2 tablespoons flour
1 tablespoon paprika (preferably Hungarian)
1 cup chicken broth
⅛ teaspoon sugar
½ teaspoon salt (optional)
½ teaspoon lemon juice
2 cups small cubes cooked veal
1 egg yolk
⅓ cup sour cream
2 tablespoons chopped fresh parsley

In a glass casserole, in the center of the oven, cook the onion and green pepper in the butter or margarine 2 minutes, or until soft. Blend the flour and paprika and stir into the vegetables. Gradually stir in the chicken broth, cooking 30 seconds, adding more, and stirring until you have a smooth sauce. This whole process should take about 1½ minutes of cooking time. Stir in the sugar, salt, lemon juice, and veal. Cook 3 minutes. Stir. Blend the egg yolk and sour cream and stir into the casserole ingredients, a tablespoon at a time. Cook 30 seconds. Stir. Cook 30 seconds. The dish should be just heated through. Before serving, sprinkle the paprikash with the parsley. This is excellent with buttered noodles. *Serves 4.*

13

VEGETABLES

ABOUT TWO-THIRDS of Japanese households have microwave ovens. The Japanese favor the microwave for much the same reasons as Americans do: space, energy, and speed. Without question, however, the most important reason is the manner in which microwaves cook. The Japanese diet consists mainly of seafood and vegetables, with vegetables in the lead. They cook their vegetables fast and like them crunchy. Microwaves accomplish this better than any other medium.

Microwave vegetable cookery offers many advantages. By now you probably take the speed for granted, but we want to point out again two astounding facts that we ourselves never can seem to assimilate: You can bake a potato in 4 minutes, an acorn squash in 7. Both vegetables require approximately 1 hour in a conventional oven. Using gas or electricity, that has to make a baked potato or squash an expensive item to serve your family.

But besides saving time, thus energy and expense, microwaves also bring beauty to vegetable cookery. Natural colors are not only retained but enhanced. You will be startled and pleased by the green of cooked zucchini.

As very little water is used, there is virtually no loss of vitamins and nutrients. In conventional cooking, these are lost in the water. Microwave vegetables are good for your health.

In addition to these factors, add one that is more important to most of us than any other: taste. Vegetables cooked by microwaves are fresh-tasting and delicious. In fact, once you've eaten properly microwave-cooked vegetables, you probably will not like them cooked any other way. Many of the vegetables cook in their own moisture; others need only a touch of butter.

Cooking vegetables, however, is no more casual than any other facet of microwave cooking. They quickly can be overcooked. And, as with grades and textures of meats, there is a variance in cooking time, depending upon what kind of vegetables you are using. We found that cooking a vegetable fresh from the home garden was quite different from cooking one purchased in a market. The fresh-picked one cooks more quickly.

The watchword again is *test*. Test frequently during the cooking. For example, if the cooking time given for a squash is 7 minutes, test it after 5 minutes and again at 6.

Results are better if the vegetables are covered while cooking. A little water should be added to some vegetables, about a tablespoon. But this will be absorbed and usually no draining is necessary. Cooking with the utensil covered retains the steam, which helps cook the vegetables more evenly.

Any vegetable with a skin, such as a potato, should be pricked on both sides in several places to prevent it exploding. This also holds true for frozen vegetables in plastic packages. Prick the packages.

Stir in order to distribute the heat evenly, making sure that you start stirring from the outer edge of the dish, so that the portions there will be moved towards the center and those near the center will be moved to the outer edge.

Any vegetable that ends up dry and tough has been overcooked. Unlike vegetables cooked conventionally, those cooked by microwave will be crunchy. Thus, when you take vegetables from a microwave oven they should be firm. If they aren't, you have cooked them too long. If you want to keep them crunchy, remember that they will cook for a few minutes after they are taken from the oven. Allow for this while cooking, and give the vegetable a setting period of about 3 or 4 minutes to finish cooking.

Don't mix frozen, fresh, or canned vegetables together. Cooking times differ for each.

We do not cook frozen vegetables in their containers, but it can be done (unless the containers are aluminum foil). Halfway through the cooking period they must be stirred, or shaken, to rearrange the position so they will cook evenly.

If cooking solid-pack frozen vegetables in a dish, the icier side should be up. This permits an even distribution of heat as the water from the melted ice passes through the vegetables. If frozen vegetables are taken from a loose pack, 2 tablespoons of hot water should be added, and they should be stirred halfway through the cooking period.

Canned vegetables just need to be heated in only half of their liquid.

Cooked vegetables need only to be reheated, usually about 1½ minutes, depending upon the size of the portion being reheated. Add no liquid, and heat them covered. Because they heat internally, and not upon the surface, the fresh color will remain, as will the flavor, and, if you watch carefully, they will not dry out.

There is no doubt that the microwave oven is the best vegetable cooker in existence, worth its price for just that alone. But cook with caution.

The timing rule of thumb, as we have stated, for converting recipes from conventional cooking to the microwave is about a fourth of the conventional time. *This is not true for vegetable cookery.* For example, that much-discussed baked potato that takes 1 hour in the conventional oven cooks in 4 minutes, or only one-fifteenth of the conventional time. Many of the vegetables cook in a surprisingly short time. Thus, you have the same old problem that confronts you in every phase of microwave cookery: You will be tempted to overcook, to give the peas, squash, or cabbage "another minute or two." Don't do it.

ACORN SQUASH WITH MADEIRA AND BUTTER

Speed-cook; 7 minutes

One 1-pound acorn squash
2 tablespoons butter or margarine

1 tablespoon Madeira wine
Salt and pepper to taste

Cut the squash in half, but do not scoop out the seeds and the stringy fibers. Cook on a paper towel in the center of the oven 4 minutes. Remove the seeds and fibers. Place 1 tablespoon of butter or margarine and ½ tablespoon Madeira in each squash half. Cook 3 minutes. Season with salt and pepper. (When cooking 2 squash, cook about 13 minutes.) *Serves 2.*
Variation: This easily can be turned into a unique accompaniment to the Thanksgiving turkey. Just before serving, half fill the squash cavities with canned, drained whole cranberries.

HONEY ACORN SQUASH

Speed-cook; 7 minutes

One 1-pound acorn squash
½ teaspoon salt (optional)
¼ teaspoon mace

1 teaspoon brown sugar
2 teaspoons honey

Pierce the whole squash straight through in several places with an ice pick or skewer. Place on a paper towel. Cook 3 minutes. Turn the squash over and cook 2 minutes. Cut the squash in half and remove the seeds and stringy fibers. Blend the salt, mace, brown sugar, and honey and spoon into the squash cavities. Cook 1 minute. Turn position of the squash. Cook 1 minute. *Serves 2.*

BUTTER BEANS IN TOMATO SAUCE

Speed-cook; 6 minutes

1 small green pepper, cored, seeded, and chopped
1 small white onion, chopped
1 tablespoon butter or margarine
One 10½-ounce can condensed tomato soup
¼ cup water

1 teaspoon prepared mustard
1 tablespoon vinegar
1 tablespoon brown sugar
Two 16-ounce cans butter beans, drained
Salt and pepper to taste

In a glass casserole, cook the green pepper and onion in the butter or margarine in the center of the oven 2 minutes, or until soft. Stir in the soup, water, mustard, vinegar, and brown sugar. Cook 3 minutes, or until hot. Stir in the butter beans. Cook 1 minute, or until hot. Season with salt and pepper. *Serves 4 to 6.*

ITALIAN GREEN BEANS

Speed-cook; 10 minutes

1 large onion, chopped
1 garlic clove, minced
1 small green pepper, seeded, cored, and chopped
2 tablespoons olive oil
4 small ripe tomatoes, peeled, seeded, chopped, and drained in a strainer

1 pound green beans, cut into 1-inch pieces
½ teaspoon sugar
¼ cup chicken broth
Salt and pepper to taste

In a glass casserole, in the center of the oven, cook the onion, garlic, and green pepper in the oil 2 minutes or until soft. Stir in the tomatoes, beans, sugar, and chicken broth. Cook, covered, 4 minutes. Stir. Cook 4 minutes. Let set, covered, 3 minutes. Season to taste with salt and pepper. *Serves 4 to 6.*

WAX-BEAN CASSEROLE

Speed-cook; 15 minutes

Two 10-ounce packages frozen
   wax beans
½ teaspoon pepper
⅛ teaspoon dried thyme
One 10½-ounce can condensed
   cream of chicken soup

1½ teaspoons soy sauce
One 3½-ounce can french-fried
   onions

In a glass casserole, place the frozen beans, icy side up. Sprinkle with pepper and thyme. Cook, covered, in the center of the oven, 6 minutes. Stir. Cook 6 minutes. Blend the soup and soy sauce and stir into the cooked beans. Stir in half the french-fried onions. Cook 2 minutes, or until hot. Sprinkle on the remaining french-fried onions. Cook 1 minute. *Serves 4 to 6.*

BROCCOLI WITH GRUYÈRE

Speed-cook; 9 minutes

1 pound fresh broccoli (about two-
   thirds of a bunch)
3 tablespoons water
Salt and pepper to taste

2 tablespoons butter or margarine,
   melted
⅓ cup grated Gruyère cheese

Divide the thick stems of the broccoli by cutting from the top down, right through the stems, so you will have thin-stemmed (about ½ inch in diameter) stalks of broccoli. Peel the stems and score the ends. Arrange them in a glass baking dish with the buds in the center, stems pointing outward. Add the water and cook, covered, in the center of the oven 8 minutes, turning the broccoli over after 4 minutes. Let set, covered, 3 minutes. Test for tenderness. It should be crisp but tender. Sprinkle the salt, pepper, and melted butter or margarine over the broccoli, then the cheese. Cover and cook 1 minute or until the cheese melts. *Serves 4.*

Variations: Substitute white wine for the water for an interesting flavor. Another simple, tasty sauce for broccoli is made by blending ½ cup mayonnaise, the juice of ½ lemon, and ½ teaspoon seasoned salt. Spoon over hot or cold cooked broccoli.

BRUSSELS SPROUTS WITH TOASTED ALMONDS

Speed-cook; 8 minutes

1½ pounds (2 pints) brussels
  sprouts, cleaned
3 tablespoons water
3 tablespoons butter or margarine

1 tablespoon lemon juice
¼ cup toasted slivered almonds
Salt and pepper to taste

Place the brussels sprouts in a glass casserole. Pour in the water, cover, and cook in the center of the oven 4 minutes. Stir. Cook 4 minutes. Let set, covered, 5 minutes. Drain well. Stir in the butter or margarine, lemon juice, salt, and pepper and sprinkle with the toasted almonds. *Serves 4 to 6.*

CAULIFLOWER IN QUICK CHEESE SAUCE

Speed-cook; 7 minutes

½ teaspoon salt (optional)
1 medium head of cauliflower
  (about 1 pound), cut into florets
2 tablespoons water

One 11-ounce can condensed
  cheddar cheese soup
3 tablespoons heavy cream
½ cup buttered bread crumbs

Sprinkle the salt into a glass casserole, then add the cauliflower florets. Add the water, cover, and cook in the center of the oven 3 minutes. Rotate the casserole half a turn. Cook 2 minutes. Drain. In a large glass measuring cup, blend the soup and cream. Cook 2 minutes, or until hot. Pour the sauce over the cauliflower. Sprinkle with the bread crumbs and place under the broiler of a conventional stove until the crumbs are brown. *Serves 4 to 6.*

CARROTS IN CONSOMMÉ

Speed-cook; 10 minutes

1 medium onion, chopped
2 tablespoons chopped fresh
  parsley
2 tablespoons butter or margarine
⅛ teaspoon mace

8 medium carrots, scraped, cut
  into ½-inch pieces
¼ cup canned condensed
  consommé

In a glass casserole, cook the onion and parsley in the butter or margarine 2 minutes, or until the onion is soft. Stir in the mace, carrots, and consommé. Cover and cook in the center of the oven 4 minutes. Stir. Cook, uncovered, 4 minutes. Let set, covered, 5 minutes. *Serves 4.*

CARROTS MARSALA

Speed-cook; 6 minutes

3 tablespoons butter or margarine
Pinch of dried thyme
Salt and pepper to taste

10 small, slender carrots, scraped
  and cut into 1-inch pieces
¼ cup Marsala

Put the butter or margarine, thyme, salt, and pepper in a glass casserole. Place the carrots on top of the seasonings. Cook, covered, in the center of the oven 2 minutes. Stir, coating the carrots with the butter or margarine. Pour in the wine. Cover. Cook 2 minutes. Stir. Cover and cook 2 minutes. Let set, covered, 3 minutes. *Serves 4.*

EASY CREAMED CELERY

Speed-cook; 8 minutes

4 cups 1-inch celery pieces
  (scraped; cut on the diagonal)
2 tablespoons beef broth (beef
  bouillon cubes dissolved in hot
  water make a quick broth)

One 10½-ounce can condensed
  cream of celery soup
Salt and pepper to taste

In a glass casserole, combine the celery and beef broth and cook, covered, in the center of the oven 4 minutes. Drain. Stir in the soup; cook 4 minutes. Season with salt and pepper. *Serves 4.*

CORN ON THE COB

This summertime American favorite is spectacular cooked by microwaves. We use three techniques, all equally good:

(1) Carefully strip back the husk (do not tear it off) and remove all the silk. Brush the corn liberally with melted butter or margarine and sprinkle with

salt. Pull the husks back into place. Tie with string about the tip to keep the husks intact. Cook.

(2) Place ears in a large glass casserole. Add a tablespoon of water. Cover with plastic wrap. Cook.

(3) Wrap each ear securely in waxed paper and place in a spoke fashion on paper towels in the oven. Cook.

Cooking Times

2 ears of corn: 4 to 6 minutes; turn corn over at 2 minutes, or halfway through the cooking time.

4 ears of corn: 8 to 10 minutes: turn corn over at 4 minutes, or halfway through the cooking time.

6 ears of corn: 9 to 11 minutes; turn corn over at 4½ minutes, or halfway through the cooking time.

Very large ears will need extra cooking time. The corn should set, covered, 3 to 5 minutes after cooking.

CORN PUDDING

Speed-cook; 10 minutes

1 egg
1 tablespoon sugar
Salt and pepper to taste
1 heaping tablespoon cornstarch

One 16-ounce can cream-style corn
1 cup milk

In a bowl, beat together the egg, sugar, salt, pepper, and cornstarch. Add the corn and milk and blend well. Pour the mixture into a buttered deep glass baking dish. Cook, uncovered, in the center of the oven 5 minutes. Stir well, from the outside in. Cook 5 minutes, or until nearly set in the middle. Let set, covered, 3 minutes. This will have a surprising soufflé consistency. *Serves 4.*

OUT-OF-THE-CUPBOARD CORN SCALLOP

Speed-cook; 4 minutes

One 10½-ounce can condensed cream of vegetable soup
1 small onion, minced
½ teaspoon pepper

One 16-ounce can whole kernel corn, drained
1½ cups crushed saltine crackers
2 tablespoons butter or margarine

Blend the soup, onion, and pepper. In a glass casserole, alternate layers of corn, the soup mixture, and crushed crackers. Dot with butter or margarine. Cook in the center of the oven 2 minutes. Rotate casserole half a turn. Cook 2 minutes, or until hot. *Serves 4 to 6.*

CREAMED PEAS AND ONIONS

Speed-cook; 7 minutes

One 10-ounce package frozen peas
One 16-ounce can small white
　　onions, drained
One 10½-ounce can condensed
　　cream of mushroom soup

3 tablespoons heavy cream
¼ teaspoon pepper
¼ teaspoon dried tarragon
Salt to taste

In a glass casserole, place the peas, icy side up. Cook 4 minutes. Drain. Stir in the onions. Blend the soup, cream, pepper, and tarragon. Stir the soup mixture into the peas and onions. Cook in the center of the oven 2 minutes. Stir. Cook 1 minute, or until hot. *Serves 4 to 6.*

FAST ONIONS AMANDINE

Speed-cook; 5 minutes

One 10½-ounce can condensed
　　cream of mushroom soup
Two 16-ounce cans small white
　　onions, drained

½ cup grated sharp cheddar cheese
¼ cup toasted slivered almonds

Stir the soup in its can until smooth. In a glass casserole, place the onions and stir in the soup. Cook, covered, in the center of the oven 2½ minutes. Rotate the casserole half a turn. Sprinkle on the cheese, then the almonds. Cook 2½ minutes, or until hot. *Serves 4 to 6.*

FRESH GREEN PEAS IN WINE AND BEEF BROTH

Speed-cook; 6 minutes

2 pounds fresh peas (about 2 cups
　　shelled peas)

2 medium celery ribs, scraped and
　　thinly sliced

4 whole scallions, minced
½ teaspoon pepper
Pinch of dried thyme
2 tablespoons beef broth

1½ tablespoons dry white wine
3 tablespoons butter or margarine
2 teaspoons cornstarch
Salt to taste

In a glass casserole, place the peas, celery, and scallions. Sprinkle with the pepper, thyme, and beef broth. Cook, covered, in the center of the oven 3 minutes. Stir in 1 tablespoon of the white wine, and the butter or margarine. Cook 2 minutes. Blend the remaining wine and cornstarch and stir it in. Cook 1 minute. Let set, covered, 3 minutes. Add salt to taste. *Serves 4 to 6.*

SAUTÉED PEPPERS, ONIONS, AND MUSHROOMS

Speed-cook; 6 minutes

Here's a way to relieve the boredom of serving the same old vegetables the same old way. See Variation (below) to convert into a main dish.

2 small green peppers, cut into
   thin rings
2 small sweet red peppers, cut into
   thin rings
2 medium onions, sliced

2 tablespoons olive oil
½ pound fresh mushrooms, sliced
¼ teaspoon dried oregano
1 teaspoon salt (optional)
½ teaspoon pepper

In a glass casserole, in the center of the oven, cook the green and red peppers and onions in the olive oil 4 minutes, stirring after 2 minutes. Stir in the mushrooms, oregano, salt, and pepper. Cook 1 minute. Stir. Cook 1 minute. Let set, covered, 3 minutes. *Serves 4 to 6.*

Variation: A unique main-course dish also can be built on this recipe. Allow one hot and one sweet Italian sausage per serving. Prick the sausages. Cook for 2½ minutes on each side in half the oil, covered with waxed paper to prevent splattering. Add the remaining vegetables in order and cook as directed above.

BAKED POTATOES

Everyone loves baked potatoes. They are nutritious and delicious, and they go with just about any main dish. The only problem is that with conventional cookery it takes at least 1 hour to bake them. If they are cooked ahead, wrapped in foil, and kept warm (as the restaurants prepare them), they become soggy and lose much of their flavor.

Baked potatoes, then, are the speedy show-off microwave vegetable. We confess that any time we are demonstrating our microwave oven and its miraculous speed, we always bake a potato and offer it to the guest who is seeing the oven in operation for the first time. Beforehand we ask the guest to time the cooking. He or she is tasting the potato in less than 5 minutes. We also are able to sit down to a fish or steak dinner and decide at the last minute that a baked potato would taste just right. We have it in minutes.

Try to select blocky, nontapered, uniform-in-size baking potatoes (we like Idahoes), each about 7 ounces, which is considered a medium-size potato. If the potatoes aren't all the same size some will be overcooked. The cooking times here are for potatoes of even dimension that weigh exactly 7 ounces. Scrub them well, and pierce both sides in several places with a fork. No cooking dish is necessary. Place the potatoes in the oven, 1 inch apart, on double folds of paper towels. The towels will absorb some of the moisture from the potatoes and help prevent oversteaming.

To cook a single potato, place it in the center. Arrange 3 or more like the spokes in a wheel (with none in the hub or center position), 1 inch apart. Cooking time depends upon the size and variety of the potatoes. We have found that a New York State potato cooks faster than the russet, or so-called Idaho. Most important: When half the cooking time has elapsed, turn the potatoes over and rearrange their position. If you are cooking a potato 4 minutes, remind yourself to turn it by cooking just 2 minutes; when the buzzing stops, turn the potato and cook it another 2 minutes.

Use the same method of selection and cooking for baked sweet potatoes or yams, but reduce the time by 1 minute.

Time

1 potato:	4 to 5 minutes
2 potatoes:	6 to 7 minutes
3 potatoes:	8 to 9 minutes
4 potatoes:	10 to 11 minutes
6 potatoes:	14 to 15 minutes

If cooking the shorter time, let set 10 minutes before serving.

These are estimated times. You will have to experiment to your satisfaction, according to how well you like your potato cooked. Again we remind you that the potato will cook after it is removed from the oven. Thus, they should be firm at the end of the cooking time. If they are withered-looking before you take them from the oven, they are overcooked. To be on the safe side, the shorter cooking time should be favored; we use it and find it exactly right for our tastes and our oven.

With the speed cooking of the baked potato you will find that a whole new world of potato cookery has opened up. Bake the potatoes, then dice them, melt butter or margarine in the browning skillet and hash-brown the potatoes. Slice them and fry them in butter or margarine for cottage potatoes. Cream them. Scoop out the baked potato, place in a bowl, add butter or margarine and cream and beat into fluffy mashed potatoes. Add cheese and minced onion to the mashed potatoes, place the mixture back in the potato shells, sprinkle a little more grated cheese atop, then place the stuffed shells in the oven until the cheese melts. Make potato salads. Potato pancakes. There is almost no limit to what you can do with that 4-minute baked potato.

GERMAN POTATO SALAD

Speed-cook; 11 minutes

4 slices bacon
2 medium onions, chopped
One 10½-ounce can condensed
   cream of celery soup
2 tablespoons water
2 tablespoons vinegar
¼ teaspoon celery seed

½ teaspoon sugar
⅛ teaspoon pepper
4 medium (7-ounce) potatoes,
   baked (page 191), peeled, and
   sliced
2 tablespoons chopped fresh
   parsley

In a glass casserole, arrange the bacon slices, cover with a paper towel to prevent splattering, and cook 4 minutes. Remove the bacon, blot grease from the slices with a paper towel, and let cool. Crumble the bacon and set aside.

In the bacon fat in the casserole, cook the onions 2 minutes, or until soft. Stir in the soup, water, vinegar, celery seed, sugar, and pepper. Cook 2 minutes. Stir. Cook 2 minutes. Add the potato slices, parsley, and crumbled bacon. Cook 30 seconds. Stir. Cook 30 seconds. Stir. Serve hot. *Serves 4.*

LYONNAISE POTATOES

Speed-cook; 9 minutes

3 tablespoons butter or margarine
½ teaspoon salt (optional)
¼ teaspoon pepper
¼ teaspoon dried marjoram
4 medium-size white onions, thinly sliced

4 medium potatoes, peeled and thinly sliced
2 tablespoons hot chicken broth (a quick broth can be made by dissolving 1 chicken bouillon cube in 1 cup hot water)

Place the butter or margarine in the bottom of a glass casserole and sprinkle in the salt, pepper, and marjoram. Arrange the onions in a layer on top of the butter or margarine and seasonings. Cover and cook in the center of the oven 3 minutes. Arrange the potatoes in a layer atop the onions and sprinkle the chicken broth over them. Cook, covered, 3 minutes. Stir well. Cook 3 minutes. Let set, covered, 5 minutes. Test for tenderness and seasoning. The potatoes and onions should be crisp yet tender. *Serves 4.*

SWIFT BUT SAVORY SCALLOPED POTATOES

Speed-cook; 4 minutes

One 10½-ounce can condensed cheddar cheese soup
¼ cup heavy cream
½ teaspoon pepper
Small pinch of cayenne
4 medium potatoes, peeled, cooked, and sliced

2 medium-size white onions, minced
1 tablespoon butter or margarine
Paprika

Blend the soup, cream, pepper, and cayenne thoroughly, making a sauce. In a glass casserole, arrange alternate layers of potatoes and onions, spooning some of the sauce on each layer. Dot the top layer with the butter or margarine and sprinkle with paprika. Cook, uncovered, in the center of the oven 2 minutes. Rotate casserole half a turn. Cook 2 minutes, or until hot. *Serves 4.*

POTATO WITH BROCCOLI

Speed-cook; 12 minutes

⅛ bunch (about ½ pound) broccoli
One 8-ounce potato
3 tablespoons olive oil

1 medium onion, chopped
1 garlic clove, minced
Salt and pepper to taste

Divide the thick stems of the broccoli by cutting from the top down, right through the stems, so you will have thin-stemmed (about ½ inch in diameter) stalks of broccoli. In the center of the oven, cook the potato in its jacket 4½ minutes. Arrange the broccoli in a glass casserole with the buds in the center and the stems near the edge of the dish, and cook in the center of the oven 2½ minutes, rotating the dish at 1½ minutes. Transfer the broccoli to a bowl. Pour off any liquid in the casserole. Add the olive oil and cook the onion and garlic 3 minutes, stirring at 2 minutes. Cut the broccoli into bite-size pieces. Peel and slice the potato when it is cool enough to handle. Add the potato and broccoli to the onion in the casserole and cook 2 minutes, or until hot, stirring after 1 minute. Season with salt and pepper. Serve hot or cold. If it is served cold, stir in the juice of half a lemon. *Serves 2.*

RATATOUILLE

Speed-cook; 12 minutes

This is said to be a French dish, originating in southern France where many of the cooks are Italian, a fact the French find forgettable. We suspect that this, like the fork, was first popularized by the Italians, who are masters of many zucchini and eggplant dishes. We like it either hot or cold, and serve it with many of our meat dishes, from lamb to duck. On a hot summer day a dish of cold ratatouille, with bread and beer, makes a superb supper.

2 cups unpeeled zucchini cubes (½-inch pieces)
2 cups peeled eggplant cubes (½-inch pieces)
Flour
1½ teaspoons salt (optional)
4 garlic cloves, minced
⅓ cup olive oil

½ teaspoon dried oregano
3 medium onions, thinly sliced
2 medium green peppers, seeded, cored, and cut into thin strips
½ teaspoon dried basil
3 large ripe tomatoes, peeled, seeded, and thinly sliced

Separately toss the zucchini cubes and the eggplant cubes with flour to coat them lightly. In a large buttered glass casserole, arrange a layer of zucchini cubes and sprinkle with a third each of the salt, garlic, and oil. Cover the zucchini with a layer of eggplant cubes, sprinkle with a third each of the salt, garlic, and oil, and all of the oregano. Make a third layer with the onion slices, sprinkling on the remaining salt, garlic, and oil. Arrange a layer of pepper strips over the onions, and sprinkle on half the basil. Cover and cook in the center of the oven 4 minutes. Stir. Cook 4 minutes. Stir. Arrange a layer of tomato slices on top and sprinkle with the remaining basil. Cover and cook 4 minutes. Let set, covered, 5 minutes. *Serves 4 to 6.*

ROEDKAAL (DANISH RED CABBAGE)

Speed-cook; 17 minutes

1 head red cabbage (3 to 3½ pounds)
1 small onion, minced
2 tablespoons butter or margarine
1 small tart apple, peeled, cored, and minced
1 tablespoon flour
2 tablespoons sugar
¼ cup cider vinegar
½ teaspoon caraway seeds
2 tablespoons currant jelly
Salt and pepper to taste

Remove the outside tough leaves of the cabbage, then quarter, core, and shred the vegetable. In a glass casserole, in the center of the oven, cook the onion in the butter or margarine 2 minutes. Stir in the cabbage and apple, sprinkle with flour, stir, and cook 2 minutes. Stir in the sugar, vinegar, and caraway seeds. Mix well. Cook, covered, 8 minutes, stirring after 4 minutes. Stir in the currant jelly. Cook 5 minutes. Let set, covered, 5 minutes. Season with salt and pepper. *Serves 4 to 6.*

SPEEDY SUCCOTASH

Speed-cook; 12 minutes

History tells us that this tasty dish was created by the American Indians, who also gave us corn. It is one of our favorite vegetable combinations, which we like with microwave-cooked Milano Meat Loaf (page 115) and a baked potato (page 191).

One 10-ounce package frozen whole-kernel corn
One 10-ounce package frozen lima beans

2 tablespoons butter or margarine
1 tablespoon flour
½ cup heavy cream

⅛ teaspoon paprika
Salt and pepper to taste

Place the frozen vegetables in a glass casserole, icy side up. Cook, covered, in the center of the oven 7 minutes, stirring at 4 minutes. Drain well. Stir in the butter or margarine until it melts, then stir in the flour. Cook 1 minute. Stir in the cream and paprika. Cook 4 minutes, stirring at 2 minutes. Let set, covered, 5 minutes. Season with salt and pepper. *Serves 6.*

SWISS CREAMED FRESH SPINACH

Speed-cook; 4 minutes

2 pounds fresh spinach
1 medium onion, chopped
1 garlic clove, minced
3 tablespoons butter or margarine

2 tablespoons flour
⅛ teaspoon nutmeg
½ cup heavy cream
Salt and pepper to taste

Wash the spinach, drain well, and chop. In a glass casserole, in the center of the oven, cook the onion and garlic in the butter or margarine 2 minutes. Stir in the chopped spinach. Sprinkle with the flour and nutmeg and stir. Pour in the cream and mix well. Cover, cook 2 minutes, and stir. Season with salt and pepper. *Serves 4 to 6.*

ZESTY ZUCCHINI

Speed-cook; 6 minutes

4 medium zucchini (unpeeled), cut
   into ¼-inch.rounds
One 8-ounce can seasoned tomato
   sauce

¼ teaspoon salt (optional)
⅛ cup grated Swiss cheese
1 cup crisp garlic croutons

Place the zucchini slices in a glass casserole. Cover and cook in the center of the oven 3 minutes. Drain. Stir in the tomato sauce and salt. Sprinkle with the cheese. Cover and cook 3 minutes, or until the zucchini is tender but still crunchy. Let set, covered, 5 minutes. Sprinkle with the croutons just before serving. *Serves 4.*

SWEET-AND-SOUR ZUCCHINI STRIPS

Speed-cook; 8 minutes

This tasty Italian squash is universally loved, and its ways of preparation are endless. There even is a zucchini cookbook. Here's one dish few will have had.

1 large onion, chopped
1 tablespoon butter or margarine
1 tablespoon olive oil
1½ pounds small, firm zucchini
   (unpeeled), cut into strips the
   size of french-fried potatoes
1 teaspoon Hungarian paprika

1 tablespoon butter blended with 1
   tablespoon flour
¼ cup cider vinegar
¼ teaspoon dill weed
1 teaspoon sugar
½ teaspoon salt (optional)

In a glass casserole, in the center of the oven, cook the onion in the butter or margarine and olive oil 2 minutes. Add the zucchini strips, sprinkle with paprika, and cook 2 minutes, turning the zucchini strips twice. Stir in the blended butter or margarine and flour until well mixed, then add the vinegar, dill weed, sugar, and salt. Cover and cook 2 minutes. Stir. Cook 2 minutes or until the zucchini is tender but still crisp and crunchy. *Serves 4.*

ZUCCHINI ABRUZZI STYLE

Speed-cook; 9 minutes

1 medium onion, chopped
2 tablespoons butter or margarine
8 small slender zucchini, cut into
   ½- to ¾-inch equal-size pieces

2 eggs
Salt and pepper to taste
¼ cup grated Parmesan cheese

In a glass casserole, cook the onion in the butter or margarine 2 minutes, or until soft. Add the zucchini, cover, and cook 3 minutes. Stir. Cook 2 minutes. Let set, covered, 3 minutes. Drain off all liquid. Beat the eggs, salt, pepper, and cheese together. Stir into the casserole with the zucchini. Cook 2 minutes, stirring after each minute, or until the eggs have set. Serve immediately. *Serves 4.*

14

DESSERTS

ALTHOUGH IT won't brown most cakes or pies, the microwave oven will take the drudgery out of cooking all desserts, and can cook everything from a cake to a custard almost instantly. In addition, there now are special microwave cake, cookie, and cupcake mixes on the market that do beautifully in the microwave.

You'll also find that fruits and fruit desserts have an incomparable fresh fruit flavor that is lessened, if not lost, in conventional cookery. You can cook a cake in 5 minutes, 6 cupcakes in 3 minutes. But there are rules to review, and points to consider:

Custards

Custards are quick and easy—but also easy to overcook (they will curdle and separate). We prepare individual custard cups, and set them in a glass baking dish in 1 inch of water. This seems to equalize the cooking. It also is a good idea to stir custards from time to time to prevent them from boiling over. Undercook all custards, as they will continue to cook out of the oven.

Fruit Desserts

Test fruits and fruit desserts when half the cooking time has elapsed. Times will vary, depending upon the ripeness of the fruit and what variety it is. For example, apples take longer than peaches. Remember, too, that during the setting time the fruits will continue to cook. When using cut-up fruit, even cooking is assured if pieces are the same size.

Cakes

Cake pans should be greased only on the bottom. An even crust will result if you let the cake set 10 minutes in the pan before cooking it. They rise quickly, and higher, in the microwave oven, so only fill the pan halfway. The extra batter can be used for cupcakes.

Just before you pour the batter into the pans, pass a knife through it several times to release the air bubbles. We find that doughy centers in cakes can be eliminated by setting the cake pan on an inverted saucer.

Cook just one cake layer at a time, about 5 minutes. Even cooking is also obtained by rotating the cake pan a quarter turn every 2 minutes.

It is also pertinent to note that cakes baked in differently shaped utensils have different cooking times. Here's the way we time our cakes:

> 8- or 9-inch round pan: 5 minutes
> 8 × 8 × 2-inch square: 7 minutes
> 9 × 13-inch rectangular: 10 minutes
> Deep bundt dish: 12 minutes

The cake is cooked when a toothpick inserted in the center emerges clean. The cake surface probably will be moist after cooking. Do not be tempted to cook it longer to reduce the moisture. That will result in overcooking other parts of the cake. After a brief setting period the moisture will disappear.

Let the baked cake set 5 minutes, then invert on a wire rack and let cool about 10 minutes.

We find that layer cakes are easier to ice if they are first refrigerated 1 hour. Do not try to frost or ice a cake right after cooking. The trapped heat in the cake will melt it.

All packaged cake mixes have a basic recipe, which reads approximately like this: "Combine cake mix, 1⅓ cups water, 2 eggs." It then goes on to instruct how to mix, beat, and bake. By using ingenuity, you can improve the flavor of an ordinary mix, converting it into a cake no one would believe came from a package. To stir your imagination, here are a few ideas: Instead of using water, use wine, rum, liqueurs, fruit juice, buttermilk; also add butter or margarine, flavorings, vanilla extract, almond, peppermint, grated lemon or orange rind, instant coffee, chopped nuts, chocolate chips, an extra egg. If you use sour cream, add ¾ cup plus ½ cup of water, no other liquid.

When using cake mixes, simply line the bottom of the baking dish with "brown-in" paper or waxed paper and butter the paper lightly if you are going to remove the cake. If you are going to serve the cake from the pan or dish, instead of lining the dish with waxed paper butter it. Peel the paper from the bottom after the 10-minute cooling period.

We've also discovered that it is wise to eat microwave cakes sooner than those cooked conventionally. They dry out a little faster. You'll have to experiment with your own oven to get the timing exactly right.

We cook our cakes 5 minutes per layer, but you might be better off cooking just 4 minutes. Play it safe and slightly undercook to allow for that carry-over cooking time. With a couple of cakes you'll have the hang of it and turn out masterpieces in minutes. And remember: There are unique microwave cake mixes that are perfect for the medium.

Cupcakes

Speaking of minutes, cupcakes are a sensation if you want to show off the speed of your oven.

1 cupcake: 30 seconds
2 cupcakes: 60 seconds
6 cupcakes: 2½ minutes

Cook the cupcakes in paper baking cups placed in glass custard cups. They should be filled only one-third full. When baking three or more cupcakes, place them in a circle for even cooking. Results are better if you do not cook more than 2 at a time. Overcooking can readily occur. Time is so short that it is a simple matter to bake a couple dozen in about 10 minutes.

We've discovered that once cupcakes are baked they should be removed from the glass custard cups. If they aren't, condensation formed while the cupcakes are cooling collects and can make the bottom of the cupcakes soggy.

Pies

Although pies do not brown under microwaves, they do cook well and their crusts are flaky.

Precook pie shells before filling, or they will be soggy. Flute the edges higher than you usually do. This enables the pie to hold a larger amount of filling. It also makes the stirring of the filling easier. Place the pie plate on another inverted pie plate to prevent doughy crusts. Stirring is necessary for even cooking. Stir gently from the outside (where the waves cook first), moving the cooked portion in toward the center. Stir after 2½ minutes of cooking time.

Cook the pie 2 minutes, then rest the pie 1 minute. This should be repeated until the pie is cooked. Rotate the pie a quarter turn every 2 minutes.

You'll probably have your own recipe for making a pie shell, but here's ours, with the timing. There are excellent frozen pie crusts on the market. But your own will be better.

PASTRY SHELL

Speed-cook; 3 minutes

1 cup all-purpose flour	½ cup shortening
½ teaspoon salt (optional)	4 tablespoons milk

Sift the flour and salt together. Place in a bowl and cut in the shortening with a pastry blender until you have a mixture resembling cornmeal. Sprinkle in 1 tablespoon of milk at a time, gently tossing it into the mixture with two forks. When all the milk is incorporated and the mixture well moistened, form it into a firm ball with your hands. On a lightly floured board, roll out the pastry to ⅛ inch thickness, rolling from the center to the edge. Let set 10 minutes.

Shape into a 9-inch pie plate, fluting the edges with your fingers or a fork. Cover with a paper towel, then insert an 8-inch glass pie plate, which will hold the pastry flat and prevent shrinkage.

Bake in the center of the oven 3 minutes, rotating a quarter turn every minute. Remove the paper towel and 8-inch pie plate, and let the pie shell cool before filling it.

Here are some hints to help in heating up desserts:

Rewarming 1 serving of pie, cake, or coffee cake takes exactly 15 seconds.

A trick that we have found helpful in serving ice cream: If the ice cream is brick-hard from the freezer, place it right in its container in the microwave oven and heat 15 seconds for 1 pint, 30 seconds for 1 quart. Careful—the ice cream should be softened just to the scoopable, not soupable, stage.

All sundae toppings—butterscotch, pineapple, caramel, chocolate, etc.—can be placed under microwaves 15 seconds, just to soften. They must, however, be in a glass container. If you wish to heat them longer and serve them hot, transfer them to a measuring cup for the additional heating; otherwise, the glass containers that they are sold in might break.

To defrost and warm convenience or commercial desserts will take varying lengths of time, depending upon thickness. Most should be heated uncovered. You'll learn this quickly. For example, six 15-ounce frozen blintzes should be placed in a circle, heated 5 minutes, then turned and heated another 5 minutes. A frozen 32-ounce peach or cherry cobbler, removed from its aluminum foil, should be placed in a glass container, heated 20 minutes and rotated a quarter turn every 5 minutes. Many convenience food packagers and manufacturers are printing microwave defrosting, heating, and cooking times on their wares.

But, as somebody's grandmother said, "Why buy it when you can make it?" And, with microwaves, you can make it in minutes.

GEORGE HERZ'S LEMON CUSTARD FLUFF

Speed-cook; 7 minutes

3 tablespoons butter or margarine
1 cup sugar
4 eggs, separated
¼ cup flour

¼ cup lemon juice
2 teaspoons grated lemon rind
½ teaspoon vanilla
1 cup milk

In a large bowl, cream the butter or margarine; add the sugar and cream the butter or margarine and sugar together thoroughly. In another bowl, beat the egg yolks well until light and fluffy, then add them to the butter or margarine and sugar, along with the flour, lemon juice, lemon rind, and vanilla. Add the milk and mix thoroughly. Beat the egg whites until stiff and fold into the other ingredients. When well mixed, pour into a medium-size glass baking dish. Place that dish in a larger glass dish containing hot water about 1 inch deep. Cook in the center of the oven 7 minutes, stirring from the outside in towards the center at 3 minutes and at 6 minutes. Let cool and serve right from the baking dish or, if you like, just before serving invert on a serving dish so the lemon custard will be on top and the fluff on the bottom. *Serves 6.*

BAKED APPLES

Speed-cook; 5 minutes

¼ cup brown sugar
4 large apples (unpeeled), cored

1 tablespoon butter or margarine
Cinnamon sugar

Place 1 tablespoon of the brown sugar in the cored cavity of each apple. Top each apple with ¼ tablespoon of butter or margarine. Sprinkle with cinnamon. Place the apples in a circle in a round glass dish. Cook in the center of the oven 2½ minutes. Rotate the dish half a turn. Cook 2½ minutes. Let set 10 minutes. *Serves 4.*

BUTTERSCOTCH RUM BANANAS

Speed-cook; 3 minutes

½ cup butter or margarine
½ cup brown sugar
¼ cup dark rum
4 small ripe (but not overripe)
    bananas, cut into halves
    lengthwise

4 large scoops hard-frozen vanilla
    ice cream

Combine the butter or margarine and sugar in a glass measuring cup and cook in the center of the oven 1½ minutes, stirring after each 45 seconds. Stir in the rum. Pour the mixture into a shallow glass baking dish. Arrange the banana halves in the sauce in the baking dish. Cook 45 seconds. Turn the bananas over and cook 45 seconds. Place the ice cream on four dessert plates. Spoon the sauce over the ice cream and arrange 2 banana halves on either side of the scoop of ice cream. *Serves 4.*

QUICK ELEGANT POACHED PEARS

Speed-cook; 13 minutes

1 cup sugar
2 cups white wine
¼ teaspoon allspice
1 cinnamon stick

1 small piece fresh gingerroot
4 firm ripe Bartlett pears
    (unpeeled) cut into halves and
    cored

In a glass baking dish large enough to hold the 8 pear halves, place all the ingredients except the pears. Cook in the center of the oven until the mixture almost simmers and the sugar is dissolved. Stir. Cook 8 minutes, stirring at 4 minutes. The mixture should be syrupy. Place the pears in the syrup. Cook 2½ minutes. Rotate the dish half a turn. Cook 2½ minutes. Chill before serving. *Serves 4.*

RAPID RHUBARB

Speed-cook; 5 minutes

That fresh rhubarb from your garden can be on the table as a sweet-tart dessert minutes after you have cut it.

2 cups chopped fresh rhubarb   ½ cup sugar
⅛ teaspoon salt (optional)

Place the rhubarb and salt in a glass casserole. Cover and cook in the center of the oven 2 minutes. Stir. Cook 2 minutes. Stir in the sugar. Cover and cook one minute. Let set, covered, until cool. *Serves 4.*

CHOCOLATE CAKE SURPRISE

Speed-cook; 10 minutes

When your guests ask you what makes this delicate chocolate cake so light and so moist, your answer is the surprise: "Mayonnaise!"

2 cups unsifted all-purpose flour   ⅛ teaspoon salt (optional)
1 cup sugar   1 cup mayonnaise
1 teaspoon baking soda   1 cup water
¼ cup unsweetened cocoa

In a mixing bowl, blend the flour, sugar, soda, cocoa, and salt. Stir in the mayonnaise and the water. With an electric beater, beat on low speed until all the ingredients are mixed and moistened. Beat at high speed 1½ minutes. Grease the bottom only of a medium-size glass baking dish deep enough that the batter will fill it only halfway. Cook in the center of the oven 10 minutes, rotating the dish a quarter turn every 2 minutes. Let the cake set 10 minutes to finish its carry-over cooking. The cake is done if a toothpick stuck in the center comes out clean. Let it cool completely before frosting. *Serves 6 to 8.*

MINA THOMPSON'S SOUR-CREAM COFFEE CAKE

Speed-cook; 10 minutes

Topping Mixture:

¼ cup granulated sugar
⅓ cup brown sugar

1 teaspoon ground cinnamon
1 cup chopped pecans or walnuts

Batter:

½ cup butter or margarine
1 cup white sugar
2 eggs
1 cup sour cream
1 teaspoon pure vanilla extract

2 cups all-purpose flour
1 teaspoon baking soda
1 teaspoon baking powder
½ teaspoon salt (optional)

In a bowl, combine the topping ingredients and mix thoroughly. Set aside. In another bowl, make the batter. Cream the butter or margarine and sugar, add the eggs, sour cream, and vanilla and mix well. Stir in the flour, baking soda, baking powder, and salt until well blended. Butter the bottom only of a 9-inch square glass baking dish. Pour in half the batter. Sprinkle on half the topping mixture. Add the remaining batter and sprinkle on the rest of the topping. Cook in the center of the oven 10 minutes, rotating the dish half a turn at 5 minutes. The cake is done when a toothpick inserted in the center comes out clean. *Serves 8.*

FUNG CHAN CHIN'S CLASSIC CHEESECAKE

Speed-cook; 9 minutes, 10 seconds

Crust:

8 whole honey graham crackers, crushed
¼ cup sugar

6 tablespoons butter or margarine, melted (about 40 seconds under microwaves)

Filling:

4 eggs, separated
½ cup sugar
Four 3-ounce packages cream cheese, heated in a bowl 30 seconds under microwaves

2 teaspoons pure vanilla extract
Dash of almond extract

Topping:

2 cups sour cream
3 tablespoons sugar

1 teaspoon almond extract
½ teaspoon ground cinnamon

Blend the cracker crumbs, ¼ cup sugar, and the butter or margarine. Pack evenly onto the bottom and sides of a 9-inch glass deep-dish pie plate, making a shell. Refrigerate. In a large bowl, beat the egg yolks until light and fluffy. Add the ½ cup sugar and blend well. Beat in the softened cream cheese, 1 package at a time. Blend in 1 teaspoon of the vanilla, and the almond extract. In another bowl and with clean, dry beaters, beat the egg whites until stiff. Mix in the remaining vanilla extract and fold the egg whites into the egg yolk–cream cheese mixture. When well blended, turn into the chilled graham-cracker shell. Cook in the center of the oven 6 minutes, rotating the dish half a turn every 2 minutes. Let cool 45 minutes.

To make the topping, blend the sour cream, 3 tablespoons sugar, and almond extract. Spread over the cool filling. Dust with the cinnamon and cook the cheesecake in the center of the oven 2 minutes, rotating half a turn at 1 minute. Let cool and place in the refrigerator to chill overnight. *Serves 8.*

JAMAICAN CHEESECAKE

Speed-cook; 6 minutes, 10 seconds

⅓ cup butter or margarine
6 whole honey graham crackers, crushed
Two 8-ounce packages cream cheese

3 eggs, beaten
¾ cup sugar
1 teaspoon pure vanilla extract
2 tablespoons dark rum

Heat the butter or margarine in an 8-inch round glass dish or pie plate in the center of the oven 40 seconds, or just until the butter melts. Blend the butter or margarine and the cracker crumbs in the glass dish. Pack evenly onto the bottom and sides of the dish, making a shell. Place the cream cheese in a bowl and heat 30 seconds, or just until softened. Beat the cream cheese until smooth. Stir in the eggs, sugar, vanilla, and rum, and beat until the mixture is smooth. Pour into the graham cracker shell. Cook in the center of the oven 5 minutes, rotating the dish half a turn every 2 minutes. The center will be soft. Refrigerate overnight; the pie will set as it chills. *Serves 8.*

DORIS L. MAYS' FRENCH STRAWBERRY GLACÉ PIE

Speed-cook; 10¾ minutes

1 unbaked 9-inch pie shell, frozen or your own
One 3-ounce package cream cheese, softened 15 seconds under microwaves

1 quart ripe strawberries, washed, drained, and hulled
1 cup sugar
3 tablespoons cornstarch
1 pint heavy cream, whipped

Cover the prepared pie shell with a paper towel. Place an 8-inch glass pie plate on top of the paper towel. Cook in the center of the oven 3 minutes. Remove the 8-inch pie plate and the paper towel. Cook the pie shell 1½ minutes. Let cool 15 minutes before filling.

Spread the softened cream cheese evenly over the bottom of the pie shell. Place half the strawberries on the cream cheese, distributing them evenly. In a bowl, place the remaining berries and cook 3 minutes. Mash and strain them. Return the juice to the bowl. There should be 1½ cups of strawberry juice. If necessary, add a little water to increase to this amount. Blend the sugar with the cornstarch and gradually stir into the juice. Cook in the center of the oven 1½ minutes. Stir. Cook 1½ minutes, or until the mixture simmers and is thickened. Let cool. Pour the cooled thickened juice over the strawberries in the pie shell. Refrigerate 2 hours. Decorate with the whipped cream.

PIE À LA MODE

Place 1 piece of peach or apple pie (at room temperature) on a serving plate. Top with a scoop of hard-frozen vanilla or peach ice cream. Heat 15 seconds. The pie will be warm, the ice cream only slightly softened. *Serves 1.*

HUGHBERTA NEERGAARD'S PARTY-TIME ICE CREAM PIE

Speed-cook; 6 minutes, 40 seconds

1 stick butter or margarine
1 cup all-purpose flour
¼ cup brown sugar

1 cup finely ground pecans
2 quarts ice cream of your choice

In a bowl, heat the butter or margarine about 40 seconds or until melted. Stir in the flour, brown sugar, and half the pecans, stirring until well blended. Pat the mixture onto the bottoms and sides of two 9-inch glass pie plates, forming shells. Cook one shell at a time in the center of the oven 2½ minutes, rotating the plate half a turn at 1 minute. Let cool. One at a time, place each quart of ice cream in its container on a plate and heat in the oven 30 seconds, or until slightly soft. Fill the cooled pecan shells evenly with the softened ice cream. Sprinkle with the remaining ground pecans. Freeze and serve at your leisure. *Makes 2 pies, serving 12.*

ALICE VAUGHN'S CHOCOLATE SAUCE

Speed-cook; 2 minutes, 20 seconds

No longer do you have to melt chocolate in a double boiler!

2 ounces unsweetened chocolate
1 cup sugar
⅛ teaspoon cream of tartar

One 6-ounce can evaporated milk
1 teaspoon pure vanilla extract
Pinch of salt (optional)

Place the chocolate in a large glass measuring cup. It is not necessary to heat the chocolate until it is completely melted (carry-over heat will continue to melt it). Just heat it in the center of the oven 1½ minutes, or until the chocolate begins to melt. Remove and stir well until it is thick and creamy. Blend in the sugar and cream of tartar. Add the milk gradually and heat for 30 seconds. Stir. Heat for 10 seconds. Stir. Heat for 10 seconds. Stir until well blended. Remove from the oven and stir in the vanilla and salt. Let cool. *Makes about 1½ cups sauce.*

Variation: This can be converted into a different and rich sauce for desserts by using ½ can of evaporated milk and 3 ounces of dark rum.

MEXICAN SUNDAE

This is an old favorite with people in upstate New York, but seems to be unknown elsewhere. Try it; your guests will love it.

1 very generous scoop of vanilla
  ice cream
2 tablespoons Alice Vaughn's
  Chocolate Sauce (previous
  recipe)

2 tablespoons Spanish peanuts

Place the ice cream in a serving dish. Cover with chocolate sauce. Sprinkle with the peanuts. *Serves 1.*

HOT FUDGE SUNDAE

This is an appreciated midwinter dessert.

1 generous scoop chocolate or
  vanilla ice cream
3 tablespoons Alice Vaughn's
  Chocolate Sauce (above), heated

2 tablespoons whipped cream (not
  from a push-button can!)

An easy way to heat the chocolate sauce is to place it in a measuring cup, heat 30 seconds; stir; heat 40 seconds. Stir and pour over the ice cream, then add the dollop of whipped cream. *Serves 1.*

INDEX